# Understanding and Developing
# Language Tests

# Understanding and Developing Language Tests

C.J. WEIR

PRENTICE HALL INTERNATIONAL ENGLISH LANGUAGE TEACHING

## Prentice Hall

New York   London   Toronto   Sydney   Tokyo   Singapore

To Hilya, to my parents,
and to colleagues in CALS, University of Reading

First published 1993 by
Prentice Hall International (UK) Ltd
Campus 400, Maylands Avenue
Hemel Hempstead
Hertfordshire, HP2 7EZ
A division of
Simon & Schuster International Group

Typeset in 10/12 pt Times
by MHL Typesetting Ltd. Coventry

Printed in Great Britain by Redwood Books
Trowbridge, Wiltshire

Library of Congress Cataloging-in-Publication Data

Weir, Cyril J.
  Understanding and developing language tests /
C.J. Weir.
    p. cm. — (Language teaching methodology
series) (Prentice Hall International English
language teaching)
    Includes bibliographical references.
    ISBN 0-13-947532-X : $14.50
    1. Language and languages—Ability
testing.  I. Title.
II. Series.  III. Series: English language
teaching (Englewood Cliffs, N.J.)
P53.4.W45  1993                        92-33403
418'.0076—dc20                              CIP

British Library Cataloguing in Publication Data

A catalogue record for this book is available from
the British Library

ISBN 0-13-947532-X (pbk)

1  2  3  4  5     97  96  95  94  93

# Contents

# General Editor's Preface

In contrast to the situation even a few years ago, there is now no lack of current, well-documented books on language testing, directed at teachers, researchers and curriculum administrators. One might then ask why publish a further volume? Oddly enough, among those books now available, there is a lack of a clear and practical hands-on guide to the design of language tests, intelligible to teachers and which directs itself at the exigencies of the classroom and the requirements of learners. Perhaps this lack is understandable, for to bring off such a book, one would have not only to be current with testing research but also be sensitive to the constraints of test administration and to the conditions of teaching and testing practice on the ground. Moreover, such a book would have to have credibility on the street, as it were, among those it wished to influence and inform. Perhaps the reason for the lack is that there are few testers who have all those virtues. Cyril Weir, by everyone's account, possesses these in abundance. I can think of no-one who has the track record of test development worldwide to match his and no-one who has consistently sought to make the connections clear between testing research and the practicalities of test design and test administration.

What is more, such an ability needs to be tuned to the influences that testing clearly has on curriculum design and teaching processes. Testing often controls teaching: the trick is to counter this pressure by taking testing to task and making it serve the objectives of the curriculum. This in turn implies empowering teachers to understand the often unnecessarily mysterious and arcane world of testing and to equip them, through developing competence as test designers, to ask the important questions: what is the test's view of language, what is the test's view of learning and what is the test's view of teaching?

This new book by Cyril Weir begins by asking these questions and ends by equipping its readers to answer them themselves.

Professor Christopher N. Candlin
General Editor,
Macquarie University, Sydney

# *Acknowledgements*

I wish to acknowledge gratitude to the following Examination Boards for their kind permission to reproduce samples of tests:

The Associated Examining Board (AEB)
University of Cambridge Local Examinations Syndicate / Royal Society of Arts Examinations Board (UCLES/RSA)
The Joint Matriculation Board (JMB)
London Chamber of Commerce and Industry (LCCI)
Oxford Delegacy of Local Examinations
Pitmans Examinations Institute
Testing and Evaluation Unit, CALS, University of Reading

and to the following publishers for permission to reproduce copyright material:

The Observer Magazine (article on double glazing in Example 3.9 in Chapter 3).

The framework for the testing of spoken interaction draws heavily on the work of Martin Bygate of the Centre for Applied Language Studies at the University of Reading (see Bygate 1987) and an important contribution was made by two other colleagues in the Testing and Evaluation Unit at Reading University, Don Porter and Arthur Hughes. These colleagues also provided valuable advice and encouragement in the development of the frameworks for listening, reading and writing.

I would like to acknowledge the influence of the work of Keith Morrow and Lyle Bachman. A number of the elements in my frameworks were suggested by their earlier ideas. Keith's seminal work on communicative language testing (Morrow 1977 and 1979) and Lyle's major contribution to language testing theory (Bachman 1990) have influenced my thinking and contributed to the development of the framework approach advocated in this book.

The recent work of Geoff Brindley and David Nunan on the testing of listening comprehension (Brindley and Nunan 1992) contributed to the development of the framework for testing listening in Chapter Four.

I would like to thank: all the students who have attended the courses which provided a basis for this book, particularly the Diploma in TEFL students at Reading University (1987–92); Penny Foster who produced an early version of Table 3.2 on reading activities in an academic context; the MAAL (Testing) students at Reading University who produced the listening recall test, Example 7 in Chapter 4; and Don McGovern who provided the Global Marking Scheme 1 in Section 5.3.

A large debt is owed to Charles Alderson of the Department of Linguistics and Modern English Language, Lancaster University. The content of Chapter 1, in particular the test-taking experience (1.1), evaluating faulty items (1.2) and the ensuing guidelines for test development, the dictation task Example 6, p. 123, and part of the marking exercise in

5.3, owe much to ideas initially developed by Charles and subsequently refined in working with him and other colleagues, on courses in the Institute for English Language Education, Lancaster University, and in overseas seminars.

I am grateful to Charles Alderson, Isobel Fletcher de Téllez, Paul Maw and Don McGovern for their extremely helpful comments on earlier versions of this manuscript. A special debt is owed to Chris Candlin for his generous advice and tolerance.

My biggest debt is to Don Porter, a friend and colleague in CALS, who provided constant support in completing this book, helped develop a more coherent line of argument throughout, and corrected the many 'slips of the word processor'. Also a warm word of thanks is owed to colleagues working in the ESP centre at Alexandria University in Egypt. The seminars on testing conducted with them over the last two years were among the most stimulating and rewarding I have ever been involved in. They encouraged me greatly in finishing this book.

Had I been able to put into practice all the sound advice I was given by colleagues and my students, the book would have been much improved. I would, however, have been many years older, and the publisher's patience totally exhausted. The faults that remain are mine (well, mostly mine).

# Introduction

The aim of this book is to develop a critical awareness of language tests so that language teachers can better reflect on and evaluate the public tests their students take and can construct for themselves valid, practical and reliable tests for use in the classroom. In Part I of the book the reader will be introduced to the key issues in language testing. A critical perspective will be encouraged through a hands-on examination of a series of faulty items designed to illustrate the major principles of validity, reliability and practicality. This exercise will generate a framework of general principles and specific guidelines for sound test construction.

The second part of the book focuses on testing language skills. The reader is first taken through a framework for test specification in each of the skills areas. Each framework is then followed by examples of a variety of formats available for testing the language skill under review. Close attention is paid to establishing what can be tested through each format and its positive and negative attributes, particularly in regard to the operations involved in carrying out the tasks and the conditions under which these activities are performed. The reader is also encouraged to apply the framework of general principles and specific guidelines for sound test construction from Part I of the book to these examples. The exercises on the test formats are intended to lead to a clearer understanding of what contributes to sound test construction and an awareness of the limitations and advantages of the different formats available for testing the various skills.

In test task design we must be as precise as we can concerning the performance conditions, operations and criteria for assessing the quality of output that should obtain. The analysis of a test task in terms of these features would indicate the degree to which it reflected the attributes of the activity in real life that it was meant to replicate. Furthermore unless steps are taken to identify and incorporate such features it would seem imprudent to make statements about a candidate's ability to function in normal conditions in his or her future target situation. Full authenticity of task may well be unattainable in the tests we write. It will not be possible to replicate reality fully because of the strong pulls of the other general principles of reliability and practicality we discuss below. We must weigh up what is practical by exploring the tension between test authenticity and test 'operationalisability'. We must determine to what extent compromises may be made in the trade-off between reliability and validity. The key issue facing language testers is where and how and to what extent to compromise in their own specific context. In the end, however, we need to make our tests as direct as possible in terms of real-life operations and performance conditions if we are to measure anything of value.

# List of abbreviations contained in the text

| | |
|---|---|
| AEB TEEP | Associated Examining Board's Test in English for Educational Purposes. Now administered and owned by the Testing and Evaluation Unit at the University of Reading, Whiteknights, Reading, Berks RG6 2AA, UK |
| AILA | International Association of Applied Linguistics |
| CALS | Centre for Applied Language Studies, University of Reading (UK) |
| EAP | English for Academic Purposes |
| ELT | English Language Teaching |
| ESOL | English for Speakers of Other Languages |
| ESP | English for Specified Purposes |
| FSI | Foreign Service Institute (USA) |
| IELTS | International English Language Testing System |
| ILR | Inter-Agency Language Round Table (USA) |
| JMB | Joint Matriculation Board (Northern Universities, UK) |
| JMB UETESOL | University Entrance Test in English for Speakers of Other Languages (UK) |
| LCCI | London Chamber of Commerce and Industry |
| L1 | First Language |
| MCQ | Multiple-choice Question |
| PLAB | General Medical Council's Professional and Linguistic Assessments Board (Test of overseas doctors' language proficiency) (UK) |
| RSA CUEFL | Royal Society of Arts Test in the Communicative Use of English as a Foreign Language (UK) |
| SAQ | Short-answer Question |
| SLA | Second Language Acquisition |
| TL | Target Language |
| TOEFL | Test of English as a Foreign Language, English Testing Service (Princeton, USA) |
| UCLES/RSA | University of Cambridge Local Examinations Syndicate / Royal Society of Arts (UK) |
| UCLES/RSA CEIBT | Certificate in English for International Business and Trade (UK) |

## PART I

## Chapter One

# *Issues in language testing*

### 1.1 A test-taking experience

#### EXERCISE 1A TEST TAKING

The purpose of this exercise is to put you in the position of candidates having to take a test. Below you will find four test questions. You are told how much time to spend on each of them. Follow the timing exactly. To do this you will need to have a watch on the desk in front of you. As you finish each question please jot down on a separate sheet of paper your reactions and feelings to each.

When you have finished all four test items and written your comments, examine your overall reaction to the experience. You might then like to compare your reaction with those of other teachers who have been put through a similar experience, by reading pages 4—5 below.

**Question 1: Lexical knowledge**

Match the following words with the definitions A—Z given alongside. You have four minutes for this task.

| | | | | | |
|---|---|---|---|---|---|
| 1. | pall | A. | dispute | N. | be irritated |
| 2. | flare | B. | volatile | O. | accuse |
| 3. | imbue | C. | worthless finery | P. | shrewish woman |
| 4. | impost | D. | free from blame | Q. | saturate |
| 5. | impeach | E. | calumny | R. | find fault with |
| 6. | obloquy | F. | tediously long | S. | levy |
| 7. | cavil | G. | trace | T. | show plainly |
| 8. | exculpate | H. | bestow | U. | move unsteadily |
| 9. | yaw | I. | vein of ore | V. | shabby |
| 10. | evince | J. | become boring | W. | anger |
| 11. | ascetic | K. | settle comfortably | X. | carry |
| 12. | mercurial | L. | spread outward | Y. | dismiss |
| 13. | ensconce | M. | given to self denial | Z. | metal |
| 14. | scintilla | | | | |
| 15. | termagant | | | | |
| 16. | trumpery | | | | |
| 17. | chafe | | | | |
| 18. | lode | | | | |
| 19. | tilt | After the four minutes are up, quickly write down | | | |
| 20. | vest | your reactions to Question 1. | | | |

*1*

## Question 2:   C-test

You have ten minutes to finish this test.

Displacement bo_____ marrow transpl_____ was car_____ out af_____ conditioning wi_____ busulphan cyclopho_____. In bet_____ she rece_____ an infu_____ of do_____ buffy co_____ an immunopr_____ manoeuvre us_____ while T ce_____ help i_____ still opera_____. Should a_____ recipient lymph_____ have rea_____ to t_____ normal enz_____ and trans_____ they wo_____ have be_____ destroyed. Intra_____ cyclosporin w_____ not be_____ until th_____ days bef_____ grafting.

T_____ posttransplantation per_____ was compl_____ by sev_____ predominantly cuta_____ graft ver_____ host dis_____, Gram nega_____ septicaemia, a_____ two epis_____ of inters_____ pneumonitis. S_____ continued t_____ have prob_____ with chr_____ graft ver_____ host dis_____, hypertension, a_____ fluid rete_____ for several months af_____ grafting. Succe_____ engraftment w_____ evidenced b_____ finding ma_____ chromosomes a_____ rising lev_____ of leuc_____ sphingomyelinase acti_____ after graf_____.

After the ten minutes are up quickly write down your reactions to Question 2.

## Question 3:   Cloze Elide

In the passage below a number of foreign words have been inserted which contribute nothing to the meaning of the passage. You have to read through the passage very quickly and underline these words. You have *one minute only* to complete this question. The first foreign word is underlined for you as an example.

A test should aim to fulfil three nokta conditions.
   It should test what the test writer wants soru it to test. If tests suffer from any of the faults ve you identified above it is possible that this principle may be yerine affected. Test validity presupposes the iki writer can be explicit about this and takes steps to ensure that the test varsa reflects realistic use of the particular ability to be measured.
   The cardinal principle of testing is that you should yanitini be testing what you want to test. You should therefore be very clear about what it is you want to test and try

to ensure that you tumceden test only that. Tests should be valid. As far as possible ozne your test should measure only what it is intended to test and not irrelevant ile capacities. The test writer must be clear about what an item is designed to measure kiplik and how performance on that item will be assessed before the candidates sit the test.

For example if you want to test for a knowledge of the present perfect tense in English ayni you should make every effort to ensure that is the only thing your items are testing. In item 5 no indication is given of the criteria that will be used to assess success in the birincisi task and given each task will result in a different text type it is eklenti difficult to see how comparability between students doing different tasks is likely to emerge from such an item. The test writer must be clear about what an eylemler item is designed to measure and how performance on that item will be assessed before the candidates sit the test.

In achievement testing, tests should relate closely to both the content of what has been learned and also the eylem way things have been taught. Students nurtured through the grammar translation approach are unlikely to perform uyumu well on tasks they have had no previous exposure to, such as spontaneous oral interaction. It may well be that to encourage teachers to adopt techniques that go with a new syllabus they adlarda need to be included in tests to increase the sifat likelihood of their doing so. To the extent that tests are mirrors of the teaching there will be a zarf positive washback effect from tests to teaching.

After you finish write down your reactions to Question 3.

## Question 4: Replying to a letter

You have received the following letter from a colleague in Wales. Write a suitable reply. You have thirty minutes to do this task.

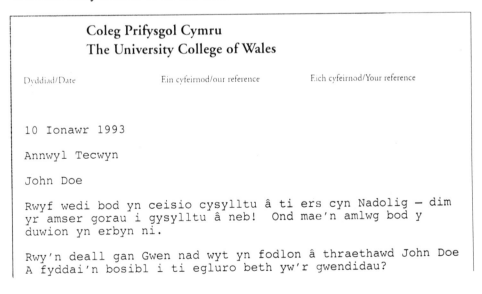

Coleg Prifysgol Cymru
The University College of Wales

Dyddiad/Date          Ein cyfeirnod/our reference          Fich cyfeirnod/Your reference

10 Ionawr 1993

Annwyl Tecwyn

John Doe

Rwyf wedi bod yn ceisio cysylltu â ti ers cyn Nadolig – dim yr amser gorau i gysylltu â neb! Ond mae'n amlwg bod y duwion yn erbyn ni.

Rwy'n deall gan Gwen nad wyt yn fodlon â thraethawd John Doe A fyddai'n bosibl i ti egluro beth yw'r gwendidau?

A fyddai'n bosibl gwella'r gendidau i gael y gwaith i fyny'r safon? Neu, a yw'r gwaith yn rhy wan i wella? Os oes pwyntiau penodol sy'n gyfrifol am y methiant, fe ddylai fod yn bosibl eu hail-ysgrifennu. Fe fyddwn yn gwerthfawrogi dy sylwadau — yn Saesneg, os bydd hynny'n gyfleus.

Llongyfarchiadau i'th gwraig am efelychu ei gŵr.

Cofion cynnes

*Dai Davies*

After the thirty minutes are up quickly write down your reactions to Question 4. Then compare your reactions with colleagues and/or with those listed below.

*Comment on the test-taking experience*

From the experience of doing these tests with groups of teachers the following were some of the reactions and feelings they expressed:

Intimidated
Confused
Surprised
Afraid
Frustrated
Useless
Detached
Embarrassed
Disappointed
Angry
Loss of confidence/demoralised/discouraged
Helpless
Anxious/pressurised

These are all conditions brought about by stress.

How would you feel if the above tests were used to comment on your ability in English if you were a non-native speaker or even a native speaker of English? How would you feel if the results were used to make a decision on your entry into a professional course of study or into a particular career?

Did you feel any desire to check the correctness of your answers with the person sitting next to you or with anybody else? The undesirable psychological states that tests can produce in candidates may lead them into behaviour patterns they would not normally exhibit. What is the difference between cooperative checking on the rightness of one's answers and the less socially acceptable 'cheating'? Both would seem to result in great part from the stress engendered by the test situation. Ways of reducing avoidable stress must be sought. We must try to identify and counteract the factors contributing to it.

What caused the feelings mentioned above?

Rubrics/instructions unclear or inadequate

Purpose of the test unclear

Time pressure

Unfamiliarity with the test type

Lack of preparation for the test: either in terms of practice beforehand or warning that it was to take place

Layout

Arcane or specialised nature of the subject matter

Level too high

Lack of interest in topics

### *Testing in the classroom: some general considerations*

Your own future will not be affected by your performance on the test tasks above. If you felt any of the emotions discussed above, imagine the pressure on students who find themselves in a situation where their future careers are dependent on test performance. What effect do you think bad testing would have on them?

As teachers we must, as far as we can, try to avoid creating negative reactions in the classroom testing we get involved in. It is all too easy to set tests which are inappropriate and beyond the abilities of our students. Your experience in understanding the letter in Welsh may well mirror that of some students faced with some texts in English. We should always test for best, i.e. give students the chance to demonstrate their optimal ability.

Classroom testing should not be divorced from the teaching that precedes it. *Achievement* testing should be firmly rooted in previous classroom experiences in terms of activities practised, language used, and criteria of assessment employed.

Achievement tests need to be pitched at an appropriate level for the students who are taking them. It must be highly demotivating not to be able to cope with most of the demands that are made on you in a classroom achievement test, either through lack of preparation, or because of the difficulty levels of the tasks set. Achievement testing must be viewed as an integral part of the learning process. The concern should be to sample from the domain specified by the syllabus and realised in the classroom. The purpose of tests of achievement should be to indicate how successful the learning experiences had been for the students rather than to show in what respects they were deficient. In this way learners might be motivated towards future learning experiences.

In classes where there is a heterogeneous mix in terms of level, a graded approach to testing may be necessary, with students being entered for an examination at a level appropriate to them as individuals, rather than the class as a whole being entered. Alternatively, test tasks accessible across the ability range might be selected and qualitative distinctions made on the resulting differential performance (as in the former RSA/UCLES tests. See Weir 1990, Appendix 3). Here all students would take the same test tasks but a different level of performance would be expected at higher levels.

The overall aim in achievement tests should be to try to get students to use language receptively and productively that they have learned during the course, but in altered contexts so that they actively have to deploy known language items (structures and lexis) in novel contexts.

The importance of the washback effect of tests on teaching cannot be ignored (see Hughes 1989, Ch. 6). Problems are always likely to arise if the achievement tests do not correspond to the teaching that has preceded them. Students nurtured in a heavily structuralist approach are unlikely to perform well on tasks they have not previously met, such as spontaneous spoken interaction tasks. If they have never had to write anything without guidance in their normal classroom activities there is no reason for them to do so in a final achievement test. If changes in testing procedure are envisaged these should always be consequent upon the prior introduction of teaching techniques and materials which reflect these changes. Where these safeguards are met, tests may prove to be invaluable instruments of change.

Changing a test is possibly the most powerful means of bringing about improvements in the learning experiences that go before it. Tests can have a most useful and powerful washback effect on teaching. By the same token, if materials are changed to reflect a new approach to syllabus, and teachers are trained in the new materials and methodology, all this enterprise may be to no avail if corresponding tests are not available.

Without appropriate tests, teachers are unlikely to change. If tests remain within a former paradigm, e.g. multiple-choice tests of grammar and lexis, then teachers may not be disposed to practise, for example, productive writing or spoken interaction in the classroom. Teachers and students are judged on test results. It would be naive to argue that they should prepare students in class for anything other than those things on which they will be tested. Thus it is crucial that achievement tests should embody the objectives of a course. In this sense they should be a reasonable sample of the important elements of the course.

If we are preparing students for a *proficiency* test, that is, a test which will provide information on a candidate's ability to perform in a future specified target situation, a similar degree of appropriateness is required in task selection. For example, if we are preparing students for an English for Academic Purposes Proficiency Test which will determine their suitability to operate in English-medium study in the future, we must also ensure that the students are adequately prepared for the tasks they will have to face.

It is important therefore to ensure that students are entered only for examinations which sample most effectively those capacities required in the future use situation. In this way the teaching that precedes the examination will benefit them when they eventually have to operate in the target situation. The more the proficiency test reflects important attributes of real-life performance the greater the potential for positive washback on the learning that precedes the test-taking experience. Everything that students do to prepare themselves for the proficiency test should be contributory to enhanced performance in the future target situation.

There would seem to be a strong argument for making tests as direct as possible. The more features of real-life use of language that can be built into tests, the more positive the washback effect and the easier it will be to make statements about what students can or cannot do in the language. It seems a waste of time to be training students in ways of improving their scores on indirect tests, such as multiple-choice tests of written expression, rather than equipping them with abilities they will need for performing in an academic context (see Hughes 1989 for an extended discussion of this).

Full authenticity of task or genuineness of text may not always be feasible in tests. In developing tests we will have to explore the tension between authenticity and what it is practical to include in a test, as well as deciding how far to compromise in the trade-off between reliability and validity. However, if we are to measure anything of value, we need to approximate as closely as we can in our tests to authentic conditions of communication. These tensions are discussed in detail below in Part II in the discussion on testing the skills and readers are invited to reflect on these issues in relation to their own testing situation. The general principles of validity, reliability and practicality are examined more fully in Section 1.3.2 below.

In both proficiency and achievement testing there is a need for a clear understanding of what test tasks are measuring and how well they are doing it. There is a need for a critical perspective both in writing test items and in scrutinising those prepared by others, including those prepared by national examining bodies. In writing achievement tests the teachers will most probably have to ensure that the tests they construct themselves meet the relevant criteria in relation both to the general mechanics of testing (see next section below) and to the frameworks for the construction of tests in specific skill areas (see Chapters 2−5 below). In selecting external tests for their students, teachers have every right to establish that examining boards meet the standards we are suggesting teachers ask of themselves.

In the following section on faulty items you will look at a number of test items to establish what is wrong with them. They each illustrate at least one fault in item design. Many of these faults can be avoided if tests are written with, or at least checked out by, colleagues. If possible try and do the exercises with somebody else, as experience suggests that test construction is an activity that is best performed in groups.

## 1.2  Evaluating faulty items

It is often useful to see how things should not be done to avoid making the same mistakes and to develop a critically reflective approach needed for writing good test items.

### EXERCISE 1B   CRITICAL EVALUATION

**1.**   Below you will find a number of test items. In most cases an indication is given in brackets of what the item writer claimed to be trying to test, for example:

**Item 1:   (Knowledge of tenses)**

The indication of what the test writer was trying to test, i.e. knowledge of tenses, did not appear with the item in the candidate's exam paper.

   Work out the answer for each item. Each item has at least one fault. Start by asking yourself in what way(s) the item writer has failed to test what was intended to be tested (in what ways is the test invalid?). Try and determine any other specific problems with an item. For example you might consider: the level of difficulty of the task or alternatives within a task; whether the task is biased in any sense; how clear the task is; the timing; the layout. You should give some thought to how each item would be marked. Are there any problems here? Would two different raters give it the same mark (i.e. is it a reliable item?) Lastly, consider how practical the item is. How easy would it be for teachers to construct similar items?

**2.**   When you have done all the items try and draw up a set of guidelines for writing test items on a separate sheet of paper. Imagine you have been asked to advise your colleagues on writing language test items. The advice you give should help them to write acceptable items. Rather than just giving vague, general advice such as 'items should be reliable', try and be more explicit and specific, e.g. make sure instructions are clear and unambiguous to other readers.

When you have finished look at the comments on the faulty items at the end of this section. An outline of general principles and specific guidelines is presented in Section 1.3.

## Item 1:   Knowledge of tenses

Select the most semantically appropriate option from those available:

John is at school today. Sally _____ the piano for half an hour because she unhappy.

(a)  play
(b)  unfortunately hasnt been able to play
(c)  Brown
(d)  will be playing

## Item 2:   Lexical knowledge

Complete the gaps with appropriate lexical items:

John was a very _____ boy. He _____ every day. He is coming _____. John speaks English very well but his sister _____ speak it at all.

## Item 3:   Knowledge of spelling

Unscramble the jumbled letters below to form English words:

MEAX
GMAEUZ
TAC
ALAVGI

## Item 4:  Working out the meaning of words from context

Read the passage below on *Estimating the Age of Trees*. Some of the words are in italics. Most of them match the dictionary definitions given. There may however be an occasional definition which has no equivalent word from the passage. If so indicate this by writing X. (NB there may be a word in italics that is not defined). Write the word from the passage by the appropriate definition.

One can make a <u>rough</u> estimate of a tree's age from the state of its <u>bark</u> and branch structure. Until it has been felled however one can only guess at its <u>exact</u> age. After it has been cut down one can get a precise estimate from the <u>concentric</u> rings which spread outwards across the stump. It is even possible to <u>tell</u> from these rings when there were <u>sunspots</u> in the tree's life.

1. not smooth, coarse in texture  _____

2. to determine  _____

3. inexact  _____

4. strictly correct  _____

5. to originate  _____

6. outer sheath  _____

7. to report  _____

8. the outside of an object  _____

## Item 5:  Writing ability

Write an essay on one of the following:

(a)  Write a spirited defence of the English public school system.
(b)  Describe what you did yesterday.
(c)  What are the shortcomings of Einstein's theory of relativity?
(d)  The funniest thing that ever happened to me.

## Item 6:   Reading comprehension

*(You are advised to spend about 15 minutes on this question)*

**5.1.**   Look at the advertisements opposite. These advertisements are numbered 1 – 10. Using these numbers, answer the following questions. The first one has been done for you.

(a)   Which companies offer AA membership or service?

**1, 6, 7, 9**

(b)   Which companies state they accept credit cards?

(c)   Which companies will bring the car to your home?

(d)   You are going abroad and want to arrange to hire a car in advance. Which company would you choose?

(e)   Where can you be certain of hiring a car which is one year old or less?

(f)   Which companies offer comprehensive insurance?

(g)   You want to hire a minibus. Which companies can you ring?

(h)   You can't drive and want to be driven in an expensive car. Which company would you choose?

(i)   Which companies give rates with unlimited mileage?

(j)   You want to hire a car for six months. Which company would you choose? Why?

Source: Oxford Delegacy.

**1**

## MINI CENTRE CAR HIRE

### For Car Hire
### Try Our Hire

If you need a car for one day, one week or even one year we are the logical choice, we offer Chevettes, Minis, Escorts, Cortinas, Marinas, Cortina Estates, Princess 1800's At very competitive rates. On hire of 10 days and over we offer a 20% discount. All cars have Comprehensive Insurance and AA Membership. No mileage charges.

For further details telephone

## High Wycombe 30007

We are Open Mon-Fri 8.30–6.30 pm
Sat 8.30–2.00 pm

West End Rd.,
High Wycombe

**2**

## Make Avis Rent A Car your first choice

For rentals in the U.K. and overseas ring

## 01-848 8733

## AVIS

**3**

(Members of the Budget Rent a Car system)

**AYLESBURY**
Dutton Forshaw
(Bucks) Ltd
Buckingham Road
Aylesbury
Bucks
HP19 3QQ
Aylesbury 84820

**HIGH WYCOMBE**
Mann Egerton & Co Ltd
111/121 London Road
High Wycombe
Bucks
High Wycombe 35440

**GOOD CARS BETTER RATES BEST SERVICE**

Budget rents the Leyland cars rarely more than 9 months old. Proper comprehensive insurance. Most credit cards accepted. That's Budget you can beat it.

**4**

## RENT-A-CAR

rent an *interesting* car from **FIAT**

- Favourable rates with unlimited mileage
- Major credit cards accepted
- Wide choice of current models under 1 year old
- Private and Business enquiries welcomed

**AMERSHAM**
Curries Garage
Hill House
Hill Avenue **Amersham 22266**

**5**

## PEARCES PRIVATE HIRE
### SELF DRIVE

Minibuses & Vans for Self-Drive
(Roof Racks Loaned Free)

*Dorchester-on-Thames, Oxford*

## OXFORD 340560

**6**

*WIDE CHOICE*
*LATE MODEL CARS*
*UNLIMITED MILEAGE*
*LOW RATES*
*AA MEMBERSHIP*

Hartford Motors
(Oxford) Ltd
Seacourt Tower
Botley Road
Oxford 46373
(STD Code 0865)

**7**

## HUMPHRIS
### RENT-A-CAR

TELEPHONE

## OXFORD 774696
(EXT 9)

* KEEN PRICES
* CURRENT MODELS
* CARS – VANS – MOTOR CARAVANS
* UNLIMITED MILEAGE
* COMPREHENSIVE INSURANCE
* RADIO IN MOST CARS
* A.A. MEMBERSHIP

**ROSE HILL, OXFORD**

**8**

## Rent-a-Car

Wide choice of cars, vans and mini buses

Competitive rates including insurance and temporary RAC membership.

## Bristol Street Motors
### RENT-A-CAR
### Tel: BANBURY 53511

**9**

### HILLTOP TRANSPORT LTD
## SELF DRIVE HIRE

SIMCA 1,000 & 1,100'S SUNBEAMS
AVENGERS HUNTERS & ALPINES
SALOONS, ESTATES VANS
DODGE 12 SEATER BUSES
A A SERVICE
DELIVERY ARRANGED

## CHESHAM 2351

**10**

### CHAUFFEUR DRIVEN
### LIMOUSINES

ROLLS ROYCE & AUSTIN PRINCESS
other cars available
including 12 seater mini bus

## OXFORD 58960
### CLIFF CARS
(Proprietor F CLIFTON)

Source: Oxford Delegacy.

## Item 7:  Listening ability

Read carefully through the following passage.

Do not fill in any of the blanks.

**Passage A**

> If we think of health care in . . . . . . . . . which give pride of place, as regards resources, to hospitals, we could easily find ourselves . . . . . . . . . more and more with no great benefit to the overall health of the . . . . . . . . .
>
> Secondly, we must curb our predilection for medicine in the form of ever more complex technology. Note I do not say . . . . . . . . . it . We must keep it and its advocates (doctors and . . . . . . . . . entrepreneurs) under control. Hospitals, with their massive costs, expensive equipment and . . . . . . . . . to technology have elbowed themselves into the centre of the medical . . . . . . . . . consuming now some 70 per cent of available . . . . . . . . . The debate concerning the . . . . . . . . . of heart transplants offers a useful lesson. It has been carried on . . . . . . . . . by doctors as if what was at . . . . . . . . . was a . . . . . . . . . technical matter instead of a . . . . . . . . . question as to the . . . . . . . . . . . . . . . . . . . of our health care resources.

You will now hear the same passage being read out on the tape recorder. Listen carefully and try to work out the words that are missing from the passage above. When the passage is finished you will have one minute to fill in the blanks.

The passage will then be played a second time. After this you will have one minute to fill in any remaining blanks.


## Item 8:  Speaking ability

Each student is required to repeat after the teacher five sentences of increasing length and complexity. The sentences are based on textbook material but are not exactly the same.

The teacher reads out each of the sentences from Form A below and gives the first student time to reply. He/she does likewise with the second student using Form B.


*Form A*
Fuad is thin.
He's very tall.
He's got brown hair.
He's a farmer from Azraq.
He lives in a nice house.

*Form B*
Ali is fat.
He's very short.
He's got brown eyes.
He's a teacher in Irbid.
He lives in School Street.

## Item 9:  Speaking

*Interview: Personal questions*

Each student is asked five different questions by the teacher after the two initial warm-up questions:

*warm-up questions (not marked):*

How are you?
What's your name?

What's his/her name? (to other person in the pair)
Can you speak English?
How would you rate your proficiency in spoken interaction in colloquial French?
When's your birthday?
What do you do this morning?
What do you do when you are bored?
When do you get up in the morning?
Are you a good swimmer?
When do you go to bed in the evening?
What do you like eating?
What do you think of nuclear disarmament?

## Comment on Exercise 1B

Below you will find comments on the faulty items you have evaluated which exemplify a reflective critical approach to test task design. These will enable us at the end of this chapter to draw up a framework of general principles and specific guidelines for use both in test construction and in evaluating tests.

## Item 1:  Knowledge of tenses: multiple-choice question format (MCQ)

A multiple-choice question test item (MCQ) is usually set out in such a way that the candidate is required to select an answer from a number of given options, only *one* of which is correct. In the example presented here, two of the four options are acceptable. Because of limited context in the stem there is often a case for more than one option being semantically acceptable in items set in this format.

The scores gained in MCQ tests, as in true—false tests, may be suspect because the candidate has guessed all or some of the answers. A candidate might get an item right by eliminating wrong answers — a different skill from being able to choose the right answer in the first place.

MCQs take much longer and are more expensive and difficult to prepare than more open-ended items. This item should have been rigorously edited to ensure that:

1. The rubric is not more complex than the item.
2. The language is concise and at an appropriate level for candidates.
3. There is no superfluous information in the stem.

4. The spelling, grammar and punctuation are correct.
5. Enough information has been given to answer the question.
6. There is only one unequivocally correct answer.
7. The distractors are wrong but plausible.
8. The responses are homogeneous, of equal length, and the item is appropriate for the test.

Item 1 fails on all of these counts.

TOEFL is an examination which until recently depended heavily on the multiple choice format. However, there are signs that even TOEFL may be moving to more direct, more communicative tasks.

An invitational conference was held by Educational Testing Service (ETS) at Princeton (see Stansfield 1986) to explore ways in which TOEFL might be made more communicative and was in itself evidence of a limited acceptance of the worth of more direct, communicative approaches to testing. A number of the participants contributed papers which argued for more domain specific tasks whereby TOEFL might fit more easily into a framework of communicative competence.

It is interesting to note that in response to requests from end users of test scores, ETS introduced a direct writing task, the Test of Written English (TWE) in 1986. This direct test of writing proficiency is not, however, compulsory in all administrations. A multiple choice test of structure and written expression is still used to make statements about a student's potential writing ability in an academic context.

The psychometric attributes of the multiple-choice format are obviously part of its attraction. The fact that it can be machine scored extremely quickly, reliably and cheaply is compelling when large numbers of students are involved. The format is not without its problems, however, and is increasingly perceived as an invalid method for assessing comprehension (particularly in the case of listening, see Heaton 1975). The General Certificate of Secondary Education (GCSE) examinations in the United Kingdom no longer employ the technique, apparently because of widespread hostile comment from teachers' organisations on its validity as a teaching and testing technique.

There is also some concern that students' scores on multiple-choice tests can be improved by training in test taking techniques and that such improvement reflects an enhanced ability to do multiple choice tests rather than any increase in language ability. This is a matter which is in need of serious investigation.

There is also some evidence (see Weir 1983) of a method effect at work in multiple choice tests. The scores obtained by candidates might be affected by the method used. This is not a problem with direct measures of language ability.

Completing multiple-choice items is an unreal task as in real-life one is seldom presented with an array of options from which to make a choice to signal understanding. Normally, when required, an understanding of what has been read or heard can be communicated through speech or writing. In a multiple-choice test the options present choices which otherwise might not have been thought of. There is no way we can tell whether a candidate would have got the right answer or made the correct response if this had not been provided as an option. The problems of guessing compound the difficulties associated with the format.

Perhaps the strongest argument against teachers concerning themselves with this format is that it is extremely difficult and time consuming to develop a sufficient number of decent items on a passage. Items need to be thoroughly trialled before we can be confident of their statistical properties, eg, facility and discrimination. Given how difficult it is even for seasoned professionals to write such items, there must be a serious question mark over their use in the classroom.

There is a very real danger that item writers become so ensnared with the intricacies of the construction of such items that they lose track of the more important issues of what constitutes an understanding of a passage or what constitutes writing or listening ability. The latter are issues which are far more worthy of our attention as teachers and testers.

## Item 2: Lexical knowledge: gap filling

The format suggests a text but there is a lack of coherence as illustrated by the tense shifting. As far as possible we should expose learners to genuine well-written texts although this may be difficult at the elementary level.

If this item is testing grammatical knowledge, some part of linguistic competence, it is not clear how to judge performance on it in terms of ability to use the language for communication. As with Item 1 it is difficult to report results other than as a quantitative score. It is not easy to make clear statements about what students can or cannot do with the language on the basis of this sort of test of grammar and/or vocabulary.

There is more than one possible answer, which in this item raises issues of validity, and of reliability of scoring. If you are hoping to elicit a specific lexical item then this open-ended format may not be the best way to do it. The importance of building in a sufficient degree of contextualisation is clear from this example. It must be clear to the candidate what is expected of him/her.

The instructions (the rubric) are not very clear and the language is more difficult than the test item itself ('appropriate lexical item'). It is not clear how many words are required. All of these points will affect the reliability of the test; they will limit the extent to which one could depend on the results.

In the last gap the candidate has to come up with the correct verb as well as the correct tense. The candidate also has to know the positioning of the negative between the auxiliary and the main verb. Item 2 might be testing grammatical knowledge as well as vocabulary as stated.

## Item 3: Knowledge of spelling: unscrambling letters

This takes an excessive amount of time to work out and even if you can do it you are left wondering whether it was worth doing anyway. Is it a test of spelling or of mental gymnastics? It is analogous to doing a crossword, which involves some sort of acrostic ability. If you do not know the word, how can you spell it anyway? When in real life do we have to do such exercises? What language-using capacities do such tests predict? How does one gauge difficulty level of decontextualised linguistic items?

The instructions are potentially more difficult than the items. In addition they are ambiguous as the candidate may infer that he/she is to form as many words as he/she can from each set of jumbled letters. It illustrates clearly the need to weigh the time a test takes to do against the information on language ability that it provides. The cost effectiveness of this test type is questionable.

### Item 4:   Working out the meaning of words from context: short-answer questions

The problem here is that it is not clear what is being tested. There are two possible options for some items but not for others. As with most of the examples presented in this faulty items section, no clear example is provided.

The only way we could be sure of what the items are testing (and this is true for all items, even good ones) is to ask students what they are doing in order to complete the items.

If it is supposed to test working out the meaning of unknown words through the surrounding context then this only seems to work for a few of the items. Some items cannot be worked out by recourse to the context, e.g. *tell*. Matching words with dictionary definitions is not the same thing as working out the meaning of words from context.

Is it an economic use of time to measure such a restricted part of the reading skill? Under which skill would you report the results of these items — reading or writing? If they contribute to a reading profile, how does this exercise relate to normal reading? When do we ever read a passage and then examine a set of definitions to see which of the latter do not have a lexical equivalent in the former?

This item raises the issue of how we decide which lexical items in a passage to select. Which lexical items contribute most to the meaning of a passage? On what principled basis should we select them?

In this manufactured example the rubric is more complicated than the task. In no sense is it 'candidate friendly'. It is also misleading as the words are underlined, not italicised as identified in the rubric. This alone might create unnecessary stress in candidates and is a glaring example of poor proofreading.

### Item 5:   Writing ability: essays

This writing item offends most of the criteria normally associated with communicative testing. Why is no addressee specified? What is the purpose of each task? If the tasks produce different text types are they therefore not comparable? No information is given on length or on time to be taken. Are the tasks of the same level of difficulty conceptually, lexically, structurally or discoursally? If not, then unequal demands are being placed on candidates by different questions.

Essay (a) is likely to be culturally biased as well as being dependent on differing knowledge bases. (b) is likely to place fewer demands on candidates than the others. (c) is likely to be biased in favour of those with some sort of scientific background. (d) is going to involve creating a text out of the candidate's head.

Some of these items are potentially non-authentic and do not reflect the way we use language for expository transactions in real life. They are functionally inadequate. For example, how would one generalise from performance on (b) or (d) how this candidate might perform in an academic course of study? Would writing this descriptive narrative give you any indication of an ability to write a laboratory report? We need to ensure that test tasks involve discourse processing and creation as similar as possible to those obtaining in the real-life target situations of the candidates taking the tests.

No guidance is given as to the criteria by which they will be marked so candidates may lose marks unnecessarily, say by an undue concern for accuracy as against coherence. Given that each task will result in a different text type it is difficult to believe they are testing the same writing ability. As a result it will be difficult to compare the performances of students who have completed different tasks even if the same assessment criteria could be used in marking the written products. The test writer must be clear about what an item is designed to measure and how performance on that item will be assessed before the candidates sit the test.

## Item 6:  Reading comprehension: short-answer questions

This is a very early example of a reading task from one of the more innovative examining boards who have since produced some excellent tasks (see Example 3.5 in Chapter 3 below, p. 86). This particular example from the 1982 paper approximates more to an authentic task but there are too many texts and too many questions testing the same thing. Having repeatedly to read through the advertisements can be demotivating. Furthermore, in real life we would normally scan such a series of advertisements with certain criteria in mind in order to select a single company. There is an important issue of task purpose here. Does the task reflect a realistic purpose? Does the discourse processing accord with what we normally do in real life?

Text and task may be irrelevant to certain groups of students. In certain cultures there are no credit cards that will do nicely (question(b)) and one might not be able to make the cultural leap in (c) that one would not expect to have to catch a bus to the garage to pick up the limo.

A difficulty with this item for the candidate is that because an example is given in which there are four answers an expectation might be built up that there are four required in questions (b), (c), (e), (f), (g) and (i). No indication is given to the candidate that this is not the case for other questions requiring more than a single choice. A good deal of time might be wasted by searching for advertisements to bring the answers up to four on these. One must be careful not to set up false expectations in the test taker.

The rubric could be improved also as it does not fit neatly with question (j) which is not homogeneous with the other questions. It is not clear either how much is required as an answer for (j) or how its adequacy would be judged. Given the different number of answers to the other questions it is not clear if they are differentially weighted. Some candidates might be penalised if they wrongly assumed they were all worth the same and so spent an equal amount of time on each.

The time to do this item is stated but it may be a bit short, given the number of times one is expected to work through the text.

### Item 7:   Listening ability: listening recall

The difficulty here is in explaining what the item is testing. The rubric is also fairly complex and it is not clear whether the invigilator should prevent candidates (if possible) from writing when they first listen. First the candidate has to read the passage although the task is stated to be a test of listening. A constant problem we will meet is: if we want to test one skill, how can we do it without other skills interfering in the measurement? In this case would the students' listening score be affected by their reading ability? It is not made clear to the candidates how many words are missing.

### Item 8:   Speaking ability: sentence repetition

It is difficult to say with any degree of precision what this item is testing. It appears to most teachers to be testing an ability to decode and repeat sounds with some involvement of short-term memory. Is it just testing an ability to repeat and if so how far does this accord with our construct of listening? Is it more a test of listening than speaking? Is this a problem? A lot of interest is being generated in this technique because it is so practical and early evidence suggests its use may well be justified. The technique is examined more closely in Chapter 2 below.

### Item 9:   Speaking: interview: personal questions

This is one of the most traditional formats for testing spoken language ability. Its major drawback is that the interaction is mainly controlled by the examiner and there is no possibility for spontaneous development of the discourse on the part of the candidate. There is no opportunity for the candidate to ask questions in this one-way 'interaction'. It only bears a limited resemblance to normal spoken interaction. We will examine this technique in more detail below in the chapter on speaking (see pp. 56−61).

Only one-word answers are needed for some of the questions here and the item lacks most of the normal features of spoken interaction. For example, both participants would normally contribute to an interaction and share the responsibility for keeping it going.

There is a lot of topic switching which may put undue pressure on candidates at the lower levels. Such frequent switching is not usual in conversation. Moreover, because of the predictable nature of some of the questions this could lead to rote memorisation of answers in preparation for the test.

In addition, a number of the items might well be too difficult in terms of both propositional content and linguistic structure for the students. This item also raises the serious issue of task dimensions. How do we ensure equivalent input for different candidates? Describing what you like eating is not really making the same demands on candidates as giving views on nuclear disarmament.

An attempt will now be made to try to generalise from the experience of evaluating the faulty items. In Section 1.3 below the general principles which guide all test construction are outlined and suggestions included for specific guidelines for writing test items. These guidelines have been arrived at with the help of colleagues in many countries around the world working on the faulty items as you have done. Do not worry therefore if you do not have all the points made below in your own list of guidelines. The points below are the product of a lot of people's ideas.

## 1.3    General principles and specific guidelines for test construction

### 1.3.1    *Testing as a group activity: the need to moderate tests*

The one inescapable guideline is that test writing should not be a solitary activity. Others will see problems with your tests that may have completely escaped your attention. They may interpret rubrics or items in a different way. They may find other errors that you cannot see because you are so close to the items, having spent a long time constructing them (see Item 4 especially). Whenever possible you should give tests, instructions and marking schemes to interested colleagues for their comments. Get them to do the test to see if they have any problems or if they produce any alternative, unanticipated answers. By doing the test they should be able to make reasonable statements about what they think the items are testing. They may feel that you are not testing what you want to test through a particular item. This is vital information and is part of the essential validation of the test.

All tests need to be thoroughly moderated before they are administered. The discussion of tasks and criteria of assessment is in fact a key contribution to achieving valid and reliable testing procedures.

### 1.3.2    *General principles*

The group moderating the test might first consider the extent to which it meets a number of general principles that should underlie all good test design: tests need to be valid, reliable and practical. These general principles are briefly examined below (see Weir 1990, Chapter 2 for an extended discussion of their nature and relationship to one another).

### Validity

A test should test what the writer wants it to test. It should be valid. Test validity presupposes that the writer can be explicit about what is to be tested and takes steps to ensure that the test reflects realistic use of the particular ability to be measured. As far as possible a test should limit itself to measuring only what it is intended to test and not extraneous or unintended abilities. To the extent that we succeed in this the test will be valid. If tests suffer from any of the faults identified in the faulty items section above it is possible that test validity may be threatened.

It is considered axiomatic in the approach advocated below that test writers should try to ensure that what students are asked to do in tests approximates as closely as possible to real-life language use. They should be set tasks which involve realistic language activities performed under appropriate conditions. Formats selected should incorporate as many important real-life features as possible. Full authenticity of task or genuineness of text will not, however, be attainable in the tests we write. It will not be possible to replicate reality fully, amongst other things because of the strong pulls of the other general principles of reliability and practicality we discuss below. However, we need to make our tests as valid as possible in terms of activities and performance conditions if we are to say anything meaningful about candidates' abilities in using the language. The key task for teachers, testers and researchers in the immediate future is to determine which of the features we have identified matter.

The major focus of Chapters 2—5 below is on establishing frameworks for constructing test tasks in the various skill areas which can help us to identify more closely what we want to test. The aim is to try and make an initial identification of important features of real-life use of language which might be considered for incorporation into test tasks.

To the extent that tests can have a beneficial influence on the teaching that precedes them, there can be a positive washback effect from tests on teaching. It is important therefore that tests sample as widely as possible relevant, criterial and communicative items from the syllabus or from the future target situation where this can be specified. The more representative the sample of tasks from the desired domain, the better the washback effect. The purpose of the test must be clear to all students taking it and teachers preparing candidates for it. The more it enhances the achievement of desirable language objectives the greater its contribution to successful teaching and the more all concerned will see the value of testing in the curriculum.

## Reliability

Validity is the starting point in test task design. However, for a test to be valid it must also be reliable. If a test is reliable you should be able to depend on the results it produces. If you gave the test again you would hope to get much the same results, although various factors might intervene to render this unlikely. If you gave your students an equivalent test that you have confidence in, the two tests should give you a similar picture of students' language abilities.

Marker ('rater') reliability makes an important contribution to overall test reliability. If we have different markers for a writing test will they arrive at the same results? What steps can we take to ensure that different markers will give the same picture of somebody's ability, so that they can maintain consistency in their own standards of marking from the first to the last piece of written work? The closer the agreement in these matters, the more reliable a test. The test must be reliable. Without reliability the validity of a test is impaired. A test cannot measure what you want it to measure if the score for a given ability fluctuates randomly.

Reliability is often connected with taking enough samples of a student's work. The more evidence we have of a student's ability the more confident we can be in the judgements we make concerning this ability. In Item 5 the students only have to do one writing task. If we gave the test again would we get similar results? To what extent can we depend on the results of one camera shot of writing ability?

We want sufficient information from a test to be able to depend on the results. This argues for a longer test but we must also remember the candidates. If it is not possible to spread the testing over a few days and we have to test for a long period on one day we might affect the results if some candidates become overtired or bored. Equally if a test were spread out over several days, the time spent might be considered unreasonable by candidates and administrators alike.

Though reliability is an essential principle to be met in test task development, reliability on its own is insufficient. Reliability without validity is pointless. Item 7 generates a lot of items and hence has every possibility of being a 'reliable' test, but it is difficult to say what it is testing and how this item relates to listening ability. A similar comment could be made in relation to response elicitation (Item 8). A test may be reliable, but if it is difficult to say what it is testing, because it is an indirect indicator of a particular ability, then its value is limited. To make worthwhile statements about a candidate's ability we have to make our tests as direct as possible. The more the test incorporates criterial features of real-life language use the easier it is to go from the test to make statements about a candidate's proficiency in the language.

If the test is not well administered unreliable results may occur. Precise steps should be laid down to ensure that the test is administered in exactly the same way whoever is in charge or wherever it takes place. This requires that exam invigilators are provided with a clear and precise set of instructions and are familiar and comfortable with all aspects of the test before administering it; test conditions, especially rooms in listening tests, should be of equivalent standards and suitably equipped (chairs, desks, clock, etc.); test materials and equipment should be carefully screened for any problems before the test is administered; procedures for dealing with candidates' cheating should have been sorted out in advance with the invigilators; all administrative details should have been clearly worked out prior to the exam, in particular ground rules for late arrivals, the giving of clear test instructions, ensuring candidates have properly recorded names and other necessary details. An example of a set of instructions for invigilators is provided at Appendix B.

As well as ensuring that tests are well administered and that we elicit sufficient data to enable us to make judgements about candidates' language abilities, many of the points emerging in the faulty items, if taken note of, would help make our tests more reliable (see Section 1.3.3 on moderation of tasks). Rubrics should be clear and candidates in no doubt as to what is required of them by each item; mark schemes should be comprehensive and markers standardised to these (see Section 1.3.4 on the moderation of the mark scheme and more specifically Section 5.3 on the marking of writing); all candidates should take the same items (see Item 5 above); they should be familiar with and preferably practised in the formats in the test.

### Practicality

Consideration must also be given to practical matters. How much data does the test provide on the candidates for the amount of time spent on designing it, administering it and marking it and processing the results? In other words how cost effective is the test? Item 3 is not efficient in this sense as it takes quite a time to complete for very little useable information. Teachers cannot afford to spend too much time in writing tests or take days testing students and marking scripts. Resources are often limited.

The context for the implementation of tests is a vital consideration. What resources are available? How much paper is available? If you can confine answers to one side of A4 this helps with copying/printing which in many countries can itself be a major hurdle to improving testing procedures. In terms of both paper and reprographic facilities colleagues in many countries face severe problems. What rooms are available? Often resources are limited and equipment such as tape recorders (or even electricity) may not be available. The tests selected should not strain the existing resources. Classroom tests should not require costly specialised equipment or unusual conditions, or highly trained examiners or markers. This means that we have to be sure that the tasks we are using are the most efficient way of obtaining the information we need about the test takers. The test must be practicable.

Examining boards have produced some excellent examples of information transfer tasks, such as reading tests where candidates transfer information onto an elaborate diagram (see Weir 1990, Appendix IV for examples of these). However, there is an important general issue underlying the use of such pictorial stimuli and that is the criterion of replicability. Many textbooks on testing include attractive examples from the examining boards using information transfer techniques, but unfortunately the graphic ability or draughtsmanship required to produce such material is beyond the range of most teachers (and testers!). As we will discuss below this means that the format is not as readily accessible to teachers as these textbooks might imply.

There is often a great deal of pressure on teachers to make tests as short and hence as practical as possible but this should never be allowed to put at risk test validity. It inevitably happens that, in the operationalisation of tests, certain authentic features of real life are sacrificed. The problem remains that, unless the tasks we use allow us to make the statements we want to make about performance, then we are wasting our time. There is a danger in employing practical but indirect tasks such as Item 7 because we cannot clearly state how the item relates to the construct of listening comprehension. If we cannot show how our tests relate to the skill being measured, it is going to be difficult to say what the pass score should be or what is an adequate performance on the test. The same comment holds true for Item 8 as a measure of speaking. The less direct the test, the more difficult it will be to translate test scores into behavioural specifications. If compromises are to be made we should attempt to minimalise any threat to validity.

As well as the general considerations of validity, reliability and practicality, the group should moderate the draft tasks, paying close attention to the specific guidelines below.

### 1.3.3  *Moderation of tasks: specific guidelines*

It is essential that tasks and marking schemes are subjected to a rigorous process of moderation before they are used. Using Murphy (1979) as the informing source, a number of important features of the test which should be considered at the moderation stage are discussed below.

### Level of difficulty

Are the tasks set at an appropriate level of difficulty?

If there is a variety of tasks/items testing a particular ability, try and put easier tasks/items first, as this will encourage all students to try their hardest and show their best. If you start with the most difficult task the weakest will soon give up. Within tasks it may not always be possible to begin with the easier items as one would want to preserve the sequential ordering of items in relation to their occurrence in the text (see Hughes 1989: 130).

### Discrimination

Will the paper discriminate adequately between the performances of candidates at different levels of attainment?

Even in achievement tests one might wish to include some of the more difficult elements from the syllabus which will be achievable perhaps by only the best students in the class. For obvious reasons the number of these would have to be limited so as not to demotivate the others, and one would ideally want them to come at the end of a test.

### Appropriate sample

Does the test assess the full range of appropriate skills and abilities, as defined by the objectives of the syllabus and course book units?

Each test is a sampling from a domain. In achievement testing this is defined by the content of the course and the methodology that has been employed in the classroom. However, though the boundaries may be clearer in achievement testing, a decision still has to be made in terms of what to sample. In Items 1−4 above the key decision is which lexical or structural items should be selected. How does the test writer determine the sample of the domain?

In most cases syllabus designers and course book writers do not state what is criterial in their courses, nor provide any other assistance in testing achievement. The teacher, therefore, is faced with the task of selecting what he/she believes to be criterial, in the course that has been taught, for inclusion in the test. What is included will be used for making wider statements about a student's ability in relation to all that has been taught or learnt.

What is included in an achievement test should be seen by students as worthwhile and a reasonable sample of what has been learnt. Where a future use of the language is specifiable, the test should match this as far as possible. Sampling should try to cover a wide range of the important test activities and conditions discussed in relation to skills tests below. To the extent that the future target situation is specifiable it should be feasible to match tests to future language use and make tests as direct as possible.

### Overlap

Is there an excessive overlap in structures, skills or communicative tasks being assessed in different parts of the test (see Item 6)? Try to avoid making tasks overlong or repetitive. Tests should avoid visual and mental overload.

**Clarity of task**

The test tasks should be unambiguous, giving a clear indication of what the examiner is asking. All tests must be carefully proofread and glaring mistakes eliminated (see Item 4 above). No candidate should be able to misinterpret the task. Avoid trick questions or anything designed to mislead.

The test rubric should be candidate friendly, intelligible, comprehensive, explicit, brief, simple and accessible (see Items 4 and 6). The rubric should not be more difficult than the text or task. In monolingual situations where complex instructions are involved it is preferable to give them in the candidates' first language though there may be strong views against this in some countries. It would be difficult, however, to argue that a test should aim to test comprehension of a rubric. Tasks might usefully be explained verbally in the mother tongue to pupils at the start of each sub-test.

If a new technique is to be employed (e.g. listening recall, Item 7 above) candidates should have been given sufficient practice in it before coming to the test proper. In achievement tests they should have practised it in class; in proficiency tests samples should be available beforehand in practice books or briefing documentation.

In general it is helpful to give candidates a clear sample item as an example before the test proper. This should reduce the possibility of candidates' scores being adversely affected by unfamiliarity with the particular test format adopted. Candidates' best performances will not be elicited in any type of test if the format is unfamiliar to them.

**Questions and texts**

In comprehension tasks the difficulty should not lie in the questions but in the text, that is the language of the questions should be easier than the text. Conversely, the questions should not be so simple or obvious, or answerable from world knowledge, as to make it possible to look first at the questions in a comprehension test and complete these successfully without recourse to the text. You should always get colleagues to read your test questions without reading or listening to an accompanying text. Any items they can get right without the text are dubious.

In general one should avoid interdependence of items, i.e. answering one question should not be dependent on ability to answer another. If the items are not independent then one may not get an accurate estimate of the ability being measured.

**Timing**

Can the tasks be answered satisfactorily in the time allowed (see Item 6)? A reasonable amount of time must be provided for the majority of the test takers to be able to complete the task. Remember the test-taking experience at the start of this book. If too little time is made available, stress will result and we will not be eliciting the student's best performance. It must be clear to candidates how much time should be spent on each part of a test. The amount of time should also reflect the importance of this element in the part of the course or the domain being tested. Where feasible, setting appropriate time limits is best done empirically. In other words, trial a test on a similar group to get a reasonable estimate or relate to similar tasks that have been taught during a course.

The time to be spent on each task should be clearly indicated on the test paper and the invigilators should encourage students to comply with the instructions.

**Layout**

Those moderating the test might consider the format and the layout of the question papers. These should be candidate friendly. This is important because a badly laid-out question paper could be the cause of considerable problems for both candidates and examiners. If the candidates have to turn over pages to answer questions based on an earlier text this will create problems. If a test is not clearly printed the effect may be similarly disruptive.

**Bias**

A test may be biased through training in particular techniques such as answering multiple-choice questions (MCQ) or cloze where the method involves the candidate in language processing which bears little resemblance to the way language would be produced or understood in real life. In addition to bias resulting from people being familiar with and practised in a test technique such as MCQ, bias can also result from experiential, cultural or knowledge-based factors (see Items 5 and 6). This is often a problem when tests written for students of English studying in Britain are taken by students abroad. We should avoid specific testing of cultural or subject knowledge in language tests and to this end avoid any texts which may give an unfair advantage to a particular section of a test population.

Conversely, we should avoid texts and tasks that may be so obscure that test takers have no existing schemata (frames of reference) into which they might naturally process information and thereby comprehend. All are thus disadvantaged and the validity of the test impaired as it fails to reflect normal discourse processing. The nature of texts and tasks and students' familiarity with them all need serious consideration.

### 1.3.4  Moderation of the mark scheme: specific guidelines

As well as having a clear idea of what they are expected to do and how to set about it, candidates should be given a clear idea of how they will be judged (see Items 5–9). If different parts of the test are weighted differently then the timing or marks to be awarded should reflect this and be evident to the test takers so that they can allocate their time accordingly. The criteria by which their answers will be judged also need to be made apparent, e.g. if accuracy is important in answering comprehension questions this must be made clear (see Items 5 and 6). This information should be available to candidates and their teachers prior to the examination.

The adequacy of an answer to an item must be measurable. This means that the tasks set must be constrained so that answers of vastly differing quality do not result and create problems for marking and reporting of results (see Items 5 and 6 above).

As you construct each test, draw up a mark scheme. Decide how you are going to mark an item and assign the relative weighting of that part as you create tasks. Ensure that the number of items reflects the weighting for the skill in the specification. It is important that the test writer is clear about how the test is to be marked before candidates sit it. If there is to be more than one marker then a full answer key must be provided. (This should ideally contain all possible acceptable answers.)

Work out how the examiner will record the marks. This is especially important for an oral test where the interlocutor might also be the marker. In productive tasks the marking criteria must be clearly laid out and the examiners standardised to these. Examiners should all be trained to mark answers applying the same criteria in the same way. Ground rules for accepting alternative answers from those prescribed would need to be established in advance.

While the tasks are moderated the people involved should consider the appropriateness of the marking scheme. Murphy (1979) is a valuable source for drawing up a list of questions which might be asked of the marking scheme.

The following are examples of the types of questions moderators might address:

- Does the mark scheme anticipate responses of a kind that candidates are likely to make? For example, what variations in spelling might be accepted in responses in listening and reading tests? Does the mark scheme allow for possible alternative answers?
- Does the marking scheme specify performance criteria to reduce as far as possible the element of subjective judgement that the examiner has to exercise in evaluating candidates' answers, especially in production tasks?
- Are the marks allocated to each task commensurate with the demands that task makes on the candidate? In listening tasks should all parts be weighted equally? In writing tasks for beginners how many marks should be given to a copying task? How many to gap filling, etc . . .? Does the mark scheme indicate clearly the marks to be awarded for different parts of a question or the relative weighting of criteria that might be applicable?
- Has the mark scheme minimised the examiner's need to compute the final mark for a candidate?
- Are the abilities being rewarded those which the tasks are designed to assess? For example, if candidates have to write down their answers in a listening test and we take marks off for errors in writing, then writing has become an element of the task.
- Can the marking schemes be easily interpreted by a number of different examiners in a way which will ensure that all mark to the same standard? Are the criteria for the marking of an essay sufficiently explicit to avoid differences in interpretation?

### 1.3.5  Standardisation of marking: specific guidelines

Even if examiners are provided with an ideal marking scheme, there might be some who do not mark in exactly the way required. The purpose of standardisation procedures is to bring examiners into line, so that candidates' marks are affected as little as possible by the particular examiner who assesses them.

Examiners might well be requested to attend a standardisation meeting before beginning marking proper. Here the marking criteria would be discussed to ensure the examiners understand the criteria that are to be applied. The marking scheme is examined closely and any difficulties in interpretation are clarified. Tape or script libraries may be set up to provide examples of performances at the prescribed levels.

At this meeting the examiners have to conduct a number of assessments. In respect of an oral test this might involve listening to and/or watching audio tape or video tape recordings of candidates' performances on the test, at a number of different levels.

The examiners are asked to assess these performances and afterwards these assessments are compared to see if they are applying the same marking standards. The aim is to identify any factors which might lead to unreliability in marking and to try and resolve these at the meeting (see Section 5.3 below for an exercise on this).

In the case of new examiners there might also be extensive discussion with the supervisors about how to conduct an examination, how to make the candidate feel at ease, how to phrase questions, what questions to ask in an interview situation, the type of prompts they might give to weaker students and how to react to candidates.

Once the standardisation has been completed there must still be checks. In tests of writing, sample scripts should be sent in to be re-marked by the supervisors so that the process of ensuring reliability can be continued. Supervisors may sometimes sit in unannounced on a number of oral tests, observe how they are conducted and subsequently discuss the allocation of marks with the examiner. They might discuss how improvements could be made either in technique or in marking.

In this chapter we have reviewed the general principles and specific guidelines which need to be considered in test task design. These are summarised in Table 1.1. It will be important to refer back to this checklist in Part II of the book when we consider testing the various skills and examine in detail the test formats we might employ. Applying this checklist to any tests you want to give to your students will help you determine if any improvements need to be made.

Table 1.1
*Framework 1: Summary checklist of general principles
and specific guidelines for test construction*

**General principles**

| Testing as a group activity | Reliability |
|---|---|
| Validity | Practicality |

**Specific guidelines**

| *Moderation of tasks* | *Moderation of mark scheme* | *Standardisation of examiners* |
|---|---|---|
| Level of difficulty | Acceptable responses/variations | Agreement on criteria |
| Discrimination | Subjectivity in productive tasks | Trial assessments |
| Appropriate sample | Weighting (items/tasks) | Review of procedures |
| Overlap | Computation | Follow-up checks |
| Clarity of task | Avoidance of muddied | |
| Questions and text | measurement | |
| Timing | Accessibility/intelligibility of | |
| Layout | mark scheme | |
| Bias | | |

## 1.4   The communicative imperative

Wherever feasible we would want test tasks to be as direct as possible, incorporating as many of the criterial features of real-life language use as we can. The first step to achieving this is to ensure that the conditions under which activities are performed in the test reflect those that obtain in the real-life situation. Contextualisation of items is important in enhancing authenticity. Given that our aim is to teach our students to communicate through English, the more directly we can incorporate criterial features of real-life use into our test tasks by getting candidates to perform authentic activities (operations) in realistic contexts (conditions), the more positive the washback effect is likely to be on the teaching that precedes the test. If the test tasks reflect real-life tasks in terms of important identified conditions and operations it is easier to state what a student can do through the medium of English.

In classroom achievement testing the starting point must be to make our tests reflect as closely as possible what and how our students have been taught. In so far as we try to employ language activities in the classroom which will help develop the communicative abilities of our students, then this is a priority for testing as well.

In proficiency testing we are interested in measuring the language capacities necessary to function in a specified target situation in the future. Examples of such are tests of English for Academic Purposes designed to measure whether students have the proficiency necessary to cope with the linguistic demands of academic courses taught through the medium of English. Again the sensible option is to try and ensure that our test tasks mirror salient features of the real-life situation; so we should make them as realistic and as direct as possible in terms of the conditions and operations we can identify as important.

In Chapter 1 of the companion volume to this book, *Communicative Language Testing* (Weir 1990), an attempt was made to describe a communicative approach to language testing and the reader is referred to that chapter as useful background reading.

The starting point in the design of any test is to know what it is we want to test. At the very least a test writer (in this case you, the teacher in the classroom) must be explicit about what the skill to be tested consists of. However primitively, we must, therefore, attempt to write theory-driven tests. If we are going to use the results of tests to make statements about a student's capacity to listen, read, write or speak in a specifiable language situation then we have to be as sure as we possibly can that the behaviours that are elicited and assessed in the test match these capacities. The student must be asked to employ as closely as possible the skills we are interested in under the conditions that would normally obtain.

If we are preparing students for specifiable language use then we must be clear about the operations students will have to perform in that target situation, the conditions under which those tasks will be performed and the quality of output (level of performance) that will be necessary. In this way we may come closer to ensuring the validity of our tests. The analysis of a test task in terms of these features would indicate the degree to which it reflected the attributes of the activity in real life that it was meant to replicate. Furthermore, unless steps are taken to identify and incorporate such features it would seem imprudent to make statements about a candidate's ability to function in normal conditions in his/her future target situation.

We also have to ensure that the sample of communicative language ability in our tests is as representative as possible. What and how to sample with our tests is a key issue in language testing. If we are to extrapolate from our test data and make statements about communicative language ability in real-life situations, great care needs to be taken with the tasks we employ in our tests. The more closely we can specify what needs to be tested, the more representative our sampling in tests might become. The possibility of making our tests longer to achieve this should not be overlooked.

In the first half of each chapter below you will be expected to reflect critically on the nature of the skill under discussion. For example, in Chapter 2, Exercise 2A asks you to think about the operations you feel the skill of speaking involves. If you can be explicit about the nature of a skill you wish to measure, you are more likely to test in a valid fashion. In addition you will be asked in each chapter to give some thought to the conditions under which tasks are performed and the level of achievement that is expected on each. After each exercise a commentary is provided. A summary framework is then provided at the end of each section to act as a checklist when you are developing tests yourself or commenting critically on tests produced by other people.

In the second half of each chapter you will be given examples of formats commonly used for testing a particular skill. You will be asked to think critically about each format. You will be asked to consider *what* is being tested in each. This will involve evaluating each task in terms of the operations involved, the conditions under which the task is performed and how level is assessed. You will also have to consider *how* the skill has been tested in each format. To do this you will need to refer back to Table 1.1 above. The guidelines will apply to most of what we do, whatever skill or combination of skills we are testing.

# PART II

## Chapter Two
# *Testing spoken interaction*

## 2.1   A framework for testing spoken interaction

The most useful starting point for designing test tasks is to see where the theory and available descriptions of spoken language interaction can help us. We need to establish the important features of spoken interaction that might be built into our language tests so that we have a readily available framework to help us in their construction. We will consider in some detail those features of spoken interaction that available theory would suggest including in a test.

A three-part framework is proposed, covering: the operations (activities/skills) that are involved in spoken interaction such as informational routines, e.g. telling a story, and the improvisational skills that might be called into play when the performance of these routines breaks down, e.g. requesting clarification (see 2.1.1 below); the conditions under which the tasks are performed, e.g. time constraints, the number of people involved and their familiarity with each other (see 2.1.2 below); and the quality of output, the expected level of performance in terms of various relevant criteria, e.g. accuracy, fluency or intelligibility (see 2.1.3 below).[1]

The purpose of developing such a framework is to offer a tentative checklist of points in each of its three parts that might usefully be considered in the construction of language tests which lay claim to be assessing the construct of spoken language interaction. Although we may lack a fully comprehensive and accessible working model of language use, we should be able to describe the performance conditions, operations and criteria for assessing quality of output that are appropriate for our tests. The analysis of a test task in terms of these features would indicate the degree to which it reflected the attributes of the activity in real life that it was meant to replicate. The categories included in the framework are hypothesised as being important, but only in the light of empirical research will it be possible to state with confidence which are the most important variables.

### 2.1.1   Operations

Either on your own or with colleagues, try to establish what you already know about testing spoken interaction by answering the questions in the exercises at the start of each section. When you have completed the exercise read carefully through the commentary that follows.

## EXERCISE 2A   OPERATIONS

What types of tasks in spoken English do your students need or want to practise?

For example, taking part in an interactional routine such as buying goods in a shop or in information giving such as describing an activity you have completed.

*Comment on Exercise 2A*

We will look first at the nature of speaking as a skill drawing largely on Bygate (1987) as our informing source. In order to be able to speak a foreign language, it is obviously necessary to understand some grammar and vocabulary (i.e. operate at the microlinguistic level in terms of Table 2.1 below) and have an idea of how sentences are put together. However, we spend most of our time actually using sentences to perform a variety of language functions and in so doing spend little time reflecting on the accuracy of our own or others' speech.

To test whether learners can speak, it is necessary to get them to take part in direct spoken language activities. We are no longer interested in testing whether candidates merely know how to assemble sentences in the abstract: we want candidates to perform relevant language tasks and adapt their speech to the circumstances, making decisions under time pressure, implementing them fluently, and making any necessary adjustments as unexpected problems arise (see Example 2.1, pp. 53−4).

There would seem to be a very strong case for testing spoken language performance directly, in realistic situations, rather than testing hypothetical knowledge of what might be said. If we wish to make statements about capacity for spoken interaction we are no longer interested in multiple-choice pencil and paper tests, that is, indirect tests of speaking where spoken language is conspicuously absent. To test speaking ability we should require candidates to demonstrate their ability to use language in ways which are characteristic of interactive speech.

The more direct we can make a test and the more we can incorporate contextual and interactional features of real-life activity into our tests, the more confidently we can extrapolate and make statements about what candidates should be able to do in that real-life context. The fewer features of the real-life activity we are able to include and the less direct the test, the more difficult it will be to translate performance in the test into statements about what candidates will be able to do with the language.

Bygate offers a useful description of how speakers organise in routines what they have to communicate. They have a repertoire of both informational and interactional routines which reflect their familiarity with certain kinds of communication. Routines are normally recurring patterns of organisation of communication, and can be found firstly in the organisation of information, and secondly in the organisation of interaction. As well as these, we need to be aware of improvisational skills which are brought into play when an interaction falters. In specifying what is to be tested either for achievement or for proficiency purposes, the test developer will need to identify what are the salient routines for the audience in question and what improvisational skills might be expected of them.

An outline of these is provided below, based on Bygate (1987). In making decisions on what activities to test it would be useful to refer to a listing of what has been taught or is necessary in the target situation.

*Routine skills*

### Information routines

These routines are conventional ways of presenting information, and are best seen as frequently recurring ways of structuring speech, such as descriptions, comparisons, instructions, telling stories.

They can be either expository routines — involve factual information which is typically concerned with questions of sequencing or identity of subject — or evaluative routines — involve drawing of conclusions, usually requiring expression of reasoning, explanations, predictions, justifications, preferences and decisions. These are normally made in connection with expository routines. Both types of informational routines can be catered for in test tasks such as oral presentations which cater for long turns, but they may also form part of interactional routines and may be tested through information gap tasks, role play or interview.

### Interaction routines

This kind of routine can be found in interactions such as buying goods in a shop, or telephone conversations, interviews, meetings, discussions, decision making, etc., which on the whole tend to be organised in characteristic ways.

*Improvisation skills*

The routines described above, if sufficiently grounded through previous experience, are normally available to us when we take part in a spoken interaction and allow us to select from a known repertoire at the planning stage. However, if something goes wrong with the communication of these established routines, improvisational skills are called for. A concern with these is only just starting to feature in some current language-teaching materials and most language tests have yet to take account of them. If teachers consider these to be important and teachable then we will need to think seriously how we might test a candidate's ability to improvise when communication is in danger of breaking down. As a first step in this process we will briefly examine the nature of this improvisational ability.

Most communication problems which occur in spoken interaction are normally solved through these 'improvisational skills'. Bygate (1987) describes how these consist of the ability to check on specific meanings, to alter wording, to correct mistaken interpretations, to enable speakers to make themselves understood and to deal with any communication problems that arise. Bygate identifies two major kinds of improvisational skills: negotiation of meaning and management of interaction.

## Negotiation of meaning

This is concerned with the way participants contribute to understanding during an interaction. It includes the procedures which speakers follow to ensure that understanding takes place. These might include conversational adjustments to maintain contact and knowledge of clarification procedures. Bygate describes how negotiation of meaning may involve the speaker indicating purpose, showing friendliness, checking that the other person has understood, establishing common ground, responding to requests for clarification, etc. The listener may similarly indicate agreement, understanding and uncertainty, or may request clarification.

This set of skills, then, focuses on the negotiation of meaning and covers broadly the monitoring of understanding. It may be that these can be built into a test, e.g. by the examiner feigning lack of understanding, thus forcing the candidate to clarify, etc., or it may be that they are taken account of only if they occur naturally in the discourse. Only through attempting to operationalise the testing of this ability will it become clear how practical this may be.

## Management of interaction

Unlike oral presentation tests, interaction-based tests allow participants a good deal more freedom of action, e.g. in deciding who is to speak next and what the topic is going to be. Participants can intervene as and when they desire. There is a need for at least one of the participants to take on responsibility for managing the interaction. Among other things, tests of this type might involve agenda management and turn-taking.

### Agenda management

This is concerned with control over the content and involves the participants' right to choose the topic, or introduce topics they want to talk about into the conversation. It also covers the question of control over the development or duration of the topic. This is more likely to occur in multi-participant test tasks such as group discussion, but it can be built into student—student information gap activities where one participant is given special responsibility for managing the agenda.

### Turn-taking

This refers to the question of who speaks when and for how long. It may include knowing how to signal that one wants to speak, recognising the right moment to get a turn, and knowing how to let the other person have a turn.

Where this is going to be assessed in the performance of test tasks it is important that the students are clearly aware of the features of turn-taking they will be expected to exhibit. This is perhaps best done in the form of explicit published assessment criteria for this element of spoken interaction.

### Summary

Speaking (in short turns) involves the reciprocal ability to use both receptive and productive skills in a continual encoding and decoding of developing message(s). This form of communication involves due observance of accepted routines and the continuous evaluation and negotiation of meaning on the part of the participants. Management of interaction may well be required with opportunity for agenda management and the need for conventions of turn-taking to be respected by participants. A summary checklist of the interactional skills we might want to think about including in our tests is included as Table 2.1. The test tasks we employ need to reflect the target situation in terms of the operations described above. In addition we need to try and ensure that the conditions under which the operations are performed similarly accord with that target situation as far as is possible within the logistics of the testing situation.

Table 2.1
*Summary checklist of spoken interaction skills*

**Routine skills**

*Informational* — frequently recurring patterns of information structure: conventional ways of organising speech:

(a)    expository: narration, description, instruction, comparison, story telling, giving directions, explanations, presentations.
(b)    evaluative: drawing of conclusions, justifications, preferences.

*Interactional* — typical ordered sequences of turns as in: telephone conversations, service encounters, meetings, discussions, interviews, conversations, decision making.

**Improvisation skills**

*Negotiation of meaning*
Use of discourse processing strategies to evaluate communicative effectiveness and make any necessary adjustments in the course of an event.

*Speaker may*: check understanding, ask opinion, respond to clarification request, check common ground.

*Listener may*: indicate understanding through gesture or summarising, indicate uncertainty, use elicitation devices to get topic clarified, express agreement/disagreement.

*Management of interaction*
*Agenda management*: choice of topic, introduce topic, develop topic, bring it to a close, change topic.
*Turn taking*: who speaks, when and for how long.

### 2.1.2  Conditions

In the discussion of spoken interaction above we have focused on the operations we might expect to see in many tests of spoken interaction. Of equal importance are the conditions under which these tasks are performed.

## EXERCISE 2B    PERFORMANCE CONDITIONS

What are the characteristic features of spoken interaction in terms of the context or the performance conditions under which the operations discussed above normally take place?

For example, in a conversation between two friends (familiar, peer/peer) one would expect both participants to contribute to the interaction (reciprocity) and there would normally be no long silences (normal time constraints).

Are there any practical problems in building such authentic contextual features into your tests?

For example, it may be difficult in a heterogeneous group to pair students of similar ability. Another constraint of operationalisability might be getting all students to contribute equally in an interaction, e.g. in a group discussion involving more than two participants.

*Comment on Exercise 2B*

Speaking involves the ability to use language to satisfy two particular demands which we should try and ensure are present in our tests of spoken interaction. The first is that of processing conditions, i.e. speech takes place under time pressure. In England only a relatively limited amount of silence is tolerated (in other countries, e.g. Finland, there may be far greater tolerance of silence between turns) and smoothness of execution is seen as evidence of fluency in the language. If it took an inordinate amount of time for a customer at a ticket sales counter to explain what he or she wanted, the other customers in a long queue behind might well feel that the condition of normal processing was not being met, and react accordingly. Giving prominence to normal time processing in language tests might encourage more practice in operating under this important condition in the language classroom.

It will also make a difference to what is said if the speaker has time to prepare in detail, as against having to speak extemporaneously. It is possible to distinguish between long and short speaking turns. Short turns are more common: usually more spontaneous loosely-strung-together phrases, rather than neat sentences. Long turns, e.g. oral presentations or lectures, require more planning decisions, and thus often tend to be more prepared. In tests where long turns are a feature, a decision has to be made as to how much planning time candidates should be allowed: three months, thirty minutes, two minutes, etc.

The second demand is that of appropriate reciprocity conditions. These are concerned with the dimension of interpersonal interaction, the relation between speaker and listener. The concern here is with the question of who has speaking rights and with the sharing of responsibility in the maintenance of an interaction.

The degree of reciprocity/participation in a developing interaction varies, depending on whether it is a lecture, interview, conversation, etc. In some situations, such as a formal lecture, only the speaker normally has speaking rights and takes on almost total responsibility for keeping the speech going. In a conversation, both participants normally have speaking rights, rather than the initiator alone.

In a reciprocal exchange the speaker must adjust vocabulary and message to take the listener's reactions into account. This process affects all participants involved in an interaction in that they share the responsibility for making communication work, with the consequence that each participant may be required to be flexible in communication.

In most speaking situations, the person we are speaking to is in front of us and able to put us right if we make a mistake. He/she can also generally show agreement and understanding — or incomprehension and disagreement. Speakers have to pay attention to their listeners and adapt their messages according to their listeners' reaction. If the listeners signal that they have perfectly well understood, it would be odd if the speaker persisted in explaining.

Clearly, if we wish to test spoken interaction, a valid test must include reciprocity conditions. This contrasts with the traditional interview format in which the interviewer asks the questions and the interviewee answers. So if we are interested in the candidate's capacity to take part in spoken interaction there should be reciprocal exchanges where both interviewer and candidate have to adjust vocabulary and message and take each other's contributions into account. This means that the candidate must be involved in the interaction to a greater extent than that of merely answering questions. It is worth noting that there may well be cultural problems here with some candidates, as what might be appropriate in terms of this condition may well vary from culture to culture.

### Further conditions in the testing situation

The important role of context as a determinant of communicative language ability is paramount. Language cannot be meaningful if it is devoid of context (linguistic, discoursal and sociocultural). The context must be acceptable to the candidates as a suitable milieu for assessing their spoken language ability. The conditions under which tasks are normally performed should obtain as far as is possible in the test. A conscious effort should be made to build into tests as many real-life conditions as are feasible and considered worthwhile by the test writers and their peers.

In this section we describe briefly some further conditions which need to be given due consideration and which will provide the milieu for the performance of various operations in our tests of spoken language interaction. Obviously the extent to which we can specify the conditions below will be dependent on familiarity with the target situation of the candidates taking the test. The problem of effective sampling from an unspecified domain is much more difficult. The closer we can identify which of these are salient features of the target situation, and the more we can include these in our tests, the more generalisable will be the results of our tests.

It may not prove possible or necessary to build all these conditions into a test. Only through teachers experimenting in the classroom will we discover what is feasible and, more crucially, which conditions are criterial. It may well be that some of these conditions will not be so important in certain contexts and to this extent compromise between authenticity and practicality will be made easier.

## Purpose

An important element to consider amongst the conditions is that of purpose. The purpose of the speakers will help to define the structure and focus of the interaction, as well as some outcome towards which the participants will be required to work.

It is highly unlikely, however, that any one test can accommodate the wide variety of conditions and operations that different situations might demand. It is argued that appropriately differentiated tests need to be made available for evaluating different groups of candidates with different target situation needs. To measure language proficiency adequately in each situation, account should be taken of why the language is to be used, where, how, with whom, on what topics, and with what effect.

The test writer needs to make it clear to candidates why they are doing the task (beyond demonstrating ability in a variety of features of spoken language). A good example of this can be found in the test for overseas doctors administered by the General Medical Council (the PLAB test) in Britain. Candidates might have to give a correct diagnosis on the basis of information provided by another medic, or elicit crucial symptoms from a patient before suggesting a particular course of action. In every sense there is a real purpose for these activities that matches very closely what they will have to do in real-life interaction.

Achieving such realism in tests for general English students may not be so easy, but the emphasis must still be on giving the interlocutors as realistic, and as needs-based a purpose as possible. Full authenticity of task may not be achievable, but we need to make our tests as valid as possible if we are to measure anything of value. The more we compromise the more difficult it will be to make meaningful statements about what candidates can or cannot do on the basis of test results.

## Interlocutors

The number of people involved in the interaction in the test should accord wherever possible with the situation in real life that one wishes to make statements about. Should it be a dialogue or a group discussion? The complexity of the task can be related in part to the number of people involved in an interaction and to the status of those involved, because of the demands this may make on formality.

It may well be easier for a candidate to speak to people with whom he/she is familiar. It may be easier to speak to a single peer rather than to an unknown authority figure such as an unfamiliar examiner. The more relaxed the candidate is, the greater the sample of language that might be elicited. The tester needs to consider with whom the candidates will be using English in their future target situations.

There may also be a gender effect in operation. Most students interact more easily with a female examiner. Women are likely to be better at keeping a conversation going whereas men are more prone to interrupt. The sexes of the participants should perhaps also correspond with those whom candidates are likely to have to interact with in real life. Obviously in certain contexts some of these features may be difficult to operationalise and in those cases testers may well have to compromise.

## Setting

The setting for the task also needs to be given due consideration. If the candidates are placed in a setting, say for a role play which is not likely to reflect their future language-using situations, validity is impaired to that extent. It is not possible to take all candidates into the dining room of a hotel in the country where the target language is spoken so as to enable them to use the language in a natural setting — as was done in some British army foreign language examinations after World War I. However, every attempt should be made within the constraints of the test situation to simulate reality as closely as possible.

Full authenticity of setting is obviously not attainable in the classroom, but the settings selected for testing and teaching should be made as realistic as possible, even if this means that the students have to imagine them on the basis of carefully designed rubrics. The roles allocated to students should certainly be within their experience and appropriate to their age and culture.

## Channel

The channel for communication can have an obvious impact on the performance. For example, it may place greater burdens on candidates if they have to simulate a telephone conversation with an interlocutor in a different room, as against carrying out a face-to-face conversation in the same room. It may be crucially important, say for air traffic controllers or business people, that they can cope with spoken interaction whilst being denied face-to-face contact.

Again, one has to resort to the demands that will be placed on candidates in the future target situation to inform judgements on the conditions that should obtain. This information is usually available from the tester's own experience of the target situation, but should always be checked out with reliable informants or, failing that, through some limited form of empirical needs analysis.

## Input dimensions

This is perhaps the least definable part of our framework and it may be problematic to put it into operation. We are concerned here less with the candidate's contribution to the interaction than with the speech of the interlocutor which the candidate has to process.

What is said to the candidate by the other participant(s) will influence his/her own performance. We need to take into account potential sources of variance in performance caused by features of the language used by the interlocutor, e.g. rate of utterance, accent of the examiner, clarity of articulation of the examiner, length of discourse (long turns by one interviewer may be more difficult to process than shorter turns by another).

To give candidates an equal chance to demonstrate their ability, it would seem that we should at least address the issue of how we might ensure that the size, complexity, referential and functional range of the other participant's contribution to the interaction should not be widely dissimilar from candidate to candidate. In other words the examiner/interlocutor's contribution to the interaction must be standardised as far as is possible. In peer/peer interaction we must try to balance the contribution of both participants in terms of the relative contributions.

The performance conditions discussed in this section are summarised in Table 2.2. We next turn to the third part of our framework which is concerned with the assessment of the quality of output arising from the performance of specified activities/operations performed under certain conditions.

Table 2.2
*Summary checklist of performance conditions (speaking)*

---

*Processing under normal time constraints*
Tolerance of silence in short turns. Planning time in long turns.

*Degree of reciprocity/participation in developing interaction*
Equal speaking rights. Shared responsibility for continuance of the interaction.

*Purpose*
Reason for doing it (beyond demonstrating xyz features of spoken language).

*Interlocutors*
*Number* of participants in the interaction: dialogue, group discussion.
*Status*: the social/professional status in real life of those involved: student, teacher, examiner, etc. Register: formal/informal.
*Familiarity:* participants known or unknown to each other.
*Gender:* male or female examiners/interlocutors for male or female students.

*Setting*
Physical.

*Role*
Appropriate to age and experience: friend/friend, undergraduate/supervisor, student/teacher.

*Topic*
Specificity, switching, familiarity, interest.

*Channel*
Telephone, face to face.

*Input dimensions*
Realistic task dimensions:
*Size*: processing appropriately sized input.
*Complexity*: language used, subject talked about.
*Range*: topics covered, lexical fields.

---

## 2.1.3  Level
*Problems in assessing spoken language*

### EXERCISE 2C   LEVEL OF PERFORMANCE

Having decided which spoken language tasks to include in your test, what problems are likely to be met in trying to rate spoken language ability?

For example, how long will it take? How can it be done reliably? What criteria should be used?

*Comment on Exercise 2C*

There are enormous practical constraints on the large-scale testing of spoken language proficiency. These include the administrative costs and difficulties and the sheer logistics of testing large numbers of candidates either individually or in very small groups. The extent to which the demands of validity can be met through direct tests of spoken language ability will depend on the particular situation test developers find themselves in. It may also be the case that what is relevant for teaching purposes may not necessarily be efficient, practicable, or cost effective for inclusion in tests.

Nor must we forget that the problems of assessing speech reliably are even greater than those for assessing writing reliably because the interaction, unless captured on tape or video, is fleeting and cannot be checked later. The importance of double marking for reducing unreliability is undeniable.

Despite these problems with reliability and practicality the essential task for the test designer is to establish clearly what operations the candidate is expected to perform and the conditions under which these tasks are to be carried out. Appropriate criteria for assessing the product arising from the elicitation procedures have to be agreed upon at this test design stage. These criteria need to reflect the features of spoken language interaction the test task is designed to generate.

It would be useful if the criteria employed in the assessment of language production on tasks could be related in a principled way to the criteria for the teaching of a skill: after all, conditions, operations and assessment should be relevant factors in helping the development as well as the summative assessment of skilled performance. If this relationship between teaching and testing could be strengthened, the important washback effect of test tasks on the teaching that precedes would be enhanced.

*Assessing quality of output: criteria*

The third element that needs to be considered in test task design is how we are to measure the quality of the output which results from the spoken language tasks we adopt.

The relationship between a task and the criteria that can be applied to its product, is an essential factor in taking decisions on what to include in a test of spoken or written production. Tasks cannot be considered separately from the criteria that might be applied to the performances they result in. Having established suitable tasks and appropriate assessment criteria to accompany them, consideration needs to be given as to how best to apply the criteria to the samples of task performance.

Just as in the rating of written tasks, so too in the measurement of spoken language there is a need to establish clear criteria for assessment and to standardise examiners in their use of these criteria. For a practical exercise relating to these procedures see Section 5.3 below. This exercise deals with the rating of writing tasks but much of the advice given is equally appropriate for assessing performance on spoken language tasks.

Normal spoken interaction is performance based, i.e. it involves memory limitations, distractions, shifts of attention and interest, and errors. We must not lose sight of this in assessing non-native speakers. Native speaker speech is characterised by compensation features such as self-correction, false starts, repetition, rephrasing and circumlocutions.

The processing conditions of oral language result in these common features so they should not feature in assessment scales to the detriment of candidates.

The assessment of spoken language is potentially more problematic than the rating of written scripts, given that no recording of the performance is usually made. Whereas in writing the script can be reconsidered as often as is necessary, assessments have to be made in oral tests, either during or shortly after the test. If the examiner is also an interlocutor then the problems are further compounded.

In oral testing, as in the assessment of written production, there is a need for explicit, comprehensive marking schemes, close moderation of test tasks and marking schemes, and training and standardisation of markers (refer back to Chapter 1, Section 1.3 above where these procedures are discussed extensively). They will all make a contribution to the reliability of the marking. In Chapter 5 the assessment of written production is considered in some detail and sample scripts are made available for rating practice. If videos can be made of candidates performing test activities these can subsequently be used for training and standardisation of marking in a similar fashion. The procedures outlined in Chapter 5 for rating written scripts are (*mutatis mutandis*) for the most part applicable to the assessment of spoken production.

In order to measure the quality of spoken performance, we first need to establish criteria of assessment. What follows is a set of suggestions for criteria that might be considered for assessment of the output of communicative spoken interaction tasks. Criteria are proposed for each of the three parts of our framework of operations: handling routines, handling improvisational skills and handling microlinguistic skills.

Testers may not wish to evaluate all three of these areas or to cover all of the suggested criteria even within a single area. This is a choice that has to be made individually in each testing context.

### Assessing the handling of routine skills

It is the effectiveness with which appropriate messages are communicated that is normally of interest in testing spoken interaction. To what extent can the candidate demonstrate an ability to meet effectively the demands of required informational or interactional routines?

It might be argued that if appropriate conditions and operations have been built into a test task these in themselves will serve to define what constitutes a certain level of performance, e.g. if candidates can perform routines abc under conditions xyz, this is what they can do. Different configurations might be established for different levels. The examiner decides whether or not candidates can successfully perform a given operation under a given set of conditions.

If it was necessary to be more specific about this functional effectiveness in performing routines the examiner might make specific assessments in terms of the following:

(i) Normal time constraints would have to be observed in all required routines. Fluency, as overall smoothness of execution of the task, would be assessed.

(ii) In addition one might want to comment on the discoursal coherence, that is, the internal organisation of the stages of the discourse. This may be especially relevant in longer turns.

(iii) Appropriateness: this would include the sociocultural ability to take into account setting, topic, role relationships, formality required (e.g. the *tu/vous* distinction). Due observance of the norms of interaction in terms of silence, proximity and dealing with encoding difficulties might be looked for.

If the task leads to the deployment of improvisational skills then we might also wish to develop criteria to take account of proficiency in the use of these.

### Assessing the handling of improvisational skills

This might involve the examiner taking a decision on overall effectiveness in two important improvisation abilities:

(a) Ability to negotiate meaning in cases of comprehension or production difficulties manifested on the part of the candidate or his/her interlocutor.
(b) Ability to manage interaction (agenda and turn taking) actively and flexibly. This is particularly important where speakers can be expected to be active participants.

If it was necessary to be more specific about the effectiveness in deploying improvisational skills the examiner might make detailed assessments in terms of the following:

(i) Fluency: that is, smoothness of execution. Ability to negotiate meaning would, for example, include the ability to use communication strategies with ease when in difficulties.
(ii) Appropriateness: this could include, for example, the degree of politeness and suitability of timing in turn taking or suitability of the language used in request for clarification or disagreement.

There may also be occasions, for example when the level of the candidates is quite low, that the examiner might need to make assessments at the microlinguistic level.

### Assessing the handling of microlinguistic skills

If the focus was on linguistic proficiency at the utterance level the examiner might wish to use the following criteria:

(i) Accuracy focusing on both intelligibility and grammar.
(ii) Range: adequacy and variety of vocabulary employed; adequacy and variety of structures employed.

In Table 2.3 we summarise the criteria that might be used to evaluate the various aspects of spoken interaction described above for assessing the handling of routines and the handling of any necessary improvisation and for operating at the microlinguistic level.

Testers also need to decide whether they will treat these criteria separately in an analytic scheme (lots of separate impressions) or try to collapse them into some form of global impression banding (see Tables 2.4 and 2.5 for some published examples of these). The decision on whether to use an analytical or a global impression band scale will largely

Table 2.3
*Summary checklist for assessing quality of output*

| *Handling Routines* | *Handling Improvisation* |
|---|---|
| Effectiveness | Effectiveness |
| Fluency (smoothness of execution) | Fluency |
| Appropriateness | Appropriateness |
| Coherence: organisation of discourse in long turns | |

*Handling Microlinguistic Skills*

Accuracy
Range

Table 2.4
*Analytic marking scheme (speaking)*

## Criteria of assessment

*Appropriateness*
0   Unable to function in the spoken language.
1   Able to operate only in a very limited capacity: responses characterised by sociocultural inappropriateness.
2   Signs of developing attempts at response to role, setting, etc., but misunderstandings may occasionally arise through inappropriateness, particularly of sociocultural convention.
3   Almost no errors in the sociocultural conventions of language; errors not significant enough to be likely to cause social misunderstandings.

*Adequacy of vocabulary for purpose*
0   Vocabulary inadequate even for the most basic parts of the intended communication.
1   Vocabulary limited to that necessary to express simple elementary needs; inadequacy of vocabulary restricts topics of interaction to the most basic; perhaps frequent lexical inaccuracies and/or excessive repetition.
2   Some misunderstandings may arise through lexical inadequacy or inaccuracy; hesitation and circumlocution are frequent, though there are signs of a developing active vocabulary.
3   Almost no inadequacies or inaccuracies in vocabulary for the task. Only rare circumlocution.

*Grammatical accuracy*
0   Unable to function in the spoken language; almost all grammatical patterns inaccurate, except for a few stock phrases.
1   Syntax is fragmented and there are frequent grammatical inaccuracies; some patterns may be mastered but speech may be characterised by a telegraphic style and/or confusion of structural elements.
2   Some grammatical inaccuracies; developing a control of major patterns, but sometimes unable to sustain coherence in longer utterances.
3   Almost no grammatical inaccuracies; occasional imperfect control of a few patterns.

*Intelligibility*
0   Severe and constant rhythm, intonation and pronunciation problems cause almost complete unintelligibility.
1   Strong interference from L1 in rhythm, intonation and pronunciation; understanding is difficult, and achieved often only after frequent repetition.
2   Rhythm, intonation and pronunciation require concentrated listening, but only occasional misunderstanding is caused or repetition required.
3   Articulation is reasonably comprehensible to native speakers; there may be a marked 'foreign accent' but almost no misunderstanding is caused and repetition required only infrequently.

*Fluency*
0  Utterances halting, fragmentary and incoherent.
1  Utterances hesitant and often incomplete except in a few stock remarks and responses. Sentences are, for the most part, disjointed and restricted in length.
2  Signs of developing attempts at using cohesive devices, especially conjunctions. Utterances may still be hesitant, but are gaining in coherence, speed and length.
3  Utterances, whilst occasionally hesitant, are characterised by an evenness and flow hindered, very occasionally, by groping, rephrasing and circumlocutions. Inter-sentential connectors are used effectively as fillers.

*Relevance and adequacy of content*
0  Response irrelevant to the task set; totally inadequate response.
1  Response of limited relevance to the task set; possibly major gaps and/or pointless repetition.
2  Response for the most part relevant to the task set, though there may be some gaps or redundancy.
3  Relevant and adequate response to the task set.

Source: TEEP, CALS, University of Reading.

Table 2.5
*Interview assessment scale: global impression marking scheme*

| Band | |
|---|---|
| 9 | Expert speaker. Speaks with authority on a variety of topics. Can initiate, expand and develop a theme. |
| 8 | Very good non-native speaker. Maintains effectively his own part of a discussion. Initiates, maintains and elaborates as necessary. Reveals humour where needed and responds to attitudinal tones. |
| 7 | Good speaker. Presents case clearly and logically and can develop the dialogue coherently and constructively. Rather less flexible and fluent than Band 8 performer but can respond to main changes of tone or topic. Some hesitation and repetition due to a measure of language restriction but interacts effectively. |
| 6 | Competent speaker. Is able to maintain theme of dialogue, to follow topic switches and to use and appreciate main attitude markers. Stumbles and hesitates at times but is reasonably fluent otherwise. Some errors and inappropriate language but these will not impede exchange of views. Shows some independence in discussion with ability to initiate. |
| 5 | Modest speaker. Although gist of dialogue is relevant and can be basically understood, there are noticeable deficiencies in mastery of language patterns and style. Needs to ask for repetition or clarification and similarly to be asked for them. Lacks flexibility and initiative. The interviewer often has to speak rather deliberately. Copes but not with great style or interest. |
| 4 | Marginal speaker. Can maintain dialogue but in a rather passive manner, rarely taking initiative or guiding the discussion. Has difficulty in following English at normal speed; lacks fluency and probably accuracy in speaking. The dialogue is therefore neither easy nor flowing. Nevertheless, gives the impression that he is in touch with the gist of the dialogue even if not wholly master of it. Marked L1 accent. |
| 3 | Extremely limited speaker. Dialogue is a drawn-out affair punctuated with hesitations and misunderstandings. Only catches part of normal speech and unable to produce continuous and accurate discourse. Basic merit is just hanging on to discussion gist, without making major contribution to it. |
| 2 | Intermittent speaker. No working facility; occasional, sporadic communication. |
| 1/0 | Non-speaker. Not able to understand and/or speak. |

Source: B.J. Carroll, 1980, *Testing Communicative Performance*.

rest on the degree to which one can describe in behavioural terms the different levels of proficiency that student performances will result in.

Given that our understanding of the continuum of proficiency in speaking is currently limited, we might be better served for the moment by analytical scales where assessments are made in terms of each criterion separately. Until we have a clearer idea of how criteria configure at different levels of proficiency the assumption that students improve at an equivalent rate in each criterion is unproven. We do not yet know whether different people remain static on a given criterion at any particular point on the scale, or whether there is any similarity between individuals. It would seem imprudent to rely on band scales which collapse criteria together and assume that students progress equally in all criteria as they move up the band scale (see Table 2.5).

If we apply analytical criteria to the spoken product of test tasks the issue still remains of what the profile of achievement of a successful candidate is. In other words we have to be explicit about the level of performance expected in each of the specified criteria (see Table 2.4). In addition, there is a question mark hanging over analytic schemes, as to whether they result in repeatedly assessing the same thing, the halo effect. One potential advantage of the analytical approach is that it can help provide a profile of a candidate's weaknesses and strengths which may be helpful diagnostically, and also make a formative contribution in course design.

The criteria in each of the three areas in Table 2.3 need empirical validation in the particular contexts testers find themselves in. First the tester would need to specify appropriate tasks in terms of conditions and operations and decisions could be taken iteratively on the criteria that are applicable to the output generated and the levels of performance within each of these. The dimension of practicality cannot be ignored here and the criteria developed would need to be readily deployable by teachers. It would have to be established how many criteria teachers could reliably handle. The criteria developed would need to be accessible to other teachers and the number of levels within each criterion would have to represent real distinctions in the performance of actual candidates.

It may well be that in any one situation not all the criteria suggested for assessing the routine skills, improvisation skills and microlinguistic skills would be applied by the assessors. The criteria used would depend on the nature of the skills being tested and the level of detail desired by the end users. The crucial question would be what the tester wants to find out about a student's performance on appropriate spoken interaction tasks. This is the crucial issue of test validity. Once the tester is clear about what to find out, then decisions on the appropriate level of analysis to be applied to the output from test tasks are easier to make.

So the starting point as always is test validity. What does the tester want to find out? In addition he or she needs to consider carefully what will be an efficient, practical way to elicit and assess these data. Finally, sound testing procedures have to be established to enable the tester to elicit and assess the data in as reliable a fashion as possible.

## 2.2  Formats for testing spoken interaction

Having established what it is that needs to be tested the test writer must decide which is the best format for operationalising the test specification. The range of formats available embraces the more direct types such as interaction between students (Example 2.1 below) and the face-to-face interview (Example 3.1 below), and the more indirect types such as response elicitation (Example 1.1 below). Directness here is a function of how closely a task relates to real-life performance (in terms of operations and conditions), and how far performance on the task can be assessed in terms which allow of direct comparison with that target performance. The more indirect the task the more difficult it will be to translate test results into statements about what candidates can or cannot do in terms of the real-life activity under review.

Below you will find a number of formats along this indirect–direct continuum. The idea is for you to reflect critically on the examples supplied of the various formats and determine the extent to which they allow the test writer to take account of the conditions, operations and criteria for assessing quality of output, discussed above, and the extent to which they exhibit good practice in test design.

The examples have been constructed for specific students in specific contexts. They are taken from a variety of levels from elementary to advanced. The particular conditions or operations in some examples may well be inappropriate for your students. The purpose of the exercise is that you should become aware of these formats, their advantages and limitations. You should think critically about them so that you can decide what would be most appropriate for the students you are responsible for in your particular context, or what alterations might be necessary before you could use them.

*Test formats to be reviewed*

1. **Indirect**
   1.1   Sentence repetition
   1.2   Mini-situations on tape
   1.3   Information transfer: narrative on a series of pictures

2. **Interaction Student with Student**
   2.1   Information gap exercise

3. **Interaction Student with Examiner or Interlocutor**
   3.1   The free interview/conversation
   3.2   The controlled interview
   3.3   Role play
   3.4   Information gap

## EXERCISE 2D   EXAMINING TEST FORMATS

Look at the examples of formats for testing speaking. For each format make notes on:

(a) What operation (s) each item is testing. Refer to the list of operations in Table 2.1 above. It may well be that you think an item is testing more than one operation. Try to decide in these cases what the major and minor focus(es) of the item are.

(b) What you think the advantages and disadvantages of testing speaking through this format are. You may wish to comment on the operations involved, the conditions (see Table 2.2) under which the task is performed, or the criteria you would employ in judgement of level (see Table 2.3). It is also useful to refer back to the general principles and specific guidelines for test construction developed in Part I of the course (see Table 1.1, page 27 above). This will also enable you to comment critically on any deficiencies in test construction the task may exhibit.

After each test format there is a commentary.

*1   Indirect formats*

**Example 1.1:   Sentence repetition**

The candidate is required to repeat each utterance exactly as it is heard. The utterance will be heard only once. If the candidate fails to repeat the statement and then the question at a given level try him on the next level up. If he gets both wrong, stop the test. The mark awarded is the number of the level at which the candidate gets both statement and question correct.

*You will hear a series of statements and questions. Each statement or question will be spoken once only. Repeat exactly what you hear to the examiner.*

1. Hello.
   What?
2. Sit down.
   You OK?
3. I'm a pupil.
   Who are you?
4. My school is here.
   Are you a pupil?
5. My parents live in Dakar.
   Where do your parents live?
6. Dakar is the capital of Senegal.
   What is the capital of Egypt?

7.  In my family there are eight people.
    Are there eight people in your family?
8.  I have got one sister and three brothers.
    How many brothers does your mother have?
9.  Both my father and my mother work in Dakar.
    Do your father and your mother work in Dakar?
10. My sister has got two friends in the twelfth grade.
    Has your sister got three friends in the ninth grade?
11. There are many nice trousers in the shops around the market.
    Are there any nice shoes in the shops around the market?
12. You can also see many green and red dresses at the market.
    Can you also see many black and yellow trousers at the market?
13. My brothers and me like football, and we play at home with friends.
    Do you and your brothers like playing football on Saturdays with their friends?
14. Someone in this class can tell me if there is a clinic in Dakar.
    Does anybody in this class know if there is a clinic in Freetown?
15. Ali is with Yemi and Fatou but he doesn't like the people at the police station.
    Does the boy who is with Ami and Sira like the people at his school?
16. The food in the nice motel was very expensive so we bought some yams in the market.
    What do you do when food in the one motel is too expensive to buy any lunch?
17. It's very cold and dark in here and I think there is somebody over there in that corner.
    Because it is dark and we are afraid there are ghosts in the room why don't we shout?

## Comment on Example 1.1

When used for assessing achievement, this sub-test normally reflects a spread of the structures occurring in the units of the course being followed by the candidates. Items should move from easier to more difficult. At the construction stage this is a matter of sentence length and giving some consideration to the lexical items and structures employed. The tests need to be trialled to ensure that the items are indeed in ascending order of difficulty, so if they get item 4 right the students also got item 3 right and so on.

Although it has a value in placement when time constraints apply, and although reliability figures are good, this still remains an indirect index of someone's speaking ability (see Henning, Gary and Gary 1983 for a discussion of the merits of a version of this procedure). It is very difficult to translate performance on this test into meaningful statements about somebody's ability to speak the language. It is also difficult to say with any degree of precision what it is testing beyond short-term memory. In terms of our framework it elicits very little data on any of the operations and it involves very few of the performance conditions we might be interested in including. It seems to be functioning purely at the microlinguistic level. In terms of criteria for assessing quality of output similarly only those criteria applicable to the handling of microlinguistic skills are applicable.

Interestingly, if recorded on tape, it does have one advantage in terms of satisfying the condition of equitable input dimensions. All candidates receive exactly the same input. Because we can thus be sure that the task dimensions are equivalent for all candidates it allows reliable comparisons across and within test populations.

Though reliability is likely to be quite good, there is a possibility of some score variation by markers and this would need to be guarded against. In addition, there are obvious concerns about its validity which make it an unlikely choice for a proficiency or achievement test where you need to say what scores on the test mean in terms of what candidates can or cannot do with the language. It is difficult to say with this task what would be an appropriate level for students to achieve. The scores obtained on indirect tests of language ability do not easily lend themselves to meaningful interpretation.

Practicality and reliability are not in themselves sufficient reason for adopting a test format. A test must be a valid measure of a particular ability as well if it is to tell us anything of value.

### Example 1.2:   Mini-situations on tape

This test takes place in a language laboratory. Candidates have to respond to a number of remarks that might be made to them, or to situations that they might find themselves in when they are in Britain.

*Task 1*
*First, you will hear a number of remarks which might be made to you in various situations when you are speaking English. Some are questions and some are comments. After each one, reply in a natural way.*

Here is an example:

  Sorry to keep you waiting.
  That's alright.

Now are you ready? Here is the first.

  1. Where've you been? We started ten minutes ago.
  2. It's hot in here.
  3. Didn't you see the red light?

etc . . .

Marking: intelligibility, appropriateness . . .

*Task 2*
*You will hear descriptions of a number of situations in which you might find yourself. Say what seems natural in each situation. Here are some examples:*

  1. You are not sure of the time of the next class. How might you ask your friend for the information?

2. You are late for an appointment at the Doctor's. What might you say to the receptionist when you arrive?
3. Your examination result was not as good as you expected. You would like to discuss your work with your tutor, and you would like to see him about it as soon as possible. What might you say to him?
4. Someone asks you what sort of weather you have in your country at this time of year. How might you answer?
5. You don't know where the local Health Centre is. Ask another student the way there.

etc . . .

Marking: intelligibility, grammar, appropriateness . . .


## Comment on Example 1.2

The use of a language laboratory for testing spoken interaction at first might seem self-defeating. The absence of a live interlocutor for the candidate to interact with denies any possibility of assessing extended interactional routines or the deployment of improvisational skills. In terms of many of the performance conditions we might want to build into a test it is also noticeably deficient, e.g. especially in terms of channel, reciprocity and purpose. As a result of these limitations the quality of output can only be assessed by a restricted range of criteria.

However, this test may have some advantages in terms of the conditions the tester is able to build into it. Perhaps the main benefit of recorded material is that it is possible to expose the candidate to a wide variety of speech events (different interlocutors, settings, roles, topics) in a short space of time. Against this it might be argued that because this involves a high degree of flexibility in jumping from situation to situation we may be placing unfair demands on candidates.

This format shares the advantage of Example 1.1 that all candidates receive exactly the same input and so the task dimensions are equivalent for all. This is a desirable condition that is much more difficult to attain in the more direct tasks we will examine below.

As the candidate's responses are recorded, reliability can be enhanced. Double marking is possible and the recording can be replayed. Reliability is further enhanced by the large number of items that this format can incorporate. In normal interaction it may also be difficult to make reliable judgements about the candidate's ability to operate appropriately in a variety of situations. The tape format lends itself to this more readily. Thus in terms of sampling this format has the advantage over a number of the later examples.

A big advantage of this format is its practicality. In those situations where language laboratory booths are available as many as forty candidates can be examined at any one time. As the performances are recorded they can be marked at a time suitable to the examiner(s).

## Example 1.3: Information transfer: narrative on a series of pictures

The candidate sees a panel of pictures depicting a chronologically ordered sequence of events and has to tell the story in the past tense. Time is allowed at the beginning for the candidate to study the pictures.

THE ASSOCIATED EXAMINING BOARD
*for the General Certificate of Education*

Ordinary Level

Specimen Picture order no 1          FRENCH ORAL EXAMINATION          034/4
138/4

NOTE TO CANDIDATES. CANDIDATES ARE REMINDED THAT THE NARRATIVE BASED ON THE SERIES OF PICTURES SHOULD BE TOLD USING THE PAST TENSES. NO NOTES MAY BE MADE.

**Comment on Example 1.3**

The technique is straightforward and much favoured by school examination boards in Britain. In the study of suitable formats for a spoken component for TOEFL (Clark and Swinton 1979) this proved to be one of the most effective formats in the experimental tests. The task required of the candidates is clear. It does not require them to read or listen and thereby avoids the criticism of contamination of measurement. An important proviso is that the value of the technique is dependent on the pictures being clear and unambiguous and free from cultural or educational bias.

It can be an efficient procedure and one of the few available to get the candidate to provide an extended sample of connected speech, a long informational routine, which allows the application of a wide range of criteria in assessment including coherence as the organisation of discourse in long turns. It is also useful for eliciting the candidate's ability to use particular grammatical forms, such as the past tense for reporting.

Because all candidates are constrained by common information provided by pictures or drawings (the same dimensions of input), it is possible to make a comparison of candidates which is relatively untainted by background or cultural knowledge, given that the drawings themselves are culture free.

If the quality of the pictures is in any way deficient then the candidate may not have the opportunity of demonstrating his best performance. Differences in interpretation might also introduce unreliability into the marking.

Our comments on information transfer tasks in the reading and listening sections below provide evidence of the value of this technique in screening out the potential impact of other skills on the measurement of the skill under review. The main problem we identify of the difficulty teachers may have in being readily able to produce the visual non-verbal stimuli applies here as well. This in the end may be the biggest limitation of the use of this technique in the classroom and teachers may resort to student-prepared talks with all their associated problems as a result.

The technique is, however, non-communicative, as one might seriously question when students ever need to do this kind of thing in real life. A claim might be made for construct validity in that the technique may well be tapping into the informational routine of reporting. Describing something which has happened may well be an important operation in some occupations, but, generally speaking, this task tells us very little about the candidate's ability to interact orally or to use improvisational skills such as negotiation of meaning or agenda management. The format does not allow the tester to incorporate the important condition of reciprocity which can only be tested in a more interactive format.

## 2 Interaction student with student

In this type of test where the examiner takes no part, candidates should be more at ease and they have more opportunity and inclination to speak. They can also select in advance whom they wish to do the test with so that they are interacting with somebody they know and feel happy communicating with.

In these tasks students normally work in pairs and each is given only part of the information necessary for completion of the task. They have to complete the task by getting missing information from each other. Candidates have to communicate to fill an information gap in a meaningful situation.

As a development from this interaction an interlocutor appears after the discussion and the candidates might, for example, have to report on decisions taken and explain and justify their decisions. The interlocutor is normally known to the students and might be their teacher.

Tasks should be explained clearly to students before they start. The teacher should interfere as little as possible and only prompt where absolutely necessary. Prompts should be in L1 in monolingual situations and no direct clues should be given to pupils about what to say.

In the example given below, candidates in groups of two or more have to organise and maintain some kind of discussion in which each student is to have more or less an equal amount of speaking time. The task involves taking information from written texts and arriving at a consensus on certain matters through interaction. If it is an achievement test then the content may well have already been practised in class in a comprehension exercise and the vocabulary and structures pre-taught. The students would not have seen the actual spoken language task before the test but may well have practised on similar activities. The task is normally set up so that there is no single correct solution.

### Example 2.1:  Information gap exercise

The situation is that one of the candidates (student B) has won a competition and the prize is £90. He or she would like to buy a camera. The two candidates are asked to decide between four cameras and decide which is the best camera to buy. Student A has information on two cameras and student B has information on another two. They have to exchange this information verbally (only) and decide which camera to buy. Tell them they have ten minutes to complete the task.

*Student's prompt sheet A*
You will find below information on two cameras, A and B. Your friend has information on two more cameras, C and D. Your friend has won some money in a competition and wants to buy a camera. Using the information you both have, you must help him/her decide which camera to buy. Make sure you check all the information before deciding. When you have finished discussing, you should tell your teacher which camera you would buy, and why. Wait for the other person to start the conversation.

|          | Price (£) | Weight (grams) | Size   | Flash |
|----------|-----------|----------------|--------|-------|
| Camera A | 90        | 250            | small  | +     |
| Camera B | 80        | 300            | medium | +     |

*Student's prompt sheet B*
You have won some money in a competition and want to buy a camera. You have £90 to spend. You will find below information on two cameras, C and D. Your friend has information on two more cameras, A and B. Using the information you both have, you

must decide which camera you would buy. Make sure you check all the information before deciding. When you have finished discussing you should tell your teacher which camera you would buy. You must take the responsibility for starting the discussion and reaching a decision. You only have ten minutes for this.

|  | Price (£) | Weight (grams) | Size | Flash |
|---|---|---|---|---|
| Camera C | 60 | 250 | small | — |
| Camera D | 80 | 550 | small | + |

*Alternative:*   It would be possible to adapt this task for use with four students at a time. Each student would be given a prompt sheet with only one of the four sets of details filled in. Each student would be asked in turn by a different member of the group about the various elements — cost, weight, etc. — and the other students would complete the details on their own sheets. In this way each student would get the opportunity both to ask and to answer questions. Next any student would be allowed to ask for any missing information on any of the cameras. The final stage would be a discussion on which camera should be bought. This could be structured by first having A/B talk and then having C/D talk and finally the group as a whole coming to an agreement.

Further alternatives could easily be constructed using: cars, motorcycles, watches, pens, etc . . .

## Comment on Example 2.1

Tasks of this type can be interesting and incorporate real materials from everyday life. The students have to solve a problem, report conclusions to a third party and support these in argument, thus covering both interactional and informational routines.

The task is interactive and as such comes much closer than most other tasks under discussion to representing real communication. It recognises the unpredictability of communicative situations and demands an ability to generate original sentences and not simply the ability to repeat rehearsed phrases.

As a normal feature of the interaction elicited by this example, candidates use question forms, elicit information, describe, make requests, make comparisons, give opinions, state preferences, give explanations, persuade, come to decisions, etc. They perform a range of the operations we identified earlier as occurring in normal spoken interaction.

The interaction is here purposeful and unpredictable. Negotiation of meaning is required to arrive at a suitable outcome and the tasks are designed to encourage cooperation and a desire to arrive at a consensus. Because the candidates' contributions are unpredictable, they are less likely to have been rehearsed beforehand, as happens in many traditional interview situations. The candidates have to monitor and respond to the discussion spontaneously. An appropriate level of explicitness is required in order to decide on the best choice of camera.

Some improvisational skills may well be called upon, e.g. candidates may need to indicate purpose, check on understanding, ask the other person for forgotten information, ask for and give opinions, check common ground, clarify by summarising, indicate understanding by gestures and other paralinguistic means, indicate uncertainty and/or lack of comprehension, express agreement or reservation, negotiate meaning by making and/or responding to clarification requests in order to succeed in the task, correct misinterpretations, and make themselves understood.

The task allows candidates to develop the activity in their own way and each participant has to respond and adjust to interlocutor feedback. There may well be agenda management even when done in pairs and this can easily be built into the task explicitly through the test instructions. In classroom testing it is perhaps best if one candidate is given a primary responsibility for this as in the example above (this role can then be swapped around during the course). Candidates need to ensure adequate cooperation and participation from their partner in the task in order to complete it.

The task will certainly involve turn taking and candidates will have to signal when they want to speak, recognise the right moment for taking a turn, know how not to lose their turn, recognise others' signals of a desire to speak and know how to let other people have a turn. The candidates could be warned in advance which aspects of negotiation of meaning and agenda management would be monitored in any assessment of improvisational skills.

Additionally, by providing students with all the information they need one is attempting not to disadvantage those with lack of knowledge about the topic.

In terms of the conditions under which the task is performed there can be few test tasks which represent the act of communication better than this particular type as it fulfils most of the criteria for what makes a test communicative: that it should be purposeful, contextualised and interactive. Normal time constraints obtain, allowing performance to be assessed for fluency in terms of smoothness of execution. Both participants have a responsibility for keeping the interaction going until the objective is realised, so reciprocity is a marked feature of this task with both contributing, taking what the other person says into account and reacting to it. The role, setting and purpose are reasonably realistic for most teenagers and the task has the advantage of allowing them to interact with peers who are familiar to them. The task dimensions were appropriate for the original target group for the test and were closely checked against the course book and previous learning experiences in the classroom in terms of the length of the discourse, its propositional and linguistic complexity and the range of structures and lexis that were needed.

Perhaps the biggest advantage of this task type is a practical one, namely its replicability. Such tasks can easily be reproduced by teachers in a multiplicity of forms by varying the details of the items to be discussed. With a word processor this would take very little time and would make a valuable contribution to test security.

The topic may affect performance, and fluency of contributions in particular. The familiarity of the candidates with each other could also have an effect. The contributions of individuals may vary as a result of these factors and though this is true of real-life discussions it may affect the assessment of certain individuals if they say relatively little.

There is a potential problem with the reciprocity condition if one of the participants dominates the interaction, as the other candidate may have a more limited opportunity to demonstrate communicative potential. Similarly, if there is a large difference in proficiency between the two, this may influence performance and the judgements made on it.

There is also a problem if one of the candidates is more interested in the topic or the task, as the interaction may become one sided as a result. If candidates are being assessed on their performance in a single situation on a task such as this, and extrapolations are made about their ability to perform in other situations from this, the resulting extrapolation may be equally one sided.

Practical constraints on this type of task include the time available, the difficulties of administration and the maintenance of test security where parallel forms are not readily available.

There also needs to be some suspension of disbelief as the natural tendency would be for candidates to show each other the information each is given as a prompt.

In terms of our framework, this format comes much closer than any of the others to allowing the test writer to build in a wide range of the conditions and operations which currently appear to characterise spoken interaction.

## 3   Interaction student with examiner or interlocutor

### Example 3.1:   The free interview/conversation

In this type of interview the conversation unfolds in an unstructured fashion and no fixed set of procedures is laid down in advance.

### Comment on Example 3.1

Because of its face and content validity in particular, the unstructured interview is a popular means of testing the oral skills of candidates. These interviews are like extended conversations and the direction is allowed to unfold as the interview takes place. The discourse might seem to approximate more closely to the normal pattern of informal social interaction in real life, where no carefully formulated agenda is apparent.

The candidate is able to take the initiative, change the direction of the interaction and introduce new topics. It at least offers the possibility of the candidate managing the interaction and becoming equally involved in negotiating meaning.

The open procedure in Example 3.1 has a higher degree of content and face validity than most other techniques, apart from the role play (see Example 3.3) and the information gap exercise (Example 2.1 above). The free interview indisputably involves interaction. In general the development of the interaction will be unpredictable and processing will normally take place in real time.

The interview to a certain extent provides a predictable context (in terms of formality, status, age of the interviewer, etc.), but the interviewer will affect the context created by the attitude adopted and the role selected. The candidate will have to react to this. In addition he or she will have to interpret and produce language that is cohesive and coherent in terms of the linguistic environment of the interaction. The candidate and the interviewer will have to react to the communicative value of various utterances.

The flexibility of the interview is a major strength. The interview can be modified in terms of the pace, scope and level of the interaction. The good candidate can be pushed to the level of her/his ability in the hands of a skilled interviewer. Such flexibility of stimuli is not possible with other more structured forms of oral assessment. The assessment of speaking and listening in this integrated fashion covers what Carroll (1980) described as 'the constructive interplay with unpredictable stimuli'. The format should enable the examiner to apply all the criteria outlined above for handling routines, improvisation and microlinguistic skills if appropriate.

A particularly effective oral interview can occur when the candidate is interviewed and assessed by both a language examiner and a subject specialist who have been standardised to agreed criteria. The procedures followed in the General Medical Council's PLAB oral interview which assesses both medical knowledge and spoken English merit consideration in this respect.

One of the drawbacks of the interview is that it cannot cover the range of situations candidates might find themselves in, even where the target level performance was circumscribed as was the case of the American Foreign Service Institute (FSI) oral interview (see Hughes 1989: 110–13, and Adams and Frith 1979).

In interviews it is difficult to replicate all the features of real-life communication such as motivation, purpose and role appropriacy. The language might be purposeful but this is not always the case and there may be exchanges in which the questioner has no interest in the answer. This is particularly so when the questioner already knows the answer (a problem with asking questions on a single picture). Normally we are communicating because we are interested in what somebody is saying, rather than how he is saying it. The intrusion of the latter into a conversation might have a dampening effect. The purpose of assessment is not in itself communicative, except of course for language testers.

It is difficult to elicit fairly common language patterns typical of real-life conversation, such as questions from the candidate. Interviewers often manipulate conversations to get candidates to say things employing a variety of structures. This might reduce the authenticity of the discourse. It is unlikely, however, that a trained examiner would produce simplified language (slow rate of delivery or lexical or structural simplification) except where this is necessary with very weak candidates. This presumably would be taken into account in the assessments made.

As there are no set procedures for eliciting language, candidate performances are likely to vary from one interview to the next not least because different topics may be broached and differences may occur in the way the interview is conducted. The procedure is time consuming and difficult to administer if there are large numbers of candidates. The success of this technique is heavily dependent on the skill of the examiner. The shy, more inhibited candidate might not do as well as the more extrovert, more garrulous one.

### Example 3.2:   The controlled interview

In this format there are normally a set of procedures determined in advance for eliciting performance. The interviewer normally has decided on the questions to ask and what to find out about the candidate's language ability. He or she normally manages the interaction and retains the initiative in selecting and developing the topics. The candidate normally only speaks in response to stimuli from the examiner. The interview is usually face to face. It normally starts with personal or social questions designed to put the candidate at ease. It may then enable the candidate to speak at length about familiar topics and perhaps finish at the higher levels with more evaluative routines such as speculation about future plans or the value of an intended course of study once the candidate returns home.

(a) The first example is of a controlled interview for students at the end of their first year of learning English (about seventy hours). One member of the team acts as interviewer, the other as assessor. At the end of each test, both will agree a mark for the candidate in each section and record this against the name of the student and his roll number. The interview will take about eight minutes and the interviewer will ask each candidate at least ten questions from the list shown in Example 3.2(a) below.

(b) The second example (3.2(b)) is a structured interview format used in early pilot studies in the Spoken Language Testing Research Project at CALS, University of Reading. The students interviewed are non-native speakers at a British university. The questions and statements form semi-scripted prompts for the interviewer.

**Example 3.2(a):  Controlled interview**

*Warm up (not to be marked):*
    What's your name?
    How do you spell that?
    Have you got a pen?
    Write your name on this piece of paper.

*Test proper:*
    What class are you in?
    How old are you?
    How many sisters and brothers do you have?
    How old they?
    I am a teacher. What does your father do?
    Where do you live?
    Can you count from ten to twenty? Do so.
    Can you tell me the time? What time is it?
    Can you speak English?
    Can you speak Japanese?
    When do you get up in the morning?
    When do you go to bed in the evening?
    What day of the week is it?
    What date is it?
    When's your birthday?
    What do you do on Sundays?
    What will you do after school today?
    What did you do yesterday?

What are you going to do next week?
What do you eat for breakfast/lunch?
What do you like to drink?
What's the weather like today?
What will it be like in . . . . .?
Do you like . . . .? Why? Why not?
How far is it from . . . to . . .?
How long does it take?

## Example 3.2(b): Structured interview

---

**INTERVIEW:     NB: Jot down notes, but don't spend a lot of time writing.**

**PART 1:**

1.  Student's name: _____

    What does s/he prefer to be called? _____

2.  Country: _____ What is the home town? _____ (or does s/he

    live in a village?) In what part of the country is the home town? _____

3.  Was the student born in the same place? (If so, did the family always live there, over

    the generations? If not, how did they come to move?) _____

4.  What kind of accommodation does the student have in Reading? Is it satisfactory for
    him/her as a graduate student, or are there problems? What are these?

    _____

5.  What is the student's opinion of Reading (or other University) as a place to study his/her
    subject? Does the department have any particular strengths/weaknesses?

    _____

6.  Why did they not do their graduate degree in their own country? What is the advantage
    in studying here?

    _____

7.  What job do they expect/hope to get when they finish their degree here?
    Will it pay a good salary?/Support a good life-style?

    _____

8.  Have they encountered any problems in Britain so far? Socially/with studies?

    _____

---

**PART 2:**

(In this part of the interview, encourage the student to go on at some length; you intervene as little as possible — but react with interest to what the student has to say.)

1.    Ask the student to explain his/her field to you; what does it involve, what is it about? (+ follow-up questions that occur to you.)

2.    Is the student's chosen field of study important to his/her country in particular? What is the importance? (If not to his/her country, then to the world in general?)

3.    What is it about the subject which particularly interested the student?

4.    How did the student come to be involved in this field to begin with?

Source: D. Porter, CALS, University of Reading.

## Comment on Example 3.2

During the interview, processing can take place under normal time constraints and the purpose of the interaction is acceptable to many candidates who may well face such a role in the future. It can put the candidate in the position of having to interact with somebody he or she does not know, of higher status and of either gender. These may be conditions which need to be built into the test to reflect the future use of the language. It is possible to test the candidate's ability to perform a variety of informational and interactional routines, and the examiner is in a position to assess improvisational skills as well, for example by asking for repetition, or clarification of responses.

In Example (a) above the candidate has to be extremely flexible and cope with frequent topic shifts which may not accord with desired performance in the future. The task could be much improved if early on in the interview the examiner could hit on a topic of interest to the candidate and then elicited the desired structures in relation to that topic. Example (b) is much more satisfactory in this respect as the areas for questioning are thematically linked and relate clearly to the life situation of the student.

It still remains difficult, however, even in a semi-structured interview, to satisfy such conditions as reciprocity, as the student is mainly cast in the role of respondent and there is little opportunity for him to take the initiative, manage the agenda, or take on responsibility for keeping the discussion going. In any interview the candidate is unlikely to walk in and say to the examiner, 'there are a number of questions I'd like to put to you'. Few demands are put on turn-taking ability either when the candidate is cast solely in the role of respondent.

Example 3.2 differs from 3.1 in that it allows more chance of candidates being asked the same questions. Thus it is easier to make comparisons across performances, and reliability is enhanced. Unlike some of the more direct tasks examined above one can be more confident that the input dimensions will be reasonably similar across candidates. The open interview in 3.1 does not share this advantage and different candidates may be expected to demonstrate their proficiency under a range of different task conditions. However, even when the procedures for eliciting performance are specified in advance there is still no guarantee that candidates will be asked the same questions, in the same manner, even by the same examiner.

With carefully prepared and agreed criteria, together with a reasonable measure of standardisation to these, a reliable and valid idea of a candidate's level can be formed. This type of interview is easy to set up and administer and has high face validity and potential scoring reliability. It has been shown that with sufficient training and standardisation of examiners to the procedures and criteria employed, reasonable reliability figures can be reached with both techniques. It can be efficient in diagnosing specific weaknesses.

It is time consuming and also expensive to administer when conducted on a large scale (the advantage of the semi-direct test such as the mini-situations in Example 1.2 is obvious here).

It may be difficult for the examiner in Example (b) to concentrate on what the candidate is saying and to reply accordingly as well as listen for how he or she is communicating. Thus in the FSI oral examination there was a separate examiner and interlocutor.

**Example 3.3:   Role play: student/examiner**

---

THE ASSOCIATED EXAMINING BOARD
*for the General Certificate of Education*

O LEVEL FRENCH

*Role-playing situation, Specimen No. 2*

NOTE TO CANDIDATES   NO NOTES SHOULD BE MADE DURING THE PREPARATION TIME EITHER ON SEPARATE PAPER OR ON THIS INSTRUCTION SHEET.

*Candidate's instructions*

Study the following situation carefully and be prepared to perform in French the role indicated.
. . . . . .

You are in a train in France, during the Christmas holidays, going to visit some friends in Avignon. The examiner will play the part of the only other passenger in your compartment.

1. Ask if you may open the window a little.

2. Ask how far he/she is going.

3. Discuss the possibilities of getting a cup of coffee on the train.

4. Invite him/her to go with you for a coffee.

---

THE ASSOCIATED EXAMINING BOARD
*for the General Certificate of Education*

O LEVEL FRENCH

*Role-playing situation, Specimen No. 2*

*Suggestions for possible development by examiner*

1. Before agreeing ask why. If too hot, agree, but say it's snowing outside so you might get too cold. If no reaction to that ask what he/she thinks you should do.

2. Going as far as Dijon. What about him/her? Discuss whether he/she lives at Avignon, length of journey, and ask whether he/she won't get hungry. If candidate says he/she is hungry, you could say:

   — there is a restaurant car;
   — would he/she like a sandwich/apple?

3. Perhaps the restaurant will serve coffee, but you don't know. What about getting a drink when the train stops at Dijon? (You could say if necessary that the train stops for 30 minutes.)

4. Before accepting, suggest looking for a snack-bar on the train, and raise the question of (a) losing seats or (b) having luggage stolen if you leave it.

**Comment on Example 3.3**

A number of examining boards include role play situations where the candidate is expected to play one of the roles in an interaction which might be reasonably expected of him or her in the real world. The interaction can take place between two students or, as in this example, the examiner normally plays one of the parts. Interactional, informational and improvisational skills may be demanded.

It is important that candidates are given a role they can identify with. Different situations can be created, albeit in imaginary settings, and the candidate has the opportunity to show an ability to change register depending on the interlocutor. The technique can be valid in both face and content terms for a wide variety of situations and the purpose should be clear and reasonable. The interaction is face to face; processing takes place under normal time constraints and reciprocity is an important feature of the interaction.

It would seem to be a practical and potentially a highly valid and reliable means of assessing a candidate's ability to participate effectively in oral interaction. In the AEB example the task is contextualised and the student has to take the responsibility for initiation. Though the content is controlled there is some room for development and hence unpredictability in the discourse. It enhances reliability in that there can be comparability from one candidate to the next as both structure and content are controlled.

There is of course a danger that the histrionic abilities of some candidates may weigh in their favour at the expense of the more introverted. There is also the danger in all oral interactions that a candidate cannot think what to say. Some people may be more able or more willing to suspend disbelief than others and for some it may be culturally inappropriate. The question of role familiarity arises in this technique, in the sense that some candidates may not know what it is normal to do in certain situations. Another problem is that candidates often use the language of reporting and say what they would say rather than directly assuming the role. If the candidate is instructed to do too many things he/she may not be able to remember them all without looking at the question paper.

Practical constraints operate here as well, especially in large-scale testing operations. If it is necessary to use different role plays then great care needs to be taken to ensure that they are placing equal demands on candidates. Candidates who have taken the test should be kept separate from those waiting.

As in the information gap exercise involving teacher as interlocutor and examiner, there is a danger that the mark awarded will reflect the latter's view of his own performance as well as of the student's. This format has been found to be quite successful when done in small groups with the examiner as observer. If the examiner is not involved in the interaction he has more time to consider such factors as pronunciation and intonation. There may be a problem with reliability where the examiner has to interact and form a judgement at the same time and the same is of course true of all face-to-face tests.

**Example 3.4:   Information gap: student/examiner**

To prevent the possibility of an imbalance in candidates' contributions to the interaction, some examining boards have the examiner as one of the participants, or a common interlocutor, perhaps a teacher whom candidates would feel comfortable with.

Candidates can be given a diagram or a set of data from which information is missing and their task is to request the missing information from the examiner and provide him/her with any required data on request.

Example 2.1 above could easily be adapted for the examiner/student format.

## Comment on Example 3.4

The main advantage of this method is that there is a stronger chance that the interlocutor will react in a similar manner with all candidates, allowing a more reliable assessment of their performance.

Interacting with a teacher, let alone with an examiner, is often a more daunting task for the candidate than interacting with his peers. There is some evidence that where the examiner is a participant in the interaction, he or she is sometimes inadvertently assessing personal performance in addition to that of the candidate.

Many of the points made in relation to Example 2.1 (information gap, student/student) above, in connection with the coverage of a wide range of conditions and operations in this format, apply here as well. This information gap format enables the tester to incorporate the majority of the features regarded as important, in the earlier discussion of the framework for assessing spoken language. As such it is highly recommended that teachers investigate its use.

## Note

1. The framework for the testing of spoken interaction draws heavily on the work of Martin Bygate of the Centre for Applied Language Studies at the University of Reading (see Bygate 1987) and an important contribution was made by two other colleagues in the Testing and Evaluation Unit at Reading University, Arthur Hughes and Don Porter. The substance of the approach appeared in Weir and Bygate 1990, a paper delivered at the RELC Conference, Singapore. We would refer interested readers to Martin Bygate's book *Speaking* (1987) for an extended discussion of the nature of tasks in spoken interaction.

# Chapter Three
## *Testing reading comprehension*

### 3.1 A framework for testing reading comprehension

What is reading comprehension?

Before we examine formats we might use for testing reading comprehension we need to think about what it is that we wish to measure. There are a number of comprehensive reviews of reading in a foreign language available (see Grabe 1991 and Williams and Moran 1989) which provide details of the current state of research, and implications for the classroom. In these overviews, reading is seen as a selective process taking place between the reader and the text, in which background knowledge and various types of language knowledge interact with information in the text to contribute to text comprehension (see also Carrell *et al.* 1988 and Alderson and Urquhart 1984).

Though the exact nature of this comprehension has not been established by research, we can come closer to understanding what it might consist of by looking at the nature of the texts people have to process and the reasons for reading these. In addition we will try to identify the types of underlying skills and strategies that from our experiences in teaching would seem to contribute to an ability to carry out these activities.

Our understanding of what goes on when we read can help us to understand what is involved in reading comprehension.

### EXERCISE 3A   TEXT TYPES

Make a list of the types of text that you have read in the last 24 hours, e.g. magazines, non-fiction textbooks. Write your list on the left-hand side of a piece of paper:

    magazines
    notes
    traffic sign
    cornflakes packet
    etc.

*Comment on Exercise 3A*

Of course we may often read something just because it looks as though it might interest us, e.g. an article about a country or a place we have visited or intend to visit, and conversely we may choose not to read something because it does not appeal to us.

At other times it may not be interest that is the deciding criterion but rather the assumed usefulness of the text. If we order or buy something that comes in kit form we often read the accompanying instructions on the reasonable basis that they will help us to put the thing together.

These categories of interest and usefulness are not mutually exclusive and we may read things that we need to read that are also interesting in themselves.

Most people process written text for a purpose; this may be for pleasure in the case of a novel or to find out how something works, as in a car instructions manual. Reading for a purpose provides motivation, in itself an important aspect of being a good reader (see Grabe 1991: 378). Normally people will have expectations about the content of a text before they start reading it and often they bring to the task existing knowledge about some or all of the content.

## EXERCISE 3B   PURPOSES

Go back to the list of text types you made earlier and against each write down your purpose(s) in reading this particular text, e.g. you might read a newspaper for general information or for specific information such as what time a programme is on television. Then compare your text types and purposes against those listed below.

*Comment on Exercise 3B*

Here is a list of some text types and possible reasons for reading them. Compare them with those you have produced (see also Cook 1990).

| | |
|---|---|
| *Cornflakes packet* | to find out what you are eating |
| *Traffic sign* | to find out the way |
| *Leaflet* | to find out how to make something |
| *Brochure* | to find out specifications |
| *Guide* | to find out where something is |
| *Advertisement* | to see if something is worth buying |
| *Letter* | to see who it is from and what it is about |
| *Postcard* | to find out who it is from |
| *Form* | to find out what information is wanted |
| *Instructions* | to find out how to put something together |
| *Timetable* | to find out the time of departure |
| *Map/plan* | to find your way |
| *Newspaper* | to find out what is happening in the world |
| *Telegram* | to establish the message that has been sent |
| *Books, fiction* | to gain pleasure |
| *Books, non-fiction* | to get specific or general information |
| *Articles* | to get information for an essay |

In constructing tests it is important to include texts and activities which mirror as closely as possible those which students have been exposed to and/or are likely to meet in their future target situations. The purposes for reading them in the test should, wherever possible, match the purpose(s) for reading those texts in real life. In reflecting on these matters you have begun to consider important conditions in the design of a reading test. We need to consider what other performance conditions — i.e. contextual features — we need to embody in our reading tests.

## EXERCISE 3C   PERFORMANCE CONDITIONS

So two important decisions on conditions in the testing of reading involve the text types to include and the purpose(s) for reading them. Make a note of other performance conditions/contextual features you might need to consider in the design of a reading test.

When you have finished compare your answers with the suggestions below.

*Comment on Exercise 3C*

### Performance conditions in the testing of reading comprehension

*Purpose*
We have discussed the importance of this in detail in Exercise 3B above. The purposes for reading involved in our tasks should be as appropriate as we can make them. We recognise the difficulty in achieving full authenticity of purpose in the test situation but would nevertheless wish to make our test tasks as realistic as possible (see Grabe 1991: 378).

### Nature of the texts (+ rubrics and tasks)

*Text type*
In achievement testing you will have a number of parameters already established, i.e. the text types you have used with the students (refer to Exercise 3A above). If you are writing a proficiency test such as an English for Academic Purposes (EAP) reading test then you will need to identify what is appropriate for the audience in their future target situation and select texts accordingly. If you are looking for an article for Science students you might wish to find one that has a methods section, a results section and a discussion section as these would seem to be salient features of much scientific discourse. If you were writing a test for Arts, Humanities and Social Science students you might select one that has a fair amount of narrative, expository text or a historical dimension. Useful texts are those which expound a conventional view and then suggest modifications, criticisms of, or challenges to this established view and end with a clear conclusion.

### Further features of text selection

*Organisational*
Whatever type of text you need to select, there are a number of general features that should be taken account of. The way a text is structured would seem to affect the ease with which

it is processed (see Williams and Moran 1989: 220). At the higher levels of proficiency, having selected an appropriate text type for the candidates (narrative, descriptive, argumentative, etc.), one would ideally like it to be clearly sequenced or have a clear line of argument running through it. We appreciate that real life does not always meet these demands. At lower levels the texts selected are often by necessity artificially constructed because of the restrictions imposed by the structures and lexis available to the students. One would perhaps also look for texts which are clearly organised into sections as this will enhance the writing of test items on surveying for gist and understanding the main ideas. Other organisational features at the levels of grammar, cohesion and rhetorical structure need to be suitable for the intended candidature (see Williams and Moran 1989: 218–20 for an extended discussion of these, and also Alderson and Urquhart 1984).

*Propositional*

We ideally need to select texts which are of interest to all participants and fall within their experience. They should be at an appropriate level in terms of propositional content for the audience addressed by the writer. The relationship between the writer of the text and the reader, e.g. equal/equal, or expert/layperson, needs to be considered at the selection stage. A text written for a different audience from the candidates will not be appropriate. For lower-level general English students we need to look at the range of language forms candidates can be expected to handle. Does the text include too many unknown lexical items? For higher-level ESP students we need to examine whether the lexical range is appropriate in terms of common core, technical and sub-technical vocabulary.

The relationship between the content of the text and the candidate's background knowledge needs to be considered (see Williams and Moran 1989: 217–18 and Grabe 1991: 381). Grabe (1991: 390) notes that research has found that activating content information plays a major role in students' comprehension and recall of information from a text. The topic should be selected from a suitable genre, at an appropriate level of specificity, and should not be culturally biased or favour one section of the test population. The issue of what is a generally accessible ESP text remains with us. In those situations where we are writing tests for heterogeneous groups of students, we are by necessity forced to select texts with a wider appeal than is the case when we have a more homogeneous group. In EAP testing this leads us to areas such as health education, study skills and habits, ecology, etc.

A text should not be so arcane or so unfamiliar as to make it incapable of being mapped onto the reader's existing schemata. Neither should it be too familiar as then there is a danger that the candidate will be able to supply some or all of the answers from his existing knowledge store. Candidates should not be able to answer questions without recourse to the text. This should be checked, whichever of the formats for testing reading are employed.

Try to sample from within the range of texts the candidates could be expected to process. The information contained in the text should be at an appropriate level of abstractness or concreteness. It should not contain so much new, densely packed information that the candidates are overwhelmed.

Grabe (1991: 390) also cites research which investigated the importance of formal schemata — 'structures of knowledge about language and textual organisation' which were found to make a significant independent contribution to reading ability. He concludes that the major implication of research in this area is that students need to activate prior knowledge of a topic before they begin to read. If this is absent then they should be given 'at least minimal background knowledge from which to interpret the text'.

### Illocutionary

As well as the organisational and propositional facets of a text, the test writer needs to take into account its functional purpose, the effect intended by the writer of the text, e.g. expository, argumentative, etc. Do we need to include a variety of texts with different functional purposes? One normally improves the validity and reliability of a test by increasing the number of passages and items, but this obviously conflicts with the concern of practicality.

Having decided what types of texts (argumentative, process description, etc.) are appropriate and allow you to test specified operations, there are a number of other performance conditions to be considered by the person writing the test.

### Channel

Decisions would have to be made on the nature and amount of non-verbal information that is desirable, e.g. graphs, charts, diagrams, etc. In addition the layout or even the typeface may merit careful consideration.

### Size

The length of text that candidates have to handle must be considered. If texts are too short you may not be able to test skimming skills, you may only be able to test intensive reading; in texts of equal difficulty the longer the text, the greater the amount of time needed for reading.

### Speed

This concerns the time constraints for the processing of text and answering the items set on it. If too much time is given candidates may simply read a passage intensively, and questions designed to test ability to process text quickly to elicit specified information may no longer activate such operations.

### Complexity

Here the concern is with the difficulty of the text/tasks students are expected to handle. The difficulty of the text will be largely determined by its organisational, propositional and discoursal attributes.

### Assistance

How much help is given? A number of factors need to be taken into account, such as: the clarity of the rubrics; whether the rubrics are in the First Language (L1) or the Target Language (TL); are they spoken and/or read; do the students get the questions in advance of the passage; are they allowed recourse to a dictionary?

*Method factor/response mode*

Every attempt should be made to ensure that candidates are familiar with the task type and other environment features before sitting the test proper. Sample tests or examples in test manuals should be available for national examinations, and in the school context similar formats should have been practised in class beforehand. Careful thought should be given in monolingual contexts to whether candidates may be permitted in comprehension tests to write their answers in their mother tongue.

An important question is whether the reading task is to be integrated with the writing task, as in the example of the TEEP test (see Chapter 5, Example 7 below). How are the questions to be ordered? Does the ordering help bring the process of taking the test closer to the way readers would normally process that particular text, or at least satisfy a critical audience that it promotes one reasonable way of doing so? Should skimming questions occur first and be separated from those questions requiring closer reading of the text? Should we ignore questions on specific linguistic points such as understanding particular cohesive devices which are easy to write but difficult to interpret in terms of their contribution to the overall construct of reading? Are some items worth more than others? How explicit should this weighting be? (Timings given, points given, etc.) Should marks be deducted for inaccuracies of expression? For a discussion of these points see procedures for test task design at the end of this chapter.

Table 3.1
*Summary checklist of conditions under which reading operations are performed*

*Purpose(s)*: for reading.

*Nature of the texts* (+ rubrics and tasks): e.g. story, song, poem, play, instructions, rules, notice, sign, message, leaflet, brochure, guide, form, timetable, map/plan, advertisement, postcard, letter, telex, report, newspaper article, magazine article, academic article, textbook, reference book, novel, label, traffic sign . . .

*Organisational:*    grammar, cohesion, rhetorical organisation.

*Propositional:*    lexical range: common core, technical, semi-technical.
topic (level of specificity/cultural bias, familiarity/interest).
status of writer to reader, e.g. equal to equal, expert to layperson.
relationship between content of text and candidates' background knowledge (content and formal).
type of information (abstract/concrete).

*Illocutionary:*    functional purpose, intended effect of writer.

*Channel* of presentation: +/− visuals, layout, typeface.

*Size* of input, length of text.

*Speed* at which processing must take place (text and questions).

*Assistance*: amount of help given (clarity of rubrics, first language (L1)/target language (TL), spoken/read, questions in advance, recourse to dictionary).

*Method factor/response mode*: familiarity with task type and other test environment features. Answer in L1/TL? Selection/production. Is it integrated with writing/speaking task? Number and nature of operations to be performed within the task and test/ordering of these. Explicitness of any weighting. Explicitness of criteria for correctness.

In Table 3.1 you will find a summary checklist of the conditions appropriate to the assessment of reading ability that a test writer might want to take into consideration. The list is not exhaustive (see Bachman 1990 for additional categories) and you may wish to add points from your own list. As with other checklists in this book, not all the components will necessarily be relevant in your situation. You will need to develop frameworks which match your situation more closely.

Next we will consider in some detail the activities/operations that might be performed on the texts you select. In particular contexts it may be easier to specify what activities participants need to perform in reading. For example, when studying a subject through the medium of English, say at a British university, participants might have to carry out the activities listed at Table 3.2. These are reading activities which are commonly found in reading English for academic purposes. Read through these and relate them to your

Table 3.2
*Reading activities in an academic context*

| 1. | 2. |
|---|---|
| *SCANNING* for specific information in a text in order to: | *SKIMMING* a text or part(s) of a text to quickly establish a general idea of the content in order to: |
| **1.1**  locate the specific parts of a text you are going to read, e.g. by using table of contents, headings, index, key words in the text, etc. | **2.1**  help you to anticipate what it might contain and therefore better understand it when you read it more carefully |
| **1.2**  locate specific data encoded in a non-verbal form, e.g. in diagrams, graphs, table, etc. | **2.2**  decide whether it should be read before other texts because it is more appropriate, clearly written, concise, etc. |
| **1.3**  locate specific data in reference works, e.g. words in dictionaries | **2.3**  determine how much of it is relevant for your purpose(s) and should be read more carefully |
| **1.4**  retrieve data already encountered during reading, e.g. to check a spelling, quotation, date, etc. | **2.4**  review what you have already read in order to recall or clarify the main points |
| **3.** | **4.** |
| *READING* a text or part(s) of a text carefully *to extract all* the relevant information for the following purposes: | *READING* a text or part(s) of a text for *background knowledge* |
| **3.1**  to carry out a written assignment e.g. dissertation, coursework | **4.1**  of topic(s) covered by the course, e.g. as pre-course reading or preparation for lectures/seminars, etc. |
| **3.2**  to present a paper orally in a seminar | **4.2**  of topic(s) related to but not covered by the course, e.g. keeping up-to-date with new developments in your field |
| **3.3**  to prepare for and/or follow up lectures and/or seminars | |
| **3.4**  to answer examination questions | |
| **3.5**  to correct your own written work | |

*Acknowledgement*: to Penny Foster for original version of this table.

own experience. Do not worry if you do not teach English for academic purposes. A similar approach should be adopted in analysing all target-situation reading needs.

## EXERCISE 3D   ACTIVITIES IN AN ACADEMIC CONTEXT

Exercise 3D(a)
Which of the activities listed in Table 3.2 have you performed? Try and think what doing each activity involved. How did you succeed in carrying it out? What skills/strategies did you use?

In the section on testing speaking above, we advocated that our tests should reflect as closely as possible salient, identifiable facets of real-life operations and the conditions under which they are performed. The activities listed in Table 3.2 reflect those that students at a British university carry out in reading for academic purposes. In general, to complete an assignment students might have to read a number of articles and/or textbooks over a period of time and then write up the assignment in a number of drafts.

Exercise 3D(b)
If, however, you had to devise a test which covered these activities as fully as possible, what problems might you come up against? If you wanted to make your EAP reading test replicate as closely as possible real-world reading for academic purposes, how close could you get to this?

Refer back to the principles of test design we discussed in Part I above (Section 1.3.2). Which principles might it be difficult to satisfy? Why does the attempt to reflect real life run into problems? Make a note of your ideas under the following three headings:

Practicality            Validity                    Reliability

*Comment on Exercise 3D*

To incorporate the activities in Table 3.2 fully into a test might lead to problems in the key areas of practicality, reliability and validity that were examined earlier in the course.

**Practicality**

Reading a number of articles would take up a considerable amount of test time. If we wanted students to read textbooks in their own areas, then the time problem would be even greater and the difficulty in supplying such texts insurmountable. In real life, we read something, then put it down, come back to it, and so on; reflecting this time scale and pattern in an examination is unworkable.

**Reliability**

If students are allowed to go to libraries and to discuss the reading texts with other students, it is difficult to ensure that the tests will provide an accurate reflection of the ability of each individual student. This type of assistance and feedback may be available in real life too, but we cannot be sure that such help would always be forthcoming. Students will probably have to depend on their own efforts when they enter academic study proper.

**Validity**

What students have to do in academic life is in essence to extract information from written texts, then reformulate it for set written assignments or in timed examinations. A generalised academic writing task might include the following features: provision of topic/assignment prompt; an indication of audience expectation; specified and accessible source(s) of data; lexis constrained (to some extent) by all of the above; the need for the candidate to search for and extract data relevant to the question; the need for the candidate to reorganise and encode these data within the conventions of academic discourse so that the reader's expectations of relevance, adequacy, coherence, appropriateness and accuracy are fulfilled.

It may well be that students also incorporate ideas or facts gathered from spoken input. This further points to the integrated nature of many language activities in real life. If we include integrated activities such as extracting information from a written text and reformulating an argument or selectively summarising the information in our own words, then failure to generate a product does not tell us where the process has broken down. It may be failure in writing and/or reading that has been the stumbling block. If we want to make comments about a student's reading ability *per se*, then this may be taken as an argument for more discrete reading tests if we are to avoid muddied measurement from skills integration.

Full genuineness of text or authenticity of task is likely to be unattainable in the tests we write. We cannot fully replicate reality in language tests because of the strong pull of the other principles discussed above. However, we are still left with the need to make our tests as valid as possible if we are to measure anything of value.

The argument as to whether reading is divisible into component skills or operations which can be identified clearly, or whether it is an indivisible, unitary process, continues. Proponents of the unidimensional/indivisible view of reading would argue that by testing enabling skills we are not getting a true measurement of the construct. Following their argument, if we wanted to test EAP reading ability in a British academic context, we might indeed be happy with a reading-into-writing task and not be worried about muddying the reading measurement by having a writing output to the integrated task (see Chapter 5, Example 7).

However, given that in many places in the world employers, admissions officers, teachers and other end users of test information want to know only about a candidate's reading ability, then we must address the problems in testing this and try to avoid other constructs such as writing ability interfering with its measurement. In our present state of knowledge, if we wish to report on students' proficiency in reading, as distinct, say, from writing ability, then we are forced to break reading down into what we conceive are its constituent parts. It is accepted pedagogical practice to break the reading process down in this way and to teach the component skills and strategies to a certain extent separately. So, to that extent, it should be possible to focus on these components for testing purposes. If we can identify skills and operations that appear to make an important contribution to the reading process, it should be possible to test these and use the composite results for reporting on reading proficiency (see Alderson 1990 and Weir *et al.* 1990 for a further discussion of these issues).

## EXERCISE 3E   OPERATIONS

Make a list of the skills you think contribute to reading ability. For example, surveying quickly to get the gist of a passage would be a skill that we might wish to teach and test.

When you have done this, compare what you have written with Table 3.3. What are the differences? What are the similarities? What distinguishes the skills in either list? Are some easier than others? Are some required before you can perform others? Does the possession of one skill imply the possession of others? Should we be testing only the more global reading comprehension skills, e.g. surveying for gist, and not the more specifically linguistic, e.g. decoding the meaning of unknown lexis from context?

Table 3.3
*Summary checklist of operations in reading*

(a)  *Skimming: going through a text quickly*:
     Identifying: which part, or whether part or whole, is relevant to an established need.
     Surveying for gist.
     Scanning to locate specific information.

(b)  *Reading carefully to understand main ideas and important detail*:
     Reading carefully for main ideas and important detail (might include tracing the development of an argument, reducing what is read to an outline of the main points and important details).
     Distinguishing fact from opinion, recognising attitude to reader and topic (e.g. persuasion or explanation).
     Understanding inferred meaning: understanding text by going outside it, e.g. by making inferences, deducing meaning of lexical items from morphology and context, understanding communicative functions without explicit indicators.

(c)  At some level all of the above might include a knowledge of the following *more specifically linguistic contributory skills*:
     Understanding concepts (grammatical notions) such as: cause, result, purpose, comparison.
     Understanding syntactic structure of sentence and clause.
     Understanding discourse markers.
     Understanding lexical and/or grammatical cohesion.
     Understanding lexis.

*Comment on Exercise 3E*

If we want to test the construct of reading *per se*, then we must take steps to avoid the contamination of the measurement of this ability by the method adopted to assess it. We must try to test reading and only reading. This leads us away from integrated reading into writing tasks.

This means breaking reading down into underlying skills components that teachers and many testers believe can be taught and tested. (see Table 3.3). This does not mean that we believe that this is a *fully* valid model of what reading comprehension is (see Williams and Moran 1989 and Grabe 1991). We admit to the possibility that the sum of the parts might not necessarily equate fully with what readers would normally take away from a text. Whatever theoretical position we take, we inevitably measure reading skills (individually or in combination) as soon as individual items are written on a passage. The debate would seem to be more a question of the strength of any claims concerning which skills are being tested by which items (see Alderson 1990 and Weir *et al.* 1990), than a strong claim for treating reading as a unified skill.

Williams and Moran (1989: 224) present a balanced view of this debate and note:

> While materials writers may disagree on the emphasis to be devoted to any particular skill, there seems to be substantial agreement on the importance of such skills as guessing the meaning of unknown words, identifying anaphoric reference, identifying the main idea, and inference.

The value of automaticity in reading, particularly in word identification skills, is commented on by Grabe (1991: 379−82). He also identifies as important components of skilled reading: syntactic knowledge; knowledge of formal discourse structure (formal schemata); content and background knowledge (content schemata); and metacognitive knowledge and skills monitoring, e.g. recognising the more important information in a text, skimming, and searching for specific information.

Grabe (1991: 382) concludes:

> A 'reading components' perspective is an appropriate research direction to the extent that such an approach leads to important insights into the reading process. In this respect, it ... is indeed a useful approach.

These enabling skills are obviously still theoretical constructs, with only a hypothesised existence. Their separate nature or the extent to which they interact with other reading skills needs to be empirically investigated. One way the teacher might do this in the classroom is to get students to introspect about the processes they are using to solve questions set on the various skills (see Cohen 1984 and Faerch and Kasper 1987). In this way we can investigate whether we are in fact testing what we set out to test. In addition it may be possible to determine whether there are different routes, for example, to working out the main idea(s) in a passage.

It might eventually be possible to determine what the interactional relationships might be between the skills which we have allowed a hypothetical separate existence. At present we have little idea about the relationship between these skills or whether some skills are superordinate to others. Does possession of one skill imply the possession of other skills in some sort of hierarchical arrangement? It might be that the ability to carry out certain activities is dependent on the prior possession of other skills. It would seem improbable that students would be able to work out the main ideas of a text without some baseline competence in the microlinguistic skills (see Alderson and Urquhart 1984 and Grabe 1991: 391). It may also be the case that students find greater difficulty with some of the more specifically linguistic skills in Table 3.3 than they do in the more global comprehension areas. It may be that they can transfer the more global comprehension skills across from their L1. If this can be shown to be the case, then this has important implications for the assessment of reading skills in English for academic purposes.

The best we can do in the present state of knowledge is to ensure that if we wish to make comments about students' reading at a certain level of proficiency, then we include a range of formats and sufficient items to cover the range of skills that we believe are important and which together equate with our construct of reading.

We must be explicit about what it is we are trying to test and set down clearly the procedures we have employed to ascertain that what we are testing is what we want to test. At the very least, if we proceed in this principled manner we might make some small contribution to an understanding of what reading comprehension is.

When making decisions about which formats to use in our tests (e.g. multiple-choice questions, short-answer questions, information transfer, gap filling, etc.) it is necessary to ensure that, as far as possible, the operations the candidate performs during a test on a selected text are equateable or comparable with the operations he or she would have to perform in processing similarly appropriate texts in real life.

Obviously there will be individual differences in the way texts are processed. What we are interested in is whether there are any general procedures that we should try to incorporate into our tests which would bring the process of doing the test closer to what we might generally agree on as 'reading a text'. It is important that the formats we adopt reflect as adequately as possible what we believe reading to be even if we accept that the test does not imply a *fully* valid model of what reading comprehension is. The bottom line is whether the tasks students have to carry out in the test reflect realistic discourse processing.

The crucial question to ask of any test is: does the ability to answer these items indicate that the participant has been able to use the text to achieve a defined purpose?

Finally we must give due attention to the level of performance we will expect from candidates taking our tests.

## EXERCISE 3F   LEVEL OF PERFORMANCE

The third part of our framework for testing reading comprehension is level of performance. In testing speaking, there was a tangible product to which we could attach performance labels, such as 'fluency' and 'accuracy'. How are we going to define levels of performance in reading?

Make notes on a separate sheet of paper, on how you would establish the pass level in a test of reading in your context. When you finish compare your ideas with those suggested below.

*Comment on Exercise 3F*

Perhaps the most important question to ask of any test is: what performance constitutes a pass? In reading, we do not have qualitative descriptors to apply to a concrete product such as speech or writing. We are depending on a quantitative score and trying to translate this into a performance description. This leads us into various problems. Do students have to get all the items in the test right or half of them? Are different combinations of right answers acceptable for a pass? How are we to score the test? Are some items more important than others and therefore to be weighted more heavily?

If we set the items at a level of difficulty at which we would expect candidates to get them all right to pass, we have a benchmark to aim at. The combination of items and text should be within the capabilities of anyone we would be prepared to pass. Given the possibility of error interfering with the measurement, we might set the pass rate at around the 80% mark.

It should be clear from the above discussion that we can develop a framework for the testing of reading which will provide us with a set of parameters against which we can compare our tests and evaluate those public tests for which we may enter our students.

We have summarised our initial ideas for such a framework in Table 3.4. This checklist combines the individual checklists from Tables 3.1 and 3.3 above. We would regard this as a draft version as we feel that you will inevitably want to revise and improve on it and to amend it to fit more closely with your own particular context and needs. When constructing reading tasks, it should act as a useful reminder of the parameters you need to consider.

Table 3.4
*Summary checklist for constructing reading comprehension tests*

**Conditions**

*Purpose(s)*: for reading.

*Nature of the texts* (+ rubrics and tasks).

*Organisational*:    grammar, cohesion, rhetorical organisation.

*Propositional*:    lexical range: common core, technical, semi-technical.
topic (genre/level of specificity/cultural bias/familiarity and interest).
status of writer to reader, e.g. expert to layperson.
relationship between content of text and candidates' background knowledge (content and formal).

*Illocutionary*:    functional purpose, intended effect of writer.

*Channel* of presentation: +/− visuals, layout, typeface.

*Size* of input, length of text.

*Speed* at which processing must take place (text and questions).

*Assistance*: how much help is given (clarity of rubrics L1/TL, spoken/read, questions in advance, recourse to dictionary).

*Method factor/response mode*: familiarity with task type and other test environment features. Answer in L1/TL? Selection/production. Is it integrated with writing/speaking task? Number and nature of operations to be performed within the task and test/ordering of these. Explicitness of any weighting. Explicitness of criteria for correctness.

**Operations**

(a) *Skimming: going through a text quickly*:
Identification: which part, or whether part or whole, is relevant to an established need.
Surveying for gist (topic, overall meaning).
Scanning for specific information.

(b) *Reading carefully to understand main ideas and important detail*:
Reading carefully for main ideas and important detail (might include tracing the development of an argument, reducing what is read to an outline of the main points and important details).
Distinguishing fact from opinion, recognising attitude to reader and topic (e.g. persuasion or explanation).
Understanding inferred meaning: understanding text by going outside it, e.g. by making inferences, deducing meaning of lexical items from morphology and context, understanding communicative functions without explicit indicators.

(c) At some level all of the above might include a knowledge of the following *more specifically linguistic contributory skills*:
Understanding notions such as: cause, result, purpose, comparison.
Understanding syntactic structure of sentence and clause.
Understanding discourse markers.
Understanding lexical and/or grammatical cohesion.
Understanding lexis.

**Level**

Level is defined in relation to the conditions and operations that students can cope with.

*Acknowledgements*: D. Porter and A. Hughes (Testing and Evaluation Unit, University of Reading) for their contribution to the development of the above framework and to Bachman (1990) for a number of the facets included.

## 3.2 Formats for testing reading comprehension

### EXERCISE 3G  EXAMINING TEST FORMATS

We will now consider a variety of formats available for testing the various components of reading comprehension. Before looking at the formats below you might find it useful to refer back to the general principles and specific guidelines for test construction developed in Part I of the course.

Examine these test formats to see how far they match the frameworks (both Table 1.1 and Table 3.4) outlined above. These are examples that have been constructed for specific students in specific contexts. They are taken from a variety of levels from elementary to advanced. The particular conditions or operations in some examples may well be inappropriate for your own students. The purpose of the exercise is to become aware of the formats, their advantages and limitations, and to think critically about them so that you can decide what would be most appropriate (with modification where necessary in terms of your own framework) for the students you are responsible for in your particular context.

The examples represent some of the more useful options for testing reading ability along an indirect/direct continuum. Read the texts and complete the test items set on each. While you are completing the items, think hard about the skills/strategies you are using to answer them. For each format consider:

(a) What operation(s) is each item testing? Refer to the list of operations/enabling skills in Table 3.4 above. It may well be that you think an item is testing more than one skill. Try and decide in these cases what are the major and minor focus(es) of the item.

(b) What are the advantages and disadvantages of testing reading through this format? You may wish to comment on the operations involved and the conditions under which the task is performed. You may also wish to relate the examples to the framework of general principles and specific guidelines for test construction. After each test format you will be given a commentary.

*Indirect test types*

## Example 1:   Selective deletion gap filling

Read the passage below and find where words are missing. Choose *one* word from the list of words provided to fill in each gap. Write the word opposite the corresponding question number on the answer sheet (rubric in L1).

*Example*: Choose from the following words: down, morning, is, not, hello.

Good morning everybody. Good (1), sir.
Sit (2) everybody. My name (3) Mr Hunt.

*Answers*

1. morning
2. down
3. is

Now look at the passage below and do the same. You have ten minutes to finish this task.

*Words*: Freetown, likes, they, her, them, sings, works, is, she, go, doesn't, not, live, a, never, their, sister, but, lives, town, dog.

Yemi is in the eleventh grade and (1) seventeen years old. She does not (2) in Bamako. (3) lives in a small (4) nearby. (5) father (6) in a factory in Bamako, and her mother works in (7) hospital in the town. She has four brothers and one (8). Her sister does (9) live in Bamako. She (10) in Freetown and works in an office. Yemi's brothers live with (11) parents and (12) to school in Bamako. Yemi (13) basketball at school. She (14) English but she (15) like Mathematics.

*Answers*

| | | |
|---|---|---|
| 1. | 6. | 11. |
| 2. | 7. | 12. |
| 3. | 8. | 13. |
| 4. | 9. | 14. |
| 5. | 10. | 15. |

## Comments on **Example 1**

The format is indirect as it measures only a limited part of what might constitute reading proficiency, namely microlinguistic contributory skills (level (c) in Table 3.3 above) and does not seem to provide any evidence on a candidate's ability to extract information quickly by skimming a text or to read it carefully to understand its main ideas and important details (levels (a) and (b) in Table 3.3). After candidates take gap-filling tests they are often unable to say what the passage was about.

It is clear that this technique restricts one to sampling a much more limited range of enabling skills (i.e. a limited set of those abilities which collectively represent the overall skill of reading) than do short-answer questions on a text. Whereas short-answer questions allow the sampling of a range of reading enabling skills, gap filling is much more restrictive where only single words are deleted.

There is even some difference of opinion on what is being tested where only single lexical items are deleted. Is it testing the ability to recognise which form of the word is required and/or lexical knowledge? On its own it is an insufficient indicator of a candidate's reading ability. If the purpose of a test is to sample the range of enabling skills including the more extensive skills such as skimming, then an additional format to gap filling is essential.

To the extent that it does not match the range of operations and the conditions under which reading tasks might normally be performed by the intended target group, then the task is indirect. The more indirect tasks are, the more difficult it is to generalise from scores on this test to statements about students' reading ability. How many would the student have to score to be deemed to have met the pass grade in reading, to be deemed a competent reader?

Items are relatively easy to construct for this format, and texts may be selected to satisfy many of the appropriate conditions identified above (see Table 3.1), e.g. propositional and organisational complexity of passage, text type, size, topic, etc. There might however be some concern over the purpose of completing such a test task. The format does not have a positive washback effect on learning as it is not in itself a direct measure of the reading construct. It is difficult to see how this test relates to a normal reading process. Would the time spent on practising this particular format not be better spent on processing real texts in a more natural fashion?

The format may well have a place, though, if one is looking for a quick, efficient measure of general language proficiency for the purpose of placement of students into language classes. In this situation it may not be necessary to make precise statements about capacity in a particular skill area as long as the indirect task splits up students into homogeneous groups in the skill area required.

Tests of this type may be more happily described as tests of general proficiency rather than tests of reading, although there is some evidence from statistical analysis that a reading factor is quite strong in determining test results (Weir 1983). Example 1 is made more of a test of reading than writing by providing the answers for the candidates to select from, rather than requiring candidates to supply them. In some versions, where the number of options is equal to the number of gaps, this might create problems of its own. If a student gets one item wrong, then it means he or she is penalised twice, and guessing is encouraged towards the end of the task. The way around this is to provide a number of additional distracters within the list of correct answers.

Even where answers are not provided, with careful consideration at the moderation stage, marking should be relatively straightforward, and items can be selected which have a restricted number of possible answers. It seems reasonable in this version to accept equivalent responses in marking and not to penalise for spelling unless it cannot be understood or the spelling could be taken as another word.

Selective deletion enables the test constructor to determine where deletions are to be made and to focus on those items which have been selected *a priori* as being important to a particular target audience. It is also easy for the test writer to make any alterations shown to be necessary after item analysis and to maintain the required number of items. This might involve eliminating items that have not performed satisfactorily in terms of discrimination and facility value.

## Example 2:   C-test

In the text below the second half of some of the words is missing. If the whole word has an *even* number of letters, then exactly half the letters are missing, e.g. to = t_____; this = th_____; thi_____ = thinks. If the whole word has an *uneven* number of letters, then one more than half the letters are missing, e.g. the = t_____; their = th_____; thanked = tha_____. Try and decide what is missing and complete the words in the space provided.

*James Watt, the inventor*

James Watt was a great inventor who was born in Britain in the eighteenth century.

He was the inventor of the steam engine. Steam po_____ was t_____ first

m_____ made po_____ used f_____ transport. Bef_____ this

inve_____ we h_____ to u_____ animal po_____. He ma_____ the

fi_____ good st_____ engine.

Wh_____ he w_____ a b_____ Watt w_____ interested i_____ steam

po_____. He not_____ how t_____ steam i_____ a sauc_____ of

boi_____ water co_____ push u_____ the l_____. From th_____

idea h_____ later inve_____ the st_____ engine.

## Comment on Example 2

The C-test has emerged recently as an alternative to cloze (the mechanical deletion of every nth word in a passage) and to selective deletion gap filling, for testing comprehension of the more specifically linguistic elements in a text. This adaptation of the cloze technique, called the C-test, was developed in Germany by Klein Braley (1985, Klein Braley and Raatz 1984) based on the same theoretical rationale as cloze, viz. testing ability to cope with reduced redundancy and predict from context.

In the C-test every second word in a text is partially deleted. In an attempt to ensure solutions, students are given the first half of the deleted word. In words with an odd number of letters half the letters plus one are deleted. The examinee completes the word on the test paper, and an exact word scoring procedure is adopted.

The comments made above on the limited information provided by indirect tests apply equally here. There is some evidence that this format tests general proficiency with a slight bias to written language. It is not therefore on its own providing comprehensive information about a candidate's reading ability. It is difficult to see how it can test operations other than the specifically linguistic contributory skills outlined in Table 3.3 above.

With C-tests a variety of texts are recommended, and given the large number of items that can be generated on small texts, this further enhances the representative nature of the language being sampled. It also means that the range of conditions that candidates might be exposed to in reading can also be widely sampled (see Table 3.1, p. 69 above). There are obviously some restrictions on channel as texts with any non-verbal information are excluded and the texts used tend to be restricted in length because of the large number of items the technique generates. The serious problem it faces relates to the purpose in performing such an exercise. This technique suffers from the fact that it is irritating for students to have to process heavily mutilated texts, and the face validity of the procedure is low. It has met with public criticism of being a puzzle rather than a language test in some countries where it has been used in national examinations.

Because of the large number of items generated it is, however, extremely useful for distinguishing between students for placement purposes. Normally a minimum of 100 deletions are made and these are more representative of the passage as a whole than is possible under the cloze technique. The task can be objectively and quickly scored because it is rare for there to be more than one possible answer for any one gap.

Whereas in cloze the performance of native speakers on the test is highly variable, according to Klein Braley (1985) it is much more common for native speakers to be able to score 100% on C-tests. This may be of some help in setting cutting scores (i.e. what percentage constitutes a pass). Obviously when writing tests for very specific audiences, it is important to use native speaker specialists as the control group in trialling.

The C-test is economical, and the results obtained to date are encouraging in terms of reliability and internal and external validity. It would seem to represent a viable alternative to cloze procedure (see Alderson 1978) and selective deletion gap filling.

*Direct task types*

In *Communicative Language Testing* (Weir 1990) severe reservations were expressed about employing a multiple-choice format in the testing of comprehension either spoken or written. For the reasons stated there, no consideration will be given to this format in this course. Multiple choice is no longer employed in public examinations in Britain, and even in countries with infinitely greater numbers of candidates and logistical problems, e.g. China, there is a very strong desire to move towards more acceptable and valid methods of assessing language ability.

In testing both reading and listening comprehension we have referred to the problem of the measurement being 'muddied' by having to employ writing to record answers. In an attempt to avoid this contamination of scores, several Examination Boards in Britain have included tasks where the information transmitted verbally is transferred to a non-verbal form, e.g. by labelling a diagram, completing a chart or numbering a sequence of events.

Some British Examinations Boards, notably the Joint Matriculation Board, have produced some excellent examples of information transfer tasks (see *Communicative Language Testing*, Appendix IV). At intermediate and higher levels of proficiency, tasks are set to elicit understanding of description of process or classification. These involve transferring information from verbal to a non-verbal format requiring quite sophisticated design work and drawing ability which cannot be replicated in the average classroom.

It was noted above that replicability of tests by teachers should be an important consideration in test design. The examples we include below (3.1−3.5) involve only simple transfer of information. They are designed for lower-level students and are capable of extensive replication by teachers. They focus in the main on scanning for specific information, and they can be considered as falling under the broad umbrella of short-answer questions. The use of the technique to demonstrate an understanding of more complex and lengthier texts involving comprehension of description of process or classification will not be reviewed.

### Example 3:    Short-answer questions

### SAQ 3.1

The passage contains details about a number of people. In the chart below fill in the missing details on these people. The first details about Laila are done for you as an example.

> Laila was once a policewoman but she now teaches because she likes children. She's been teaching for five years at the same school. Nabeela was a teacher but for two years now she has worked as a reporter for Syrian Television because she makes more money there. Sadeq works for Syrian television also as a presenter. He was a famous footballer but he injured his leg. He has presented the sports programme for the last three years. Hassan has been a policeman for two years. He was a shepherd but all his sheep died in a cold winter. Jamil works with Hassan. He's been in the job for five years. He was a farmer but he wanted a more interesting job.

Key:

| Name | Job before | Job now | Years | Why in job |
|---|---|---|---|---|
| Laila | policewoman | teacher | 5 | likes children |
| Nabeela | | | 2 | more money |
| Sadeq | | presenter | | |
| Hassan | | | 2 | |
| Jamil | | | | |
| | | | | |

## SAQ 3.2

Below you will find a description of life *then* and *now* given by a father to his son. You have to separate the sentences into *then* and *now*. Read the passage and write the numbers of the sentences which refer to *then* and the numbers of the sentences which refer to *now* in the space provided. The first two are done for you.

### *Then and Now*

(1) When I was a young boy life was very hard. (2) Let me tell you that now things are a lot better. (3) We can get water from a well and we have electricity. (4) Before, people had to walk to get water from the river. (5) There was no electricity in the houses, only oil lamps. (6) I am happy because most boys and girls can go to school now and I prefer my sons to go to school. (7) Young boys had to look after the goats all day. (8) Our sisters had to cook, clean and make bread. (9) Today we have good roads in Egypt and I have a car to drive. (10) When I was young the roads were poor and I rode a donkey everywhere. (11) In the evening we can also watch television in our homes. (12) My father's family talked or went to bed when it got dark.

Then:     1 _____

Now:      2 _____

## SAQ 3.3

Read the following text and answer the questions.

You are thinking of studying at Reading University. Before you decide you want to find out certain things about the University. Read the questions and then go through the passage quickly to find the required information.

Write the letter of the paragraph where you find the information in the space provided. Number 1 is done for you as an example.

1. How old is the University?                                              __A__

2. How many students are there at the University?              _____

3. Is there a cinema on the campus?                                  _____

4. What subjects can I study?                                         _____

5. Where is Reading?                                                      _____

6. What happens if I am ill?                                          _____

7. What sports can I play?                                             _____

8. Where can I live?                                                     _____

**A.**   The University of Reading has been fortunate in its history; its traditions and roots go back into the later years of the nineteenth century, when local initiatives established schools of science and art in Reading. After a generation as a University College the University received its Royal Charter in 1926.

**B.**   Reading is the country town of the Royal County of Berkshire, at the confluence of the Thames and Kennet, some 40 miles west of London.

**C.**   The University has almost 7,000 registered students, some part-time, the great majority full-time; this will increase to almost 8,000 with the establishment, from April 1989, of the Faculty of Education and Community Studies. The numbers of full-time students in each Faculty during the Session 1988–89 were: Faculty of Letters and Social Sciences, 2,316; Faculty of Science, 1,518; Faculty of Agriculture and Food, 1,009; Faculty of Urban and Regional Studies, 939; and School of Educational Studies, 362. The proportion of men to women in the University is four to three. Some 24 per cent of the students are from overseas. There are about 2,050 postgraduate students.

**D.**   Teaching is provided by 43 departments, grouped into the five Faculties of Letters and Social Sciences, Science, Agriculture and Food, Urban and Regional Studies, and Education and Community Studies. These faculty groupings provide a flexible structure for teaching, so that in the Arts and Social Sciences and the sciences it is possible to provide a wide range of inter-related single and combined subject courses, while in Agriculture and Food and in Urban and Regional Studies, the emphasis is on a series of interdisciplinary courses applying principles and techniques drawn from a wide range of departments. In Education and Community Studies, teacher education is provided through a wide choice of subject specialisms, combining a tradition of educational innovation with the highest academic and professional standards.

**E.**   The University of Reading is a residential university. There are twelve halls of residence, all of which offer accommodation for both men and women. The halls vary in age, size and character, but all are within easy reach of Whiteknights and London Road (a circle of one mile radius encloses all the halls and the academic buildings), and provide a range of study, domestic and social facilities.

**F.** The University Health Service provides a comprehensive medical care for students. The Service is housed in a modern purpose-built Health Centre with in-patient and nursing facilities. Students who are taken ill during term may be admitted to the Health Centre and cared for until they are well. A staff of five full-time doctors provide full general practitioner care, which includes all forms of immunisation, a sports injury and physio-therapy clinic, gynaecology and contraceptive care for students and staff and their families. A fully-staffed dental service is also provided under the National Health Service.

**G.** Sport is an integral part of University life. Three levels of participation are catered for at Reading; the top performers who represent their University clubs, the middle band seeking lower level competition such as inter-hall and inter-departmental sport and the large non-competitive group who enjoy exercise in its many forms. The University enjoys good relationships with many leading clubs in the area such as the Reading Swimming Club and the Reading Athletics Club. In addition there are 'Centres of Sporting Excellence', for Athletics, Badminton, Biathlon, Cycling, Modern Pentathlon, Judo and Table Tennis within easy reach of the University.

**H.** The cultural life of the University is greatly enhanced by its having an active Department of Music which organises regular concerts and recitals for members of the University and for those living in the neighbourhood. There is a large University Choral Society and Orchestra, a Chamber Orchestra and a Chamber Choir. Also there is a Music Club, a small chamber choir known as the University Singers and a University Opera Society which gives a stage performance each year. These groups are open to members of all departments. There is a series of lunchtime Campus Concerts each term.

**I.** There are several dramatic groups; the focus of these is the University Drama Society, offering several presentations each term. The French and German Department also produce a play each year.

**J.** The Reading Film Theatre provides performances twice a week in the Palmer Building. For an annual subscription a member gets reduced entry prices, attendance at members-only performances and an advance booking scheme. The RFT aims to show films which represent 'the best of the cinema' rather than those which were immediate box-office successes.

## SAQ 3.4

Read the description of Saudi Arabia below and complete the table. The first one has been done for you as an example.

### *Saudi Arabia*

Saudi Arabia is a Kingdom in the Arab Peninsula where over six million people live, mainly in the capital Riyadh and in the cities of Dhahran and Jeddah. The area of the country is approximately 450,000 square kilometres, which is mostly desert. The head of state is a member of the Royal family who is called King Fahd. The people who live there are called Saudis and they speak Arabic. Their official religion is Islam and the important Islamic Holy Places of Mecca and Medina are in the western part of Saudi Arabia. The currency, the money which the Saudis use, is the Riyal. The weather is nearly always hot and it has a desert climate with an average rainfall of about three inches although in some years it has been as high as seven inches. It produces and exports mainly oil and some dates.

Country _____ *Saudi Arabia* _____

Capital city _____

Area _____

Population _____

Head of State _____

People _____

Currency used _____

Holy places _____

Exports _____

Climate _____

Average yearly rainfall about _____

## SAQ 3.5

2. Answer **all three** sections of this question, using the advertisements printed opposite.

### SECTION A

On the opposite page, there are nine advertisements (labelled **A – I**) for English Language Schools in New South Wales, Australia. Below are the details **(1) – (9)** of what different students might need on an English Language Course. Write the letter of the advertisement for the *most suitable* school in the appropriate box. The first one has been done for you.

Schools needed for the following:

(1) A student wishing to start studying on 9th January.                                    | I |

(2) Five engineering colleagues working in an Australian factory on a year's exchange and wishing to have lessons at their place of work.

(3) A businessman who frequently needs documents translated.

(4) A student wishing to have very intensive private lessons.

(5) A teacher wanting to take a course leading to the RSA Cert TEFLA.

(6) A Greek couple who have just emigrated to Australia.

(7) A travel agent/tourist guide needing to learn English for her job.

(8) A student who wants to stay with an Australian family.

(9) Someone who is very keen on learning with video and computer programmes.

Source: Oxford Delegacy

Remember that you may use your English-English dictionary ─────────

**Comment on SAQ/information transfer (Examples 3.1–3.5)**

Information transfer tasks are probably best seen as a useful variant of short-answer questions. Short-answer questions are generically those which require the candidates to write down answers in spaces provided on the question paper. These answers are normally limited in length either by the space made available to candidates or by controlling the amount that can be written by deleting words in an answer that is provided for the candidate. The technique is extremely useful for testing reading comprehension.

The questions set in this format normally try to cover the important information in a text (overall gist, main ideas and important details) and understanding of structures and lexis that convey this. The nature of the format and the limitations imposed by capacity at lower levels of ability will constrain the types of things students might be expected to read for in the early stages of language learning. In the first year of learning a language, reading will normally be limited to comparison and contrast of the personal features of individuals and extracting specific information from short non-personal texts. At higher levels more complex texts will be used and most of the skills in Table 3.3 involving skimming and reading carefully to understand the main ideas and important detail can be assessed.

The guiding principle here is to keep the answers brief and to reduce writing to a minimum to avoid possible contamination from students having to write answers out in full. SAQ 3.3 is a good illustration of how students can deploy a fairly demanding skill such as skimming without having to understand everything in a text which would normally be deemed to be above their level. It is a realistic task for various situations, and its interest and authenticity give it a high face validity in these contexts.

All of the conditions identified in Table 3.1 can be taken account of in this format and, in contrast to the indirect formats discussed above, the normal purposes for which people read can be more easily accommodated.

However, a good deal of care needs to be taken that the non-verbal task the students have to complete does not itself complicate the process or detract from the authenticity of the experience. In some of the more sophisticated tasks using this format, there is a danger that students may be able to understand the text but not be totally clear what is expected of them in the transfer phase. There is also a danger that in order to fit more neatly into such formats texts are sometimes expressly written for this purpose and the conditions of authentic text are accordingly not met.

## SAQ 3.6

**Summary cloze**

Read the following passage on 'The History of Money' and then fill in the gaps in the passage below.

> Money is generally accepted right across the world as payment for goods in shops or as wages paid by employers to employees. People use money to buy food, clothes and hundreds of other things that they might want.
>
> In the past many different things were used as money. Shells were one of the first things that were used. People who lived on islands in the Pacific Ocean used these shells for ornaments and if somebody had more food than they needed they were happy to exchange the extra food for these shells. The Chinese used cloth and knives. In the Philippines rice was used for money. In Africa elephant tusks or salt were used. In some parts of Africa some people are still paid in salt today.
>
> In some parts of the world a wealthy man was a man who owned a lot of animals. In East Africa a man showed how rich he was by the number of cows he owned. Sometimes wives were bought with cows. Using animals as money was difficult however because it was not easy to give change. If your animals died it also meant that you had lost all your wealth.
>
> Exchanging goods or animals was difficult. Perhaps it was a Chinese businessman who, tired of carrying lots of knives, invented coins to pay a large bill in the shops. The coins first used by the Chinese were round pieces of metal with a hole in the centre so that a piece of string could keep them together. Russia made copper coins, Nepal had leather coins and the people on Yap island had stone coins. These stone coins were huge but they were used even though they were so heavy. They were two metres in diameter.
>
> The most valuable coins were made of gold and silver and the heavier the coin the greater the value. It was still a problem though if you wanted to buy something expensive as you had to carry many coins with you. The Chinese again came up with an answer. They began to use paper money for coins which were promises to pay certain amounts of money. Now paper notes are used throughout the world.

Fill in the gaps in the passage below with an appropriate word.

The history of money is very interesting. Today money is used everywhere to buy goods and services. In the past _____ were among the earliest objects used as money. These were originally used as _____ but gradually the people in the Pacific began to use them in exchange for food and other items.

In other countries many different objects were used as money. Rice was used in the _____, whereas in Africa they used _____ which is still in use as money in certain parts of that continent today.

A person's wealth was often demonstrated by the number of _____ he owned and it was even possible in some countries to buy a _____ with these animals.

Coins came in many shapes and sizes. In Russia they were made from _____ but in _____ they were made from leather. The _____ of the coins, however, was the main factor which led to the invention of money made from _____.

## Comment on Example 3.6

A passage is selected which lends itself to summary. This may restrict the range of texts sampled to those types that lend themselves to use in this format. Gaps are then created in the summary which candidates have to complete. This has the advantage that it is clear to candidates what is expected from them, and they do not have serious problems of written expression as they are guided to the answer that is required of them.

It is often quite difficult to summarise a passage in such a way that the candidate is required to do more than transfer lexical items from the passage to the summary. It is doubtful that the full range of operations we identified for reading in Table 3.3 can be examined through this format, e.g. it is unlikely that the candidate's skimming skills are tested. In some cases the ability to work out the main ideas of a passage may be difficult to assess as well. There must also be some concern that the activity does not have a direct relationship with how students might process written discourse in real life.

It might be improved by deleting more than one word at a time, but the more this is done the more it becomes a test of writing ability as well.

## SAQ 3.7

Your Manager is giving a talk on 'Communications in Business' to a group of young business people and asks you to assist him by listing the main points from the following passage, which is about 400 words, so that he can use them as guidelines during his talk. List the points you consider most important.

---

According to the pamphlet *A Guide to the Writing of Business Letters*, published by the British Association for Commercial and Industrial Education, a business letter has two main purposes. Firstly, it enables business arrangements to be made without the need for the parties to meet. Secondly, it enables both parties to have a permanent record of these arrangements.

We should note carefully that the prime purpose is to remove the need for personal contact. It is a strong indication of the failure of such business correspondence if a meeting is necessary to remove misunderstanding. A letter is successful if the writer achieves his object. Before the letter writer begins his letter he must understand what his object is.

When the writer is clear about this object, his writing and the presentation of the writing should enable this object to be reached. The language should be simple and clear. Pompous jargon and foreign phrases have no place in business communication. Sometimes we are required by the subject-matter to use technical terms. We may use technical jargon provided we are certain the recipient will understand the terms; otherwise we must explain ourselves in non-technical language.

Simple language will help to get our message over, but we should remember that simple language alone will not solve our problems. We have our object to achieve, and we must therefore make sure that we include all the details necessary to give our reader a clear idea of what we require of him. We must also remember that businessmen are by definition busy men who do not wish to waste time on irrelevant material. Avoid ungrammatical and insincere concluding sentences like 'Assuring you of our best attention at all times.'

We can fail in our purpose through grammatical errors and careless spelling. The following example, taken from a reader's letter in the *Daily Telegraph*, illustrates this point.

'We have pleasure in informing you that your shoes are *not* available.'

No doubt the writer of this letter would argue that he left the spelling to his secretary who typed 'not' for 'now'. The responsibility for faults in letters cannot be shifted; it remains with the writer. If the writer finds that his dictation is not taken down correctly he has several solutions. He can, for example, start listening to his own dictation on tape. If the dictation is coherent he can try the excellent management exercise of training or retraining his secretary.

Source: LCCI, Second Level.

## SAQ 3.8

Situation:  Your company is going to re-locate to Docklands in London. At a recent staff meeting several members of staff asked you about how they could reach the new premises by public transport. In particular, they wanted to know about the new Docklands Light Railway.

Task:  Using the information in the leaflet that you have obtained, **write the answers to their questions in your answer book**. The questions are given below the leaflet.

Your answers should be brief, but give all the information required against the number of the question. for example:

25. Can we use DLR tickets on other train services? *25. Yes you can use them on the Underground and British Rail.*

### LEAFLET

The Docklands Light Railway (DLR) came into being when re-development in Docklands made it essential to improve public transport — both for commuters and local residents. From the start it proved popular and already needs to expand to meet an increasing demand.

All stations are monitored by closed circuit TV. In addition, mobile staff patrol the stations, which are clean and brightly lit. The destination of trains is flashed on an Electronic Indicator on station platforms, and also announced on the public address system. Every train has a Train Captain, who checks tickets and can answer queries whilst ensuring the smooth operation of the train. All stations have special lifts that take wheelchairs and space is allocated for wheelchairs on the trains. Trains were built to take wheelchairs easily. Each station is equipped with a passenger alarm (emergency use only) which, when activated by a push button, establishes immediate contact with our control room. There are emergency buttons on trains for passenger use if warranted. Whilst engineering work is in progress to improve and extend the railway (after 9.30 pm and at weekends, until further notice) a special DLR substitute bus service is operated. The railway is controlled from the Operations and Maintenance centre adjacent to Poplar Station. Queries about the railway are also handled from here (telephone 01-583 0311) or from our 24-hour information service 01-222 1234.

Single journey tickets to all DLR and Underground stations can be bought on the day from the coin-operated ticket machines in station entrance halls. You must have a valid ticket before you travel. Any passenger without a ticket will be dealt with in accordance with the regulations. This may involve payment of an additional fare 10 times the value of the fare avoided, or may lead to prosecution. London Regional Transport and British Rail Travelcards and Capitalcards are valid on DLR trains and substitute buses provided they cover the right fare zones. DLR tickets are valid on the Underground and British Railways. Group and special tickets can be bought in advance by writing to the Docklands Light Railway, PO Box 154, London E14 9QA, and on the day from the DLR Information Centres at Island Gardens stations (open 10 am to 4 pm weekdays) or at Tower Gateway station (open 10.45 am to 3.15 pm most days).

*Questions*
 1. Where are tickets checked?
 2. Who checks tickets?
 3. What can we do if there is an emergency on the station platform?
 4. How do we get tickets for single journeys?
 5. If we are planning a special journey for several people, where can we get tickets?
 6. How do we know where the trains are going?
 7. When does the railway close on weekdays?
 8. Can we use DLR trains if we are working on Saturday?
 9. Is it possible for disabled people to use the DLR?
10. What will happen if we are on a train and don't have a ticket?
11. Can we travel on the DLR without a ticket issued by the DLR?
12. If it is late at night and we need information about DLR services, how can we get it?
13. If we miss the last train, how can we travel on the DLR service?
14. While we are waiting for trains, how are we protected from thieves and other criminals who might enter the stations?
15. Can all British Rail Travelcards be used on the DLR?

(30 marks)

Source: LCCI, First Level.

## SAQ 3.9

You're thinking of having your windows double glazed. You want to consider all the aspects of the problem before making up your mind. Read the following article and draw up a list of all the points you can find for and against double glazing.

You can use words directly from the passage.

---

**Double Glazing**

Presumably you have already insulated your roof and walls if you are considering double glazing? In an 'ordinary' home you lose 25 per cent of heat through the roof and 15 per cent through the walls, so they must be your priorities unless your house is made of windows.

New buildings now have to meet new standards of insulation and are often fitted with double glazing when built, especially since the Government's Save It campaign. Usually this factory-made double glazing does not just add to the comfort but is very well designed and actually looks quite good.

Still, it's a difficult decision to double glaze an existing home, since you are going to have to spend a lot of money on what, in an ordinary small house with smallish windows, will save you about 10 per cent of the heating bill. And that's if you install sealed units.

Of course there are other benefits besides the financial one. The room will be much more comfortable. You won't get a chilly feeling when sitting near the window and draughts will be fewer. So on the whole, if the wherewithal exists, double glazing is not a foolish enterprise, though even good double glazing won't be as effective as a brick wall!

Double glazing is not just 'Double Glazing'. There are several ways of achieving it. You can install Replacement Windows with two sheets of single glass or twin sealed units. Or you can have Secondary Windows, either hinged to the existing window or sealed to it. Secondary windows are cheaper, can often be installed by the owners, but are not likely to be so efficient as replacement windows.

The simplest form of DIY double glazing is the applied frame method which means fixing a second pane of glass directly on to the original frame using beading or special frame sections. The most important thing is that the second leaf should be completely sealed, and that the seal should be long lasting.

Points to check are: that condensation will not occur between the two panes; that you will be able to open 'openable' windows (or that you're prepared to give up that luxury); that you will (or won't) want to be able to clean the windows and that you have some other form of ventilation.

If you think that by double glazing you automatically insulate against sound too — think again. To have a noise insulating effect the two leaves will need a gap of 110mm to 200mm (the wider the gap the better) so double glazing with noise insulation needs to be specially made. It is more difficult to make it look nice and to fit it into the existing window openings. This gap won't work as well for heat insulation unless thicker glass is used. So unless you live directly under Concorde's flight path it will hardly be worth insulating for sound.

(From The Observer Magazine in F. Grellet, *Developing Reading Skills*)

---

## SAQ 3.10

Situation:    The Napier Automobile Company had three models in production in the 1980s: the Blenheim GLX, a five-seater executive car, the Gladiator GTi, a high-performance four-seater and the Sprite MG, a two-seater sports car. The graph below shows the sales figures for each model from 1980 to 1990.

Task:    Using the information in the graph, complete the following account of the production and sales of Napier cars during the 1980s. For each space write a word, or a date or a number as appropriate.

**NOTE:**    **Copy the numbers 1 to 20 from the passage as a list down the page in your answer booklet and then write your answer for each numbered space.**

(20 marks)

The Blenheim was already in production in (1) . . . . . and by 1983 was selling (2) . . . . . per year. At that time it sold (3) . . . . . than any other model. However, in 1984 sales declined to (4) . . . . . but they later (5) . . . . . to 40,000 in (6) . . . . . Since then sales have remained steady and there has been a slight (7) . . . . . in recent years. Although sales of the Blenheim were low in 1984, the company's other two models, the Gladiator and the Sprite, both achieved their (8) . . . . . sales figures in this year. The Gladiator came onto the market in (9) . . . . . and within (10) . . . . . years had achieved sales of 60,000 per annum. Sales soon began to decline and by 1988 had reached (11) . . . . . a year. This model is still in production and sells about (12) . . . . . per annum. The Napier Auto Company's third model, the Sprite, was in production between (13) . . . . . and (14) . . . . . and achieved its highest sales figures in (15) . . . . . when (16) . . . . . were sold. Sales declined rapidly, however, although they picked up in (17) . . . . ., two years before production of this model (18) . . . . . At the end of the decade Napier Autos had (19) . . . . . cars in production, of which the (20) . . . . . has been the most successfull overall.

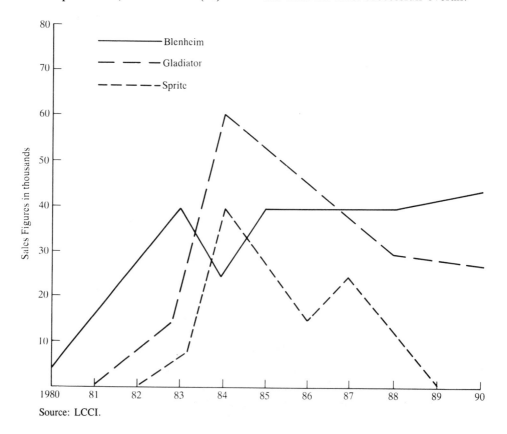

Source: LCCI.

**Comment on SAQs 3.6−3.10**

With careful formulation of the questions, a candidate's response can be brief and thus a large number of questions may be set in this format, enabling a wide coverage. In addition this format lends itself to testing the skills of surveying for gist, scanning for specific information and extracting the main ideas and important details from a text we identified as important above (see Table 3.3, p. 73). Testing these skills is not normally possible in the indirect formats of gap filling or the C-tests we looked at earlier.

Activities such as inference, recognition of a sequence, comparison and establishing the main idea of a text, require the relating of sentences in a text with other items which may be some distance away in the text. This can be done effectively through short-answer questions where the answer has to be sought rather than being one of those provided. Answers are not provided for the student as in multiple-choice questions: therefore, if a student gets the answer right one is more certain that this has not occurred for reasons other than comprehension of the text.

All of the conditions identified as suitable for consideration by the test writer in Table 3.1 above can be addressed through this format. A strong case can be made in appropriate contexts, such as EAP tests, for the use of long texts with short-answer formats on the grounds that these are more representative of required reading in the target situation, at least in terms of length. They can also provide more reliable data about a candidate's reading ability. The beneficial washback effect of this type of format on the teaching that precedes it cannot be ignored.

Answers should have to be worked out from the passage and not already known because of world knowledge or easily arrived at by matching wording from the question with wording in the text. Other guidelines considered in Part I above must be applied to all exemplifications of this format.

If the number of acceptable answers to a question is limited, it is possible to give fairly precise instructions to the examiners who mark them. The marking should allow the range of semantically acceptable answers. Mechanical accuracy criteria (grammar, spelling, punctuation) should not feature in the scoring system as this affects the accuracy of the measurement of the reading construct.

The main disadvantage to this technique is that it involves the candidate in writing, and there is some concern, largely anecdotal, that this interferes with the measurement of the intended construct. Care is needed in the setting of items to limit the range of possible acceptable responses and the extent of writing required. In those cases where there is more debate over the acceptability of an answer, in questions requiring inferencing skills, for example, there is a possibility that the variability of answers might lead to marker unreliability. However, careful moderation and standardisation of examiners should help to reduce this (see Sections 1.3.1−1.3.5 above).

The superiority of the short-answer format over all others is that texts can be selected to match conditions appropriate to any level of student, and the format allows you to test all the operations in Table 3.3 above. In the example of the TEEP test (included as Appendix 1 of *Communicative Language Testing*, Weir 1990), short-answer questions were set on the same passage across the range of skills we identified. We would certainly advocate its use for testing operations in (a) and (b) of Table 3.3, namely those involving skimming and establishing the main idea and important details.

For testing microlinguistic skills, either selective deletion gap filling or C-tests would now seem to be more appropriate and a more efficient format. If there is a desire to test at the level of contributory linguistic skills ((c) in Table 3.3) this is best done separately from tests of the other operations.

When adopting a short-answer format there are a number of procedures that can be adopted, as well as the guidelines in Part I, to enhance the validity of the test. These are referred to in the next section on procedures.

*Procedures for test task design*

There are a number of steps that we can take to try to ensure that we come closer to achieving the goals in the testing of reading that we have discussed above.

1.  We should first ask ourselves of any text what would constitute an understanding of that text. We might try to map diagrammatically the main ideas of a passage and any important detail, in a form of 'mindmapping' exercise (see Buzan 1974). This could be done in the form of a spidergram or as a linear summary. We might then try to reach a consensus with colleagues who have followed the same procedure on what are the main points and important details. We could examine whether what we have decided is important matches what colleagues consider important (see Sarig 1989 for an interesting empirical investigation of this procedure). This would be an important first step in trying to ensure the validity of our tests. In the EAP test discussed above, we would be concerned that the answers to the questions we then wrote revealed the important information in the text, and matched a good summary of the text or any abstract available of the text. An ability to answer the items should indicate that the candidate has understood the passage.

2.  In any test of extended reading serious thought might be given to 'frameworking' the task by encouraging candidates to perform a series of introductory activities designed to bring the processing of discourse in the test closer to what we would consider to be efficient reading in a real-life context. In an EAP context for example, these might take the form of instructing them to:

    (a) read an abstract if one has been provided;
    (b) look at the first and last paragraphs;
    (c) identify the section headings;
    (d) look at the titles of any graphs or charts.

    The result of this should be to ensure that the candidate processes the discourse in a way that accords more with natural processing. It should help ensure that after the test the candidate is better able to convey information about what he/she has just read. In tests that do not require these strategies, candidates may often do well on test items but be unable to tell the interlocutor what the passage was about.

3.  We need to consider closely the order the questions should come in. It may be beneficial to separate those items focusing on skimming from those catering for

more intensive reading ability. Within the skimming section we might also wish to separate surveying for gist from scanning for specific information. The items should follow the sequence as they occur in the text (see Hughes 1989: 130). In using longer texts such as articles from professional journals, questions can be located within sections if these are sufficiently long and candidates' attention is drawn to this.

If we include items testing more specifically linguistic skills should we separate these from items intended to measure more global comprehension skills? There is evidence that it is the former that non-native speakers sometimes find most difficulty with. If they can carry out the broader global skills such as understanding the main idea, should we indeed concern ourselves about the fact that they do not know the meaning of 'they' in line 46?

In skills testing it is important that students should see the questions they are going to find answers to before they actually read the text. In this way they will be able to approach the text in the desired manner. Therefore, if the questions only demand specific pieces of information, the answers can be sought by quickly scanning the text for these specifics rather than reading it through very carefully line by line.

4.  We need to ensure that the formats we select are not in themselves adversely affecting performance, e.g. do multiple-choice tests test reading and/or the ability to do multiple-choice tests? There is some evidence that in tests of reading MCQ tests only exhibit a low correlation with other measures of reading (see Weir 1983). If we use short-answer questions, are we testing the ability to write? How can we guard against this? We should mark for meaning only and through care in item construction delimit the amount of writing required in the answer. In monolingual countries, thought might be given to candidates answering in the mother tongue. What else can we compare the results of tests against? Do you get different results if you use different formats?

Formats should be familiar to the candidates and, if they are not, a practice test item should be given to familiarise them. If it is an achievement test, it should reflect the types of text and associated activities that have been practised in class. If it is a proficiency test, it should mirror future activities and text types.

The main proviso for testing within a communicative framework is that the test tasks should as far as possible involve realistic discourse processing and cover a range of enabling skills that have been previously identified as appropriate. It is important that tests developed within this paradigm should have a positive washback effect on practice in the language classroom (see Hughes 1989, Ch.6).

# Chapter Four
## *Testing listening comprehension*

### 4.1 A framework for testing listening comprehension

In many situations the testing of listening can be handled as part of the testing of spoken interaction (see Chapter 2 above). In the real world, however, there are a number of occasions when listening is not the precursor of speech, e.g. listening to lectures, railway announcements, recorded messages or television and radio programmes.

It is essential in these cases to decide on the conditions and operations that merit inclusion in a test of listening comprehension. We need to identify the situational features and important facets of interaction involved in the desired performance. It might be even more important to specify these in assessing comprehension abilities as one does not have a tangible product of speech or writing to attach behavioural labels to. To determine what is a satisfactory performance one needs to specify in some detail what it is the candidate can do (operations), under what circumstances (conditions).

### EXERCISE 4A   OPERATIONS

> Make a note of the operations you feel you might want to include in a test of listening. Compare your answer with our suggestions below.

Table 4.1
*Summary checklist of operations (listening comprehension)*

(a)   *Direct meaning comprehension:*
Listening for gist.
Listening for main idea(s) or important information; includes tracing the development of an argument, distinguishing the main idea(s) from supporting detail, differentiating statement from example, differentiating a proposition from its argument, distinguishing fact from opinion when clearly marked.
Listening for specifics; involves recall of important details.
Determining speaker's attitude/intentions toward listener/topic (persuasion/explanation) where obvious from the text.

(b)   *Inferred meaning comprehension:*
Making inferences and deductions; evaluating content in terms of information clearly available from the text.
Relating utterances to the social and situational context in which they are made.
Recognising the communicative function of utterances.
Deducing meaning of unfamiliar lexical items from context.

(c)   *Contributory meaning comprehension (microlinguistic):*
Understanding phonological features (stress, intonation, etc.).
Understanding concepts (grammatical notions) such as comparison, cause, result, degree, purpose.

Understanding discourse markers.
Understanding syntactic structure of the sentence and clause, e.g. elements of clause structure, noun and verb modification, negation.
Understanding grammatical cohesion, particularly reference.
Understanding lexical cohesion through lexical set membership and collocation.
Understanding lexis.

(d)  *Listening and writing (note taking from lecture, telephone conversations, etc.):*
Ability to extract salient points to summarise the whole text, reducing what is heard to an outline of the main points and important detail.
Ability to extract selectively relevant key points from a text on a specific idea or topic, especially involving the coordination of related information.

## Comment on Exercise 4A

In the past, emphasis was placed on the candidate's ability to discriminate phonemes, to recognise stress and intonation patterns and to record through a written (usually multiple-choice) product, what had been heard. The sum of a candidate's appropriate responses in these 'discrete' sub-tests was equated with proficiency in listening comprehension (the listening component of the General Medical Council's PLAB test is an example of this discrete point approach which is still in use).

Few people would now maintain that an ability to discriminate between phonemes implies a capacity to comprehend verbal messages. The emphasis has shifted to contextualised tests of listening comprehension, incorporating all the additional redundant features that facilitate comprehension. The concern now is with testing the communication of meaning as against structural understanding. (For further discussion of the shift see Brindley and Nunan 1992, Buck 1991, Rost 1990, Weir 1990: 51–4.)

Much of the current thinking on the nature of listening comprehension is based on earlier work on reading comprehension (see Brindley and Nunan 1992 , Dunkel 1991, and Rost 1990). Both are receptive skills and the testing of listening has many similarities with the testing of reading, not least in its invisible, cognitive nature, which makes it difficult to describe and to assess.

Accordingly, many of the elements for consideration in the operations part of our framework for testing listening comprehension were discussed in Chapter 3 when we were dealing with reading. It was noted there that such taxonomies of sub-skills have the status of hypotheses only, premised on what experience and opinion suggest are important (see Buck 1990). The operations identified for listening all need extensive validation before their status is raised and, according to Buck (1990: 95), this may be problematic because 'listening comprehension is a massively parallel interactive process taking advantage of information from a large number of sources, both linguistic and non-linguistic' and it may not be possible to separate out individual variables.

Despite these difficulties, testers need to establish the relationships between skill levels, and we must do the best job we can in the present state of uncertainty (see Brindley and Nunan 1992 for an extremely clear and thorough review of the issues involved here).

In most contemporary approaches to the testing of listening, the texts are no longer broken down into small chunks and as far as possible they retain their authenticity. This contributes to their validity as tests of listening. Although it is now usual to provide long, uninterrupted texts as stimuli in a test battery, in terms of the tasks and scoring it might still be desirable to focus on individual operations, rather than testing a global understanding of the passage through written summary.

Because of the difficulties associated with integrated testing (see discussion of this in relation to reading-into-writing tasks p. 72 above) the items set on these texts tend to focus on 'discrete skills' of the type listed in Table 4.1 (Sections (a) and (b)) above. However, as with reading, the strength of the claims for the discreteness of these skills has still to be established, and it is likely that different candidates might arrive at acceptable answers to test items by different routes, depending on individual processing (whether top down, bottom up, or interactive-compensatory processing. See Brindley and Nunan 1992: 3–4 and Dunkel 1991: 438–51 for thorough discussion of these skills.).

Reliability is, however, likely to be enhanced by having a larger number of individually focused items, rather than testing understanding of a spoken passage through an integrated writing task such as a selective summary of the discourse. In the latter case the danger of muddied measurement referred to earlier in Part I cannot be ignored.

If we wish to make test tasks more like those in real life, the unbroken, sequential nature of extended spoken discourse precludes items which focus on the more specifically linguistic skills such as understanding lexis from context or recognising the meaning value of specific features of stress or intonation (see Sections (b) and (c) in Table 4.1 above). Candidates would find it extremely difficult to backtrack and focus on specific features of discourse while listening to and attempting to understand a continuing discourse. If we wish to preserve the authentic nature of the listening material, we have to focus questions on the more global processing skills which enable us to extract meaning from a spoken text (see the skills listed under Section (a) in Table 4.1 above). These questions would reflect the sequence in which information occurred in a text and there would need to be sufficient time between them in order not to make undue demands on a candidate's processing capacity.

Where the purpose of the task is transactional, to understand the main ideas and important detail in a piece of discourse, it should be possible to establish a reasonable consensus on what students could take away from texts through mindmap exercises with colleagues (see Sarig 1989 and discussion of this in relation to reading on p. 96 above). It can then be established through trialling that candidates, whom we would pass, can extract this information. As with reading it may well be that non-native speakers can extract this global information but might not do as well on tests focusing on the more specifically linguistic items (see Section (c) in Table 4.1).

If non-native speakers do not know the meaning of a particular lexical item or connector this should not trouble us unduly. It may be unnecessary to bother with the more intensive tests of linguistic understanding discussed in Exercises 4E and 4F below. We can be reasonably sure that to cope with global processing in terms of Section (a) sub-skills, candidates will, in any case, need a minimally adequate competence in the microlinguistic skills described in Section (c).

As in testing the other skills, there is a tension between the describable and the testable in the assessment of listening. There may be a problem with operationalising certain facets from the framework above, in particular the testing of understanding specific linguistic items when comprehending extended spoken discourse. The value of approaching testing with a framework for test task design is that it makes apparent what needs to be tested and what does not. It will make clearer the features of real-life activity that we should attempt to build into tests. Attempts to operationalise frameworks in classroom testing will help establish where the problems lie, help clarify the relationships between the posited skills, and help shed some light on levels of ability.

To avoid unnecessary repetition the reader is referred to the discussion of these skills in relation to reading on pages 72−5 above. One of the main differences in listening comprehension is the effect of speaker-related conditions on these operations, for example, stress, intonation, pausing, rhythm and amount of built-in redundancy. Another difference arises from the transient nature of spoken language. Normally the listener is not able to backtrack over what has been said, as a reader can when faced with a permanent written text. Processing has to take place in real time.

## EXERCISE 4B  PERFORMANCE CONDITIONS

Given the interactive nature of most listening experiences, we need to determine which conditions it might be important to take account of in a listening test. We have already referred to speaker-related variables and the need to process serially in real time.

Make a note of any other conditions you feel ought to be taken into consideration at the design stage in a test of listening. Then compare them with our suggestions below.

Table 4.2
*Summary checklist of performance conditions (listening comprehension)*

*Purpose* of task for listener.

*Number* of speakers (monologue, e.g. lecture; dialogue, e.g. conversation; multi-participant, e.g. seminar).

*Speaker-related variables*: accent and pronunciation, speed at which discourse is uttered and has to be processed, degree of pausing, degree of built-in redundancy, attitudes, personality, degree of sympathetic adjustment in interactive tasks, speakers' status, familiarity and gender.

*Nature of the texts*: story, song, poem, play, lecture, instructions, directions, message, radio announcement, joke, conversation (face to face and telephone), interview, television documentary, focused social interaction, service encounters, news broadcast, public announcement, discussion.

*Organisational*: grammar, cohesion, rhetorical organisation, phonology.

*Propositional*:  lexical range: common core, technical, sub-technical.
topic (genre/level of specificity/cultural bias/familiarity/interest/relevance).
status of speaker to listener, e.g. equal to equal, expert to layperson.
flexibility (adapting appropriate listening strategies, recognising and responding to topic switches).
relationship between content of text and candidates' background knowledge (formal and subject).
type of information (abstract/concrete).

*Illocutionary*:    functional purpose(s), intention(s) of the speaker.
discoursal range (across texts).

*Setting*: level of formality, acoustic environment.

*Channel* of presentation: +/− visual support.

*Size* of input, length of text.

*Method factor/response mode*: familiarity with task type and other test environment features; amount of help given; clarity of rubrics, rubrics in L1/TL, spoken/read; questions in advance or questions only after candidate has heard the input material; amount of context provided, e.g. prior related reading task; number of times input heard. Answer in L1/TL. Integrated with writing/speaking task. Demands made on productive skills. Number and nature of operations to be performed within the task and test/ordering of these and time available for completion. Explicitness of any weighting in questions. Explicitness of criteria for correctness.

*Acknowledgements*: Don Porter for drawing attention to some of the skills in Table 4.1 above, and Bachman (1990) for a number of the facets in Table 4.2 (see also Brindley and Nunan 1992, Buck 1991, Dunkel 1991, Richards 1983, Rost 1990).

*Comment on Exercise 4B*

Many of the conditions we have included in Table 4.2 will be familiar to the reader from our discussion of conditions for reading tests in Exercise 3C in Chapter 3 above. The test writer will need to take account of: purpose; organisational, propositional and illocutionary features of the input; channel; size; speed of processing and method factor/response mode, especially the context in which the listening takes place, when selecting a sample of spoken discourse for a test task. Comprehension will be affected by the interaction of all these factors with the procedural demands of the operations set (see Brindley and Nunan 1992 and Dunkel 1991 for further discussion of these conditions).

In designing listening tests, the test writer has to make additional decisions on speaker-related variables such as speed of utterance, degree of sympathetic adjustment (see Rost 1990), accent and pronunciation, familiarity, status, gender and on the nature of the text types to be selected (see Table 2.1 in Chapter 2 for a listing of the routine skills and improvisational skills that the candidate might need to be exposed to). In particular the number of speakers the candidate has to understand in audio tests may have an important influence on performance (see Brown and Yule 1983). The sound quality of the input, particularly if audio-recorded, and the acoustic environment may also require close attention if validity and reliability are not to be affected adversely.

The decisions taken on these conditions are important because of the added load they can place on processing, especially given the serial nature of the listening experience, where we normally only have an opportunity to listen to something once as we process it under normal time constraints. For further discussion of these conditions, refer to the section on procedures for the design of extended listening tests below.

*Level*

Finally we need to consider *level*. As with reading, this is best defined in terms of the operations and conditions we feel students should be able to cope with if they are to be considered as passing the test we have set for a particular purpose.

## The way forward

It is clear from recent reviews of the teaching and testing of listening comprehension (see Brindley and Nunan 1992, Brown and Yule 1983, Buck 1990, Dunkel 1991 and Rost 1990) that we have a long way to go in developing satisfactory models which can provide a firm basis for construction of assessment tools. As with reading, we do not have any clear evidence on listening text and task hierarchies or on listening ability levels.

We need to investigate systematically the elements in our proposed frameworks in order to determine which are important and how they relate to each other. In our present state of knowledge, the safest approach for teachers is to try and make test tasks approximate as closely as possible to the real-life behaviour(s) they wish to say something about. Through careful sampling of listening tasks which demonstrably approximate to desired performances, in terms of likely operations and specified conditions, we can be reasonably confident that we are doing the best we can in attempting to describe candidates' language abilities. We need through empirical research to determine the types of task (identified operations performed under specified conditions) that can be carried out at various ability levels.

## 4.2  Formats for testing listening comprehension

We will now consider a variety of formats that should be useful in testing the various components of listening comprehension. Before looking at the formats below you might find it useful to refer back to the general principles and specific guidelines for test construction we developed above in Part I of this book.

You will have to examine these examples of tests designed to measure listening to see how far they match the frameworks for listening we have just examined in Tables 4.1 and 4.2. These are examples that have been constructed for specific students in specific contexts. They are taken from a variety of levels, from elementary to advanced.

The particular conditions or operations in some examples may well be inappropriate for your own students. The purpose of the exercises is to become aware of these formats, their advantages and limitations, and to think critically about them so that you can decide what would be most appropriate (with modification where necessary in terms of your own framework) for the students you are responsible for in your particular context.

The following examples represent some of the more useful options for testing listening ability along a direct/indirect continuum.

## EXERCISE 4C   THE TESTING OF EXTENSIVE LISTENING: SHORT-ANSWER QUESTIONS

The test in Example 1 below is an EAP proficiency test used to determine whether students would cope successfully with study in the UK. Also, if required, an EAP proficiency test could indicate that as postgraduate students in their own country, they should be able to understand visiting speakers or local lecturers presenting in English medium. A student able to cope with most of the questions at this level is capable of listening in English to an academic lecture.

Look at Example 1. This is an early example of a short-answer test task in listening to lectures and note taking from the Test in English for Educational Purposes (TEEP). A transcript of the mini-lecture is provided (see Appendix A). If possible get somebody to read this out to you and answer the questions set on the passage below.

(a) First consider what conditions the test writer has been able to take account of in designing this task. Secondly, think about what operation(s) can be tested through this format. Refer to the list of operations/enabling skills and conditions in Tables 4.1 and 4.2 above.

(b) Establish what you think the advantages and disadvantages of testing listening through this format are. You may wish to comment on the operations involved and the conditions under which the task is performed. You may also wish to relate the examples to the framework of guidelines for test construction from Part I.

## Example 1:   Short-answer Questions

This is another test of your ability to understand spoken English. You have to make notes and use them to answer a number of questions. You have **2 tasks** to do in approximately **50 minutes**.

### TASK ONE

You are going to hear part of a lecture on 'Issues in the Women's Liberation Movement'.

The recording is about 10 minutes long and it will be played once only.

A Lecture Outline starts on the next page of this booklet and consists of three important statements, in capitals and underlined, each followed by questions. There is a space after each question for notes and below that a space for your answer.

While listening to the lecture, make notes in the space provided (these notes will not be marked).

You will be given time after the lecture is finished to use these notes to write your answers.

Use all the information in the lecture outline. It will help you to find exactly what information you need to listen for.

LECTURE OUTLINE

STATEMENT 1. SINCE THE EARLY 1970S WOMEN'S GROUPS HAVE FORMED REGIONAL AND NATIONAL GROUPINGS, AND HAVE MOUNTED REGIONAL AND NATIONAL CAMPAIGNS.

**1.1**  These campaigns have concentrated on 4 central demands. What are they?

NOTES:   a)  _____

b)  _____

c)  _____

d)  _____

ANSWER:  a)  _____

b)  _____

c)  _____

d)  _____

STATEMENT 2. AN IMPORTANT ISSUE IN THE DEVELOPMENT OF THE WOMEN'S LIBERATION MOVEMENT HAS BEEN THAT OF THE INVOLVEMENT OF MEN IN THE MOVEMENT'S ACTIVITIES.

**2.1**  What, according to the speaker, did women particularly resent from the beginning?

NOTES:   _____

_____

ANSWER:  _____

_____

**2.2**  Why did men dominate the discussion in the early meetings of the movement?

NOTES:   _____

_____

ANSWER:  _____

_____

**2.3**  What happened at the Skegness conference in 1971?

NOTES:   _____

_____

ANSWER:  _____

_____

**2.4** What decision was taken with respect to the involvement of men in Movement activities?

NOTES:    _____

_____

ANSWER:    _____

_____


STATEMENT 3. A SECOND ISSUE WIDELY DISCUSSED IN WOMEN'S GROUPS IS THE
QUESTION OF WAGES FOR HOUSEWORK

**3.1** According to the speaker, what is the effect on the woman of the situation in which the man
goes out to work, but the woman stays at home and does the housework?

NOTES:    _____

_____

ANSWER:    _____

_____


**3.2** In what way is the housework done by a woman at home less pleasant than a man's work
out of the home?

NOTES:    _____

_____

ANSWER:    _____

_____


**3.3** What is the major difference, according to the speaker, between a woman's work in the home
and a man's work outside it?

NOTES:    _____

_____

ANSWER:    _____

_____


**3.4** The suggestion of state wages for housework is rejected by most women for three reasons.
What are they?

NOTES:    a) _____

b) _____

c) _____

ANSWER:    a) _____

b) _____

c) _____

**3.5** What is the attitude of the speaker to regarding the family allowance as a basis for a scheme of state wages for housework?

NOTES: _____

_____

ANSWER: _____

_____

Source: TEEP TEST. Testing and Evaluation Unit, CALS, University of Reading.

*Comment on Exercise 4C*

First the test developer needs to check that the discourse selected as input is valid in terms of the conditions appropriate to the particular context it is being developed for. The listening text you select for your students should take account of as many of the relevant features in Table 4.2 above as possible.

In Example 1 the text had be sufficiently long for testing academic listening in order for us to have confidence that the candidate will process the text in a similar manner to students operating in an academic context. Though the example of a short lecturette is for more advanced EAP students, there is no reason why the same general format cannot be used at other levels in general English contexts. Young children, for example, might be asked to listen to a very short story delivered by the teacher followed by a few appropriate questions. In testing proficiency for listening in general English contexts, the texts should reflect appropriate features of the future target situation and in achievement testing reflect the salient features from texts previously encountered in a course.

Due care would need to be taken of speaker-related variables such as accent, degree of pausing, adequate redundancy and speed of delivery in recording this text. The text in Example 1 is considered appropriate for postgraduate students in the Arts and Social Sciences to have to process in terms of its organisational, propositional and illocutionary features. The lack of visual referents would make it less suitable for students in Science and Engineering. The purpose for which students have to listen would seem to approximate to that of students in a lecture situation in an English-medium university. The method factors are discussed in more detail in the section on procedures for the design of extended listening tests below.

SAQs are a realistic activity for testing EAP listening comprehension if one wishes to simulate real-life activities where a written record of the main ideas and important details is made of a spoken message. The responses produced by the candidate are limited and so the danger of the writing process interfering with the measurement of listening is restricted.

If the candidate has to answer written questions while listening to continuous discourse there is a danger that some of the main ideas or important details might be missed while an answer to a previous question is being recorded. For this reason we would advocate a number of changes to Example 1 above.

It could be improved by first getting the candidates to listen to the lecture and take notes while they are doing this. Then they could be given the questions and have to answer them. This seems to accord more with what we normally do when we listen to lectures and take notes. Where students are given the questions in advance there is a danger that they will process input differently, i.e. they will be listening for specific cues indicating that the answer to the next question is coming up. This would seem to be different from processing a text to make sense of it as it unfolds.

In addition, by providing candidates with a framework of statements and questions in the example above, the tester has actually given away the main elements of the structure of the text and has reduced the number of questions relating to main ideas that could be asked. The framework of statements was originally provided partially to compensate for the additional difficulties resulting from listening to an audio recording of an unfamiliar voice.

If we want to test a candidate's ability to extract the main ideas and important detail from spoken input (see Section (a), Table 4.1 above), this would appear to be better served by candidates first making notes while listening to the lecture and then answering questions after they have finished listening.

It is crucial that test writers mindmap a text in advance of writing the questions in order to ensure they do not miss out on testing any of the main ideas or important details, where this is the purpose of the particular listening exercise. Get a colleague to read out the passage from Appendix A to you, and make notes of what you think important. Compare these with the questions in Example 1 above. As long as the initial mindmapping exercise is carried out with due care and attention then the questions the candidates receive after they have listened to the lecture and taken notes should represent a reasonable summation of the information (main points and important details) that could have been extracted from the text. It would be advisable to check this through piloting of the test and if there are any items where very few of the passing candidates have recorded an answer successfully, consideration might be given to removing the item from the test.

A number of further steps could be taken which might help improve Example 1. As with reading, it is useful to try and give some guidance on how one might go about designing and implementing test tasks in listening, as this information is seldom available in books on testing. We outline below some of the stages that colleagues in a recent test design project at the ESP Centre, Alexandria, Egypt found useful in constructing extended listening tasks. Particular attention is paid to providing some preliminary feedback on the conditions and operations they found it useful to take account of.

You will note that in several places compromises have been made, particularly in relation to the authenticity of the stimulus material. A conscious decision was taken to present the candidates with input that was well delivered and had a clear informational structure. The voice quality was to be of a high standard and distracting variables such as background noise, rapid delivery and strong regional accents were eliminated. If candidates could not cope with this type of input, we could be fairly certain that they would be even more disadvantaged when faced with the additional problems in processing, posed by badly organised lectures, delivered speedily in strong regional accents.

It was felt that given the additional burden placed on candidates by having to listen to an unfamiliar, disembodied, taped voice in a decontextualised listening experience then some compensation in terms of conditions was necessary. These seemed reasonable decisions in the overseas contexts in which they were taken. They are not, however, irrevocable, and it remains to be seen in the light of the experience of others whether such compromises in terms of conditions are correctly premised. What is important is that a framework approach enables the testers to take account of such conditions and a principled and explicit solution can be arrived at through reasoned discussion.

The procedures below are offered in the spirit of research and improvement. They are not meant as prescriptive statements to be slavishly copied. The value of documenting such experiences is that others who follow do not have to start from scratch and, through experimentation in different contexts, these guidelines can be rigorously examined and improved.

## Procedures for the design of extended listening tests

### Phase 1  Preparation

*Review available listening texts*
First review all appropriate extended listening material, available locally, in terms of conditions (see Table 4.2 above). Particular attention should be paid to the following:

1.  Organisational structure: ensure there is a sufficiently clear outline and a sufficiency of information in terms of main ideas.
2.  Sound quality: avoid extraneous noise.
3.  Length: choose an appropriate length. For a lecture it is normally at least ten minutes, whereas instructions or directions might be less than a minute.
4.  Clarity/lecturing style, manner of delivery/pacing should be acceptable and accessible.
5.  Accent should not be too pronounced.
6.  Propositional content should be suitable and accessible for the intended audience. Text should not be biased in terms either of culture or of subject matter.
7.  Adequate redundancy: there should be some degree of repetition of main ideas and sufficient narrative padding to allow the listener time to extract the main ideas. Do not use texts which have been written to be read and which consist of densely packed and close-knit argument (see Shohamy and Inbar 1991).
8.  Pausing should be sufficient to allow note taking.
9.  Speed should be normal for the context.

The starting point is either a tapescript, a tape, or preferably both, containing content suitable in terms of the conditions outlined above. Out of the many materials you will need to preview, only a limited number will be suitable. Where the sound quality is not high, both reliability and validity might be reduced and re-recording will be necessary. If one can guarantee a good recording and reasonable acoustics then a taped test is always preferable to a live delivery if the test is to be administered on more than one occasion.

*Make any revisions considered necessary*
When you have selected the text, read the tapescript to edit it. After discussion with colleagues, you might want to make changes to provide a clearer overall information structure. In order to make the structure clearer the following steps could be taken:

1. Ensure that sufficient contextualisation is available prior to the listening activity in order to activate the students' schemata (see Dunkel 1991: 442–4 for an insightful discussion of the critical role played by content and textual schemata in L2 listening comprehension). The prior reading of a passage in the same area is a positive attribute of Example 1 above (see Weir 1990, Appendix 1 for the complete version of this test).

2. A verbal introduction can be added to the revised script which might include a statement of the topic for contextualisation (but this normally removes the possibility of asking gist questions), and outline background information (limited so as not to give away all the information relating to the main ideas). The introduction is probably best spoken only.

3. In some variations of the SAQ format, as in Example 1 above, students are given a written framework of the main sections of a text but this will tend to make the task easier and to reduce the number of questions that might be asked.

4. A conclusion could be built in to reinforce the overall message.

5. An adequate degree of pausing and redundancy should be built in. With caution, one can limit the length of segments in each breath group and lengthen pauses at the end if there is insufficient redundancy written into scripted messages. Beware of making the discourse sound unnatural.

6. Consideration might be given to building an introductory phase into the test, after candidates have heard the instructions, where they are asked to make predictions about what they are going to hear. They are asked to predict the likely development of the topic. Give them three or four minutes to write out their own ideas/mindmaps before starting the test proper.

## Phase 2  Implementation

*Record the edited text*
As a result of the work in phase 1, in phase 2 record the lecture to build in the conditions which are considered appropriate for the listening experience. Try to ensure that the re-recording is made as natural as possible. Whenever possible it is important that the listening text is re-recorded before an actual audience as it contributes to the authenticity of the activity. At the very least delivering the lecture before a live audience should ensure greater listenability (see Shohamy and Inbar 1991).

Avoid passages originally written to be read. If it were possible through practice or familiarisation to deliver the lecture/talk semi-scripted rather than from a full transcript this would certainly improve its listenability (Shohamy and Inbar 1991). It might result in a more natural level of spontaneity, false starts, ungrammaticality and hesitation phenomena. This might however require a number of practice runs first before the final recording is made. Time constraints often mean that the recording has to be made largely scripted but the presence of a live audience should enable the speaker to modify the discourse interactively. It is essential that copies be made of master tapes as soon as they are recorded to avoid accidental damage.

*Establish the main ideas and important details: mindmap the text through listening and note taking*

While recording the lecture, the audience of teachers/colleagues/students should take down notes of what they consider to be the main points and important details of the talk. Very often weak points in the structure of the talk are discovered after comparing notes. Some of the more common are failure to:

1. State the topic clearly.
2. Signal the main points of the talk.
3. Ensure that each section is consistent in terms of content with the stated topic of that section.
4. Take care with the range of referring expressions employed. There must be simple repetition of new terms or concepts. The greater the variety in the number of referring expressions the more difficult it would be to process.

If the intention is to get candidates to make notes on the passage then its structure should obviously allow this.

The text might need to be revised in the light of the foregoing discussion and re-recorded (in front of a live audience!), to improve its authenticity.

The passage should then be given to students (as similar to the eventual target population as possible) to take down notes while listening to it once only. This will help determine what it is that students think important in the text. Other colleagues could also take down notes from the final version of the tape. This mindmapping is best done by teachers who did not take part in the earlier procedures so as to get a wider spectrum of opinion on the main ideas and supporting details. It would also help guard against too deep a processing of the text by those teachers who actually constructed it. The questions and notes relevant to a single listening are what we are after. So if the team actually construct the listening text and record it then perhaps it would be best to get colleagues who have had no prior experience of the text to make notes on it while listening.

*Item writing*

You should next divide into small groups to devise questions. Questions should be firmly based on the important details or main ideas that have been noted down in actually listening to the tape as described in the previous section. Never ask questions that do not appear in the notes that people have made while listening to the tape. Questions should be based on the listening experience, *not* the transcripts. The questions should reflect a consensus mindmap of the groups' views (i.e. the views of teachers, and of students deemed to be of passing level) on the main ideas and important details contained in the text, based on the note-taking experience.

In addition, it may well be that questions related to operations such as the speaker's attitude to topics and audience, and inferential questions such as separating facts from opinion, may be written when appropriate. These will not occur naturally in every text selected. If questions are asked concerning the reasons for certain decisions, then these should be based on information clearly stated in the text. One could also possibly make deductions which follow logically from information in the text.

The questions should be written in sequential order, that is they should normally follow in the sequence in which the information appears in the discourse, and there must be sufficient spacing between them. Ensure there is sufficient time to answer a question before the candidate has to listen for information to answer the next. Missing an item because of too close proximity with the preceding item could have a serious knock-on effect for later items and unreasonably deflate a candidate's score.

A chairman should distil the essence of the groups' versions on each item. A synthesised version of the questions emanating from the groups should be put on a whiteboard or OHP. Changes should then be made to the versions on the whiteboard. In case of difficulties in wording, these difficulties can be resolved on the whiteboard. It is useful to have a transcript available at this stage to refer to.

## Phase 3   Trialling and marking

*Trialling*

Trial the test on a group as similar as possible to the target audience. Check how long it takes for students to complete the test. During the actual administration of the test, a close watch should be kept on whether the majority of the candidates are able to complete the sub-test in the time allotted. Determine rogue items/candidates and revise these in the light of analysis. When the test is trialled on a representative sample care must be taken to ensure that all the scripts are numbered and that candidates write their names on the scripts.

*Marking*

In marking, a proforma test data sheet should be used. Scores for each item for each candidate need to be registered as a 0 if incorrect or as a 1 if correct. Where no attempt has been made to answer an item a dash should be recorded as this may help identify if there was insufficient time for completion of any sub-tests. Recording the data in this way will help later in any statistical analysis. Ensure that the class and the test are identified on the mark sheet.

When marking scripts in the early stages of test development it may well be that alternative acceptable responses arise in student scripts. It is essential that marking is done by the team together in the same room initially until these variations in acceptable answers are finalised. No alternative answer should be accepted until it has been agreed by the whole group and then it should be recorded on the master of the marking key. If changes are made, then previously marked scripts should be checked for acceptability on this item. In marking listening tests, no marks should be deducted for errors in mechanical accuracy such as spelling, punctuation or grammar as long as these do not obscure the intelligibility of the response.

It is essential that the data sheets reflect a reliable and consistent marking policy. The markers should be sure of this before submitting data sheets for statistical analysis. This obviously suggests the value of an initial trialling period where alternative responses are examined as rigorously as possible.

*Level*

A serious problem in testing extensive listening by use of a tape recorder is that the visual element, plus exophoric reference and paralinguistic information, is not available to the candidate and perhaps, therefore, the listening task is made that much more difficult. The listener does not normally have to process disembodied sounds from a machine in real life (apart from the obvious exceptions such as listening to the radio, telephone conversations and public announcements). Candidates might be expected to cope with additional difficulties arising from the restricted context available in a listening test. We need to compensate for this or we might seriously underestimate their ability to process spoken language. Listening is often made the most difficult part of a test because we forget the additional burdens the test task imposes on the listener. Though the utterances may be heard twice in some of the examples we include, the listener — unlike the reader — does not normally have an opportunity for multiple checking or going back to confirm his understanding.

Do not, therefore, lose sight of the fact that a disembodied voice from a tape recorder is harder to process than a speaker in front of you. Though the clear specification and appropriate implementation of operations and conditions will help in setting the pass level, we should not demand too high a level from candidates in testing this skill.

Serious consideration might be given to writing items and accepting answers in the mother tongue of candidates in monolingual situations. This might help remove some unnecessary difficulties for candidates in the task and enable the tester to be confident of specifically testing the listening construct. If the candidate has to read and write in the target language as well as listen, this might be felt to be putting undue demands on him. Further it may not be his listening ability which prevents him from answering a question. This may be a contentious issue in certain contexts but in Britain it is fairly common in foreign language examinations for rubrics, questions and answers to be written in the mother tongue.

## EXERCISE 4D   INFORMATION TRANSFER TECHNIQUES

Look at the further examples of listening tests below (Examples 2−5)

(a) Consider what conditions the test writer has been able to take account of in designing the task. Secondly, think about what operation(s) can be tested through this format. Refer to the list of operations/enabling skills and conditions in Tables 4.1 and 4.2 above.

(b) Establish what you think the advantages and disadvantages of testing listening through this format are. You may wish to comment on the operations involved and the conditions under which the task is performed. For example, what types of text do you think this format will lend itself to? You may also wish to relate the examples to the framework of guidelines for test construction from Part I.

**Example 2**

The teacher explains what the students have to do. The students listen to part of a radio programme in English on the basis of which they complete a chart. The students have to indicate on the chart which is the best camera in respect of each feature and which is the worst. They write + for best and − for worst. The students have the chart with blanks in front of them while the teacher reads the passage out. The teacher reads the passage at a normal speed. Students are advised not to write anything during the first reading. During the second reading they can write in their answers while the teacher is speaking if they wish. After the second reading the teacher allows one minute for the students to write in their answers.

Teacher reads out:

*The advantages and disadvantages of three cameras*
The best cameras are the lightest. Camera A is much lighter than camera B. Camera A weighs 250 grams and B weighs 400 grams. Camera C is the lightest of all. Most people prefer cheap cameras to the more expensive ones. A costs $90, B costs $80 and C costs $100. C is the most expensive camera. Most people like a camera to have a flash. A has a better flash than B but C has no flash at all. Size is also important. The smaller the better. C is the best in size as it is the smallest. A is the biggest camera of the three. Finally, of the three cameras B is the easiest to use and A is easier to use than C.

The students are then given one minute to complete the chart. The teacher reads the passage out again and the students are then given one further minute to complete.

*Student script*
Look at the chart below. Some information is not there. You have to indicate on the chart which is the best camera in respect of each feature (cheapest, best flash, smallest and easiest to use) and which is the worst (most expensive, worst flash, biggest and most difficult to use). Write + for best and − for worst. The first one is done for you as an example. Listen to the teacher.

*Advantages and disadvantages of three cameras A, B and C*

| CAMERA | A | B | C |
|---|---|---|---|
| Weight | | − | + |
| Price | | | |
| Flash | | | |
| Size | | | |
| Ease of use | | | |

**Example 3**

You are in Britain on holiday and you would like to see a Shakespeare play performed by the Royal Shakespeare Company at Stratford upon Avon. You telephone the Royal Shakespeare Company Theatre at Stratford to find out what plays are being performed. You need to discuss with your friends which play you are going to see so you have to take down the details you are given on the telephone. Write down the information that you need, to help your friends decide. The first one is done to help you.

Text to be read out:

> Thank you for calling. We're sorry there is no one in the office at the moment. This recording gives you information about the plays that are being performed in Stratford this week. On Monday at 2 o'clock the Three Sisters will be performed and seats are available at £5. This play can also be seen in the evening on Thursday at eight o'clock when seats are available at £10. On Wednesday there is an afternoon performance of Julius Caesar at half past two and the price of tickets is £6. Julius Caesar will be performed again on Saturday evening at 8 o'clock and tickets will be £15. We are pleased to announce that on Tuesday and Friday this week there will be performances of Hamlet, one of Shakespeare's most famous plays. On Tuesday it will be performed at 2 o'clock in the afternoon and on Friday there will be an evening performance at the usual time. Tickets will cost twelve pounds for the evening performance and six pounds for the afternoon. Should you require any more information please ring this number between ten o'clock in the morning and two o'clock in the afternoon.

*Information about plays on at the Royal Shakespeare Company*

|  | Time starts | Play | Price |
|---|---|---|---|
| Monday | 2.00 | Three Sisters | £5 |
| Tuesday | 2.00 |  | £ |
| Wednesday |  | Julius Caesar | £ |
| Thursday | 8.00 |  | £ |
| Friday |  | Hamlet | £ |
| Saturday | 8.00 |  | £ |

**Example 4**

A transcript of the tape for this test is included at Appendix D.

## PART ONE

In this part of the test you will hear a conversation and a part of a radio programme about *olive oil*. You will hear them *once*. You may take notes as you listen. Then:

  (i) On Figure 1, page 3, label the parts of the olive, using words from the conversation.

 (ii) On Figure 2, write a colour to show each stage of the olive's development.

(iii) On Table A, circle the correct letter or letters in each column.

 (iv) Complete Tables B and C.

  (v) Tick ☑ any correct answers, 1–6 below, about Ray's attitude.

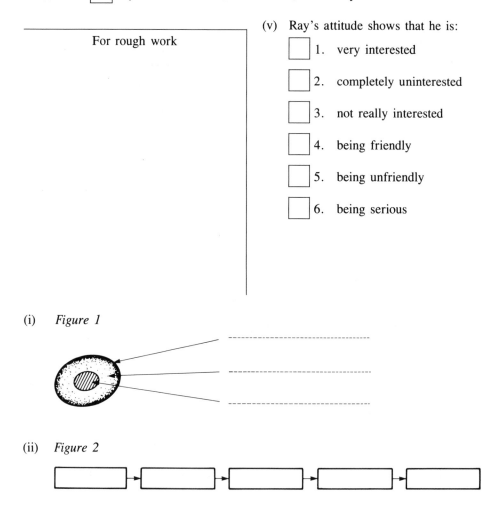

---
For rough work

(v)  Ray's attitude shows that he is:

☐ 1.  very interested

☐ 2.  completely uninterested

☐ 3.  not really interested

☐ 4.  being friendly

☐ 5.  being unfriendly

☐ 6.  being serious

(i)  *Figure 1*

(ii)  *Figure 2*

(iii)

*Table A*

| | Climate | | Conditions | | Fruition | | Life span |
|---|---|---|---|---|---|---|---|
| a. | short summers | a. | rich soil | a. | March – Sept | a. | 5–8 years |
| b. | long summers | b. | clay soil | b. | June–August | b. | 4–7 years |
| c. | hot summers | c. | poor soil | c. | July–Oct | c. | 60 years |
| d. | cool summers | d. | sandy soil | d. | June–Oct | d. | 300 years |
| e. | short winters | e. | heavy rain | e. | Sept–Mar | e. | 600 years |
| f. | mild winters | f. | light rain | f. | Oct–May | f. | 700 years |

(iv)

*Table B*

| Type | Acidity % |
|---|---|
| Pure | |
| Semi-Fine Virgin | |
| Fine Virgin | |
| Extra Virgin | |

*Table C*

| Country | Characteristics |
|---|---|
| | cloudy<br>dark green<br>sharp |
| | golden<br>mellow<br>soft |
| | clear<br>dark green<br>fruity |
| | clear<br>light<br>pale |

## PART TWO

In this part of the test you will hear a talk about the design of English drinking glasses. You will hear the information *once*, followed by a question and answer session. As you listen you should take notes. Then:

(i) Identify the glasses on page 119.
Write the name of each glass in the *large* box below each illustration.
The names are listed in Table 1 below.

(ii) Indicate the order in which the glasses were developed.
Write a number, 1–7, in the *small* box below each illustration.

(iii) Write the name of the drink served in each glass in the *circle* on each illustration.

Write AL for *ale*, CH for *champagne*, CO for *cordial*, ME for *mead*, and WI for *wine*.

(iv) Choose a *reason or reasons* for the design of each glass.
Write a letter from a—g below, on Table 1.

For rough work

*Table 1*

| Name | Reason for design |
|---|---|
| Dwarf | |
| Flute | |
| Firing Glass | |
| Mazer | |
| Passglass | |
| Ratafia | |
| Rummer | |
| Stirrup cup | |

a. because it hid the sediment.

b. because it showed how much to drink.

c. because it was easy to break.

d. because it was hard to break.

e. because it was not set down.

f. because it was set upside down.

g. because it held a strong drink.

Source: JMB UETESOL

## Example 5

Below is a map. You need to get to Forest Road. Listen to the instructions. Draw the route on the map. Mark Forest Road and any other roads that will help you find your way. You can make notes as you listen. You will hear the instructions only once.

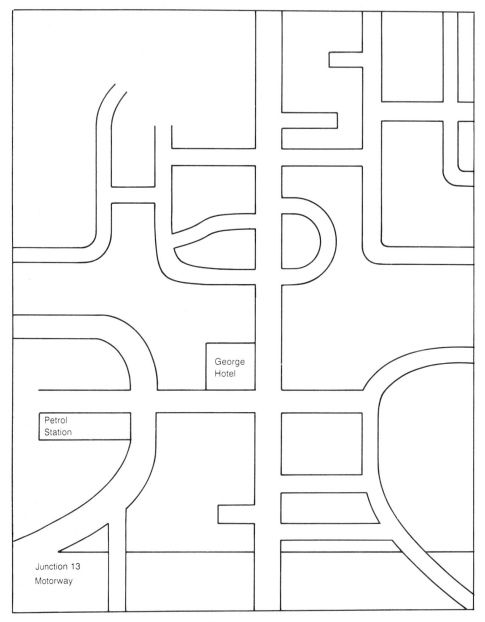

Source: Pitman Examinations, Higher Intermediate.

## Comment on Exercise 4D

In classroom testing the information transfer technique will usually involve drawing or labelling diagrams or pictures, completing tables, recording routes or locating buildings, etc., on a map. At lower levels of ability we need to keep the actual transfer operation simple, as in Examples 2, 3 and 5. The nature of the format and the limitations imposed by communicative capacity in the early stages of language learning constrain the types of things students might be expected to listen for. These are normally going to be limited to identification, comparison and contrast of the personal features of individuals, or distinguishing features of various physical items or of events as in Example 3. The students could be asked to follow a set of instructions, where the teacher reads out a set of instructions and the students complete a drawing and label it as in Example 5.

In using this format you should try to keep answers brief and to reduce writing to a minimum, so as to minimise any demands on productive skills. In the questions, cover the range of information in the text and if possible, even with short texts, try to establish what colleagues, or students in the same ability range as the intended test population, would consider important in terms of main ideas/important details to extract from the listening experience.

With more advanced students a wider range of skills can be tested through this format. It is particularly efficient for testing an understanding of sequence, process description, relationships in a text and classification. The format does not, however, lend itself easily to testing the skills of inferred meaning comprehension or determining the speakers' attitudes (see Table 4.1). If the purpose for listening to spoken discourse involves these skills then this particular format may not be suitable.

Example 4 is from the JMB Test in English for Overseas Students. A particular advantage of using this technique in testing listening is that the student does not have to process written questions while trying to make sense of the spoken input, and the amount of writing the student has to produce can be even more constrained than in SAQs.

There is, however, a problem of securing authentic texts which match with the conditions one might wish to include. There is a danger that, as in Examples 2 and 3, the text will relate more to the written than the spoken medium and listenability will be impaired. Shohamy and Inbar (1991) suggest that texts which more closely resemble spoken language are easier to process than those which exhibit more 'written' features. Care must be taken to select text types which reflect the purpose of the test (see Brindley and Nunan 1992).

Beyond the elementary level it is quite difficult to find spoken texts which fit neatly into the information transfer format. Pure classificatory texts are very rare. Whereas in reading a certain amount of editing of texts is feasible (though not necessarily desirable) and in general a greater variety of texts are more readily available, this is not the case for listening texts taken from authentic sources. It is extremely difficult to locate and record suitable authentic spoken discourse for this format at an advanced level. This must put a serious question mark against its potential validity.

In terms of the types of texts suitable for use in this format, many of those identified in Table 4.2 may be inappropriate. If these are identified as important in particular testing contexts then other formats may need to be adopted.

Teachers are most likely to use the information transfer technique at lower proficiency levels than the level of the JMB test in Example 4, not least because of the problems of replicability referred to above in the discussion of its use in reading tests. Understanding of complex classification or description of state and process are normally dealt with at the higher levels of ability. Constructing information transfer tasks to match these texts could entail a level of draughtsmanship or drawing ability normally beyond that of the average teacher. The most serious factor limiting its use in the classroom is the issue of achieving reasonably clear drawings, as most teachers simply do not have the abilities required to produce the illustrations used in Example 4. The illustrations are at the same time one of the strengths of this approach and a potential Achilles' Heel.

### *The testing of intensive listening: indirect tests*

The two tests below are indirect. They do not directly test a range of desirable operations, nor do they incorporate a reasonable coverage of relevant conditions, and would thus seem to measure only a limited part of what might constitute listening proficiency. To the extent that they do not match the operations and the conditions under which these might normally be performed by the intended target group, then the tasks are indirect. The more indirect they are, the more difficult it is to go directly from performance on the test task to statements about capacity to carry out future real-life activities.

Such techniques may well have a place, though, if one is looking for a quick, efficient measure of general language proficiency for the purpose of placement of students into language classes. In this situation it may not be necessary to make precise statements about capacity in a particular skill area as long as the indirect tasks split up students into homogeneous groups in the skill area required.

Reference was made above to the difficulty of focusing on specific listening points whilst candidates are exposed to ongoing discourse. Given the need to enhance the reliability of our test batteries it is sometimes thought advisable to include a more discrete format with the possibility this gives of including a greater number of specific items. We shall take two examples of such indirect test formats: dictation and listening recall.

### EXERCISE 4E   INDIRECT TASKS: DICTATION

Look at the first example of intensive listening below from an EAP test designed for use in placement on a presessional course at a British University.

(a) What operation(s) are the items testing? Refer to the list of operations/enabling skills in Table 4.1, page 98 above. It may well be that you think an item is testing more than one skill. Try to decide in these cases what the major and minor focus(es) of the item are.

(b) What are the advantages and disadvantages of testing listening through this format? You may wish to comment on the operations involved and the conditions under which the task is performed. What types of text do you think this format will lend itself to? You may also wish to relate the examples to the framework of guidelines for test construction.

## Example 6

LISTENING: SUB-TEST, DICTATIONS

*INSTRUCTIONS TO STUDENTS*

*Situation:*   You are in a lecture and the lecturer concludes with a brief summary. He then gives you details of an assignment you have to do, and a reference to some reading which will help in the assignment.

*TASK:*   Write down in *AS MUCH DETAIL* as you can

  i. the lecturer's summary
  ii. details of the assignment
  iii. the reading reference.

*PROCEDURE:*   You will hear the test *ONLY ONCE*. There will be pauses. During the pause you should write down what you have heard.

You will have a few minutes at the end to check what you have written.
When you hear numbers you can use figures.

*N.B.*   This is a test of your ability to grasp detail while listening in English.
      You will not be penalized for spelling or grammar mistakes. Don't worry about punctuation.

To give you some practice, you will now hear the lecturer speaking. When he's finished write down what you have heard. This will *NOT BE MARKED*.

*PRACTICE*

*DICTATION 1*

1.  whenever one surface _____

    _____

2.  moves over another surface _____

    _____

3.  a force is set up _____

    _____

4.  This force will resist movement _____

    _____

5.  It is called friction _____

6.  and will oppose motion _____

7.  Your next essay is on lubrication _____

    _____

8. This is one of 3 basic methods

9. that are used for reducing friction

10. Your essay should be a 1000 words long

11. Hand-writing must be readable

12. Please hand in your essay by 9am on Friday 14 February

13. Please read Chapter 3 on Methods of Lubrication

14. in Brown's Mechanical Engineering, 1979

15. You can buy a copy from the University Bookshop for about £10

*Comment on Exercise 4E*

**Dictation**

Given that candidates should be asked to perform operations as close as possible to those they might encounter in the target situation, this means listening to dictated material which incorporates oral messages typical of those they might have to process in this way in real life. Thus in EAP tests candidates might, for example, listen to scientific laws, references, details of assignments being dictated to them at reduced speed — all as might occur in the normal context of a lecture. Dictation tasks are likely to involve recall of details at level (a), in addition to the more specifically linguistic, contributory skills (discriminating phonological units and determining word boundaries from context) at level (c) in Table 4.1 above.

The format is restricted in terms of the number of conditions for listening that the tester is able to take account of. There are restrictions on the speaker variables (speed, pausing, built-in redundancy) as the candidate normally has to write everything down. There are also severe limitations on the organisational, propositional and illocutionary features of the text(s) that can be employed as even native speakers are restricted in the length of utterances they can handle in this format. Similarly the condition of channel can only be partially accounted for. In short, the conditions under which this task is conducted only in a very limited sense reflect the normal conditions for reception in the spoken language.

In terms of efficiency these indirect tests score highly. They are relatively easy to construct, easy and quick to administer and with adequate training they are relatively quick and easy to mark. Compare this with the considerable effort required to produce Examples 1 and 4 above.

It may be considered necessary in certain situations to improve the overall reliability of a listening battery by including a format such as dictation which can enhance this through the large number of items that can be generated as well as being partially valid for specific situations where dictation might feature as a target group activity.

Marking may be problematic if one wishes to adopt a more communicatively oriented marking scheme where a mark is given if the candidate has understood the substance of the message and redundant features are ignored. However, training and standardisation of examiners can normally overcome these problems. Using this method one mark is given for each segment that is re-encoded in a semantically acceptable form. No marks are deducted for use of recognisable standard or personal abbreviations, omissions of communicatively redundant items, e.g. articles, or mechanical errors of grammar, punctuation or spelling. The decision the marker has to make in awarding a mark is whether the candidate demonstrates that he has understood the dictated utterance or not. If yes, then one mark is to be awarded. There are no half-marks. This is a yes/no decision. If in doubt, mark it wrong! The use of a semantic scoring scheme as against an exact word system should further enhance a test's validity. One would not want to penalise for mechanical accuracy errors in a candidate's answers as to do so would interfere with the measurement of listening ability to the extent that performance is contingent on written production.

The central problem remains as to how performance on an indirect test of this type, which appears to measure only a limited part of listening ability, can be translated into a direct statement of proficiency. The tester cannot easily decide on what would constitute a satisfactory performance. Quantitative indicators of language ability do not easily translate into qualitative descriptors.

### EXERCISE 4F   INDIRECT TASKS: LISTENING RECALL

Look at the example of a listening recall test below taken from a general English placement test. In this example students are given a short period of time to read over the text, allowing for activation of their expectancy grammars. They have to fill in the blanks, having heard a tape recording of the complete passage twice. They are advised to listen the first time and then attempt to fill in the blanks during a short period allowed for writing in the answers. They hear the passage a second time and then are allowed a short period of time to write in any remaining missing words. Candidates are given clear instructions as to what is expected of them and a short practice piece is normally provided.

(a) What operation(s) are the items testing? Refer to the list of operations/enabling skills in Table 4.1 above. It may well be that you think an item is testing more than one skill. Try and decide in these cases what the major and minor focus(es) of the item are.

> (b) What are the advantages and disadvantages of testing listening through this format? You may wish to comment on the operations involved and the conditions under which the task is performed. What types of text do you think this format will lend itself to? You may also wish to relate the examples to the framework of guidelines for test construction.

## Example 7:  Listening recall

### *Aid, poverty and the poor*

Why is aid given and why is it accepted? To some extent, this is a political business. The countries who are the highest receivers of aid are countries which are in politically _____ areas. Particularly at the moment, the Middle East is _____ represented as an aid recipient. Aid is used as a means of bolstering the economies of politically _____ developing countries which are regarded as _____ so that's one reason why aid is given. It is given for political reasons to support friendly _____. It's also given for economic reasons. This is sometimes called a 'pump-priming' activity, and those of you who have _____ knowledge will know that certain kinds of pump need some water in them in order to get them going.

And _____ is also used in economics to some extent to describe the economic 'priming' of a country. For example, it may be _____tactic for the UK government to give the government of a developing country a_____ of tractors in the hope that this will generate a future flow of extra orders from _____ because they will need spare parts when the tractors _____ and they will also need maintenance equipment and so on. So it could be that there are self interest, _____, why rich countries regard it as useful to give away a certain amount of equipment.

So there are political reasons. There are reasons of economic _____. But there are also — I don't want to be entirely cynical about this — humanitarian reasons.

There is a belief that this _____ can help developing countries to grow and particularly it can help those countries do something for the _____ of their populations. So it's a mixture of reasons, in other words, _____ for a mixture of reasons.

The next question to ask, is: why do these countries request aid? Well, it is requested because _____ that it will assist the governments of those countries to build roads, to build schools, to train manpower, _____ and so on. Let me now turn to the other theme, which is poverty.

_____ that it's necessary to say much about the extent to which there are _____ between the circumstances in which people live in different parts of the world. You are already, I'm sure, _____ But I mean, if you look at it in statistical terms, the gaps, which are getting wider, incidentally, rather than narrower, between the rich countries and the poor, are _____. If we look at the notion of 'national income', the *per capita* national income in Ethiopia is currently _____ US $110 per year — that is the value of the _____ produced. The USA, on the other hand, has a *per capita* national income of US $15,390 per year. If you were to _____ in Ethiopia 100 times, it would still be less than the *per capita* income in the United States. And there are plenty _____ where the gap is almost as large. You might ask whether _____ are in fact accurate indicators of the actual _____. And you can, you know, make a comparison about the _____ to food, to material goods that people enjoy in these countries.

## Comment on Exercise 4F

Initially a mindmap is made of the passage which allows the test developer to focus on the key lexical items to be deleted from the text. The words deleted are normally content words felt to be important to an understanding of the discourse, and the blanks should occur at increasingly frequent intervals. Initially deletions are best made of individual words. Later deletions can be of longer sequences. A text of five minutes should provide about thirty items of increasing length and frequency.

The test might be improved by just listening to the complete text first, with candidates taking notes if they wish. They are then given the mutilated passage; they listen to it a second time and complete the blanks while listening, with a short amount of time being available afterwards to finish completing any blanks. There is some limited evidence that following this procedure enables the listener to comprehend more fully what the passage is about, thereby coming closer to more authentic discourse processing.

In limited trials with colleagues at the ESP Centre in Alexandria, the initial listening without the written text was felt to improve overall comprehension of the tape. It was felt that this would also have a positive washback on teaching as it is important for students to be exposed to continuous uninterrupted discourse. Students in the trialling were not necessarily aware of the benefit and many would have preferred to have the text in front of them, as they considered this would improve their scores. However, we are more interested in measuring the trait of listening than their ability to cope with the method.

During trialling, if the best students have undue difficulty with certain items then some words may be replaced to improve the efficiency of the test. Ensure that the physical gaps on the page are sufficient for students to write in the deletions without having to run on to the next line. Ensure there is sufficient time between gaps for candidates to be able to process and write down the deleted items. The closer the gaps are to each other the greater are the processing difficulties. The gaps can occur more frequently and increase in length progressively as the text develops.

Deletions should reflect items felt to be within the grasp of the aural comprehension of the students in an achievement test and reflect the appropriate target situation in the case of a proficiency test. In achievement tests the test writer should attempt to sample both the structures and lexis from a variety of units covered and as far as possible (difficult at the lower levels) try to achieve a coherence in terms of story line. If possible the items should represent an ascending order of difficulty.

Texts can be selected to fit as closely as possible with the conditions felt by the tester(s) to be appropriate, e.g. texts can be well organised, topic suitable and accessible, approximate to normal target discourse (expository, argumentative, etc.), and appropriate speaker variables can be built in. There may however be problems in terms of the short length of the texts that are suitable for this format.

It is best to select material with as high a degree of listenability as possible and formal texts written to be read are best avoided. A normal speed of delivery for the discourse type selected should be followed. Like dictation, this technique can be administered rapidly and scored objectively. It also allows the tester to focus on items which are deemed to be important (as in selective deletion gap filling).

The test may well be useful as an initial screening device when the objective is to divide large groups of students into broad ability bands rather than to say anything precise about specific listening capabilities. This type of test has advantages in large-scale testing operations in that it is easy to construct, administer and mark. Decisions must, however, be taken in advance as to whether answers will be marked by an 'exact word' approach or an 'acceptable alternative' approach. Mark schemes would need to be prepared accordingly.

The major drawback of this format for the tester is the difficulty in saying with any degree of certainty what is being tested. Where only one word is deleted, it may not be testing anything more than an ability to match sounds with symbols, aided by an ability to read the printed passage containing the gaps. Careful construction is needed to ensure that the students cannot fill in the blanks simply by reading the passage without having to listen at all. The tester should ensure that pupils cannot get answers from reading alone by giving the text in advance, as a reading exercise only, to another group of students. In the event it is unlikely to involve much beyond the microlinguistic skills at the level of contributory meaning comprehension outlined in Table 4.1 above.

As such it is difficult to report on what test scores mean. Performance at the microlinguistic level gives no clear idea of how a candidate might perform on more global comprehension tasks. We cannot tell from this format or from dictation, whether a candidate could understand the main idea(s) of a text, recall important detail without the benefit of a gapped script, understand the gist of a passage, or determine the speaker's attitude to the listener. Thus, though such indirect tests are related to listening ability they cannot be said to be representative of it.

The big danger of using such indirect formats in tests is the poor washback this will have on the teaching that precedes the test. Time spent in practising for such indirect tests could be much more profitably spent in preparing candidates for the real-life listening activities they will later have to cope with. The more test tasks reflect such activities in terms of appropriate operations and conditions, then the more positive the washback of testing on teaching is likely to be.

# Chapter Five
## *Testing written production*

### 5.1  A framework for testing written production

A current concern in writing theory and practice is with the new 'pedagogical orthodoxy' of process writing where the main interest is in what writers do when they write. This approach sees writing as an exploratory, generative, collaborative, recursive process rather than as a linear route to a predetermined product. From this viewpoint, writers rarely adhere to a preconceived plan or model and, in attempting to approximate meaning, writers discover and reformulate their ideas (see Kroll 1990 and Raimes 1991, for an informed assessment of the current status of research and practice in second language writing).

The pure form of the process approach has not won widespread acceptance in academic writing instruction, although classroom methodology has adapted certain of its features. There has, conversely, been a strong move to genre-based writing in EAP courses. The concern here has been with content and satisfying the demands of the academic discourse community, rather than with the writer and writing process itself. The content-oriented approach is more concerned with the effect of the text on a reader drawn from the target discourse community, than with the personal discovery, writer-focused type of writing favoured in the process approach.

In academic contexts, the concern in most subject areas is that a candidate can perform academic writing tasks which satisfy the academic community, such as essay exams. These have little to do with a process orientation.

Similarly, the practical constraints on language testing, particularly as regards the time available, have resulted in test tasks in which the candidate is asked to display his or her ability to produce a piece of written work, composed under restricted time conditions. Little interest has been shown by examining boards in tasks which focus on the composing process itself, where a number of drafts might be involved and a number of people might provide feedback to the writer en route to a finished product.

Concerns about the reliability of tests have meant that the collaborative element, central to the process approach, has largely been ignored. This stems from a desire for the written product to be assessed as the work of a particular candidate alone, who may differ in proficiency from his or her contemporaries. If the candidate has received a large amount of support, in terms of feedback, there is no guarantee that this would be available in the target situation. A manager is unlikely to get a great deal of help in the creative process of writing a business letter from a secretary or colleague, or a postgraduate student from his/her hard-pressed contemporaries.

In this chapter there is an attempt to establish what might be good practice to follow in the testing of writing. We shall start by considering what features of real-life performance we might try to take into account in specifying what is to go into our writing tests. We will consider these under the usual headings of:

Conditions
Operations
Quality of output.

## EXERCISE 5A    PERFORMANCE CONDITIONS, OPERATIONS, LEVEL OF PERFORMANCE

Either on your own or with a colleague make a note of:

(a)  What conditions you might take into account in the design of a writing task for students in your own situation. When you have finished look at Table 5.1 below. Not all of these conditions will be relevant to your situation, but many will. Is there anything you would like to add from or to your own list (e.g. size of output/length: how much would we expect students to write)?

(b)  What operations might be included in writing tasks at various levels of ability (e.g. describing a process or writing a letter of thanks).

When you have finished look at Table 5.2 below. Not all of these operations will be relevant to your situation, but many will. Is there anything you would like to add from or to your own list?

(c)  What criteria might you use to make decisions on levels of performance on the above operations under specified conditions? How far do you agree with criteria listed in Table 5.3 below?

*Comment on Exercise 5A*

As with testing the other language skills, it is useful to start by considering a framework of the features we might wish to take into account in designing writing tests. In the second part of the chapter we will examine in closer detail the available options, along an indirect/direct continuum, for testing this ability.

The intention in the first part of the chapter is to examine the important conditions, most generalisable operations and appropriate criteria of assessment, of which test writers might take account. We list in Tables 5.1 and 5.2 the interactional and situational features of writing which we might consider for inclusion in test tasks, and in Table 5.3 criteria for assessing the quality of the written product. The categories provided in the framework are hypothesised as being important, but only in the light of research will it be possible conclusively to state which of these are the most important variables (see Hamp-Lyons 1990 and 1991, Raimes 1991 and Ruth and Murphy 1988, for details of current research in these areas).

To produce a certain text type a candidate would have to control various functions from the list below. A division is made for descriptive purposes between social/service texts and academic texts, with particular focuses on interactional and informational operations. However, it is quite likely that a number of informational routines (in particular description and narration) may be called on in completing some of the interactional tasks.

The reader will be familiar, from the earlier discussion of reading in Chapter 3, with many of the operations and conditions laid out in Tables 5.1 and 5.2. To avoid unnecessary duplication the reader is referred to pages 64–77 for comment on these.

Table 5.1
*Summary checklist of performance conditions (writing)*

---

*Purpose*: realistic

*Text type* required: form, letter, message, note, notice, postcard, report, speech, set of directions/ instructions, article, written assignment, summaries, memo, poem, story, etc.

Demands which construction of the text(s) places on the writer *vis à vis*:

*Organisational*: grammar, cohesion, rhetorical organisation.

*Propositional*: lexical range: common core, technical, sub-technical.
type of information (abstract/concrete).
cognitive demands.

*Illocutionary*: functional range (within texts).
range of tasks/text types required in test.

*Topic*: level of specificity. Personal/non-personal. Relationship between content of output text and candidates' background knowledge. Information given or invented; response to information provided or self-initiated.

*Channel* of presentation: plus or minus visuals; layout; typeface.

*Addressee*: known/unknown; relationship between writer and audience, e.g. equal to equal, expert to layperson; knowledge of audience's attitudes, beliefs and expectations.

*Setting*: where it is written — examination hall or at home.

*Time available*: speed at which processing must take place, length of time available to write, normal time constraints; whether it is an exam or hand-in assignment, and the number of revisions/drafts allowed (process element).

*Size* of output, length of text.

*Amount of support given*: plus or minus dictionary. Clarity of rubrics: L1/TL.

*Method factor/response mode*: familiarity with task type and other test environment features. Length of prompt. Integration with reading task: single or multi-source. Verbal and/or non-verbal input.

*Stated or unstated criteria of assessment*: (these relate to level but affect conditions to the extent they are known to the candidates or not).

---

Table 5.2
*Summary checklist of operations (writing)*

---

**Interactional** in social and service texts (adapted and developed from RSA/UCLES list. See Weir 1990, Appendix III: 149—70):

*Expressing*: thanks, requirements, opinions, attitude, confirmation, apology, wants/needs/lack, ideas, information, complaints, reasons, justifications, etc.

*Eliciting*: information, directions, service, clarification, help, permission, etc.

*Directing*: ordering, instructing, persuading, advising, warning.

**Informational** in academic texts (acknowledgement to Keith Johnson for early version of this list):

*Describing phenomena and Ideas* which might involve:
Definition
Classification
Identification
Comparison and contrast
Exemplification
Summary

*Describing process* which might involve:
    Purpose
    Describing means, results, process, change of state
    Sequential description
    Instructions
    Summary

*Argumentation* which might involve:
    Stating a proposition
    Stating assumptions
    Induction
    Deduction
    Substantiation
    Concession
    Summary
    Generalisation
    Speculation/comment/evaluation

*Microlinguistic level:*

    Handwriting
    Handling: grammar,vocabulary, cohesive devices, discourse markers

## Operations

Two different approaches for assessing writing ability have been adopted in the past (see Hamp-Lyons 1991, Raimes 1991). Firstly, writing can be divided into more specific 'discrete' elements, e.g. grammar, vocabulary, spelling, punctuation and orthography, and attempts can be made to test these formal elements separately by the use of objective tests. These tests would be indirect in that they would only be measuring parts of what we take to be the construct of writing ability (see Examples 1–4 below). What they test may be related to proficient writing as statistical studies have demonstrated, but they cannot represent what proficient writers can do (Hamp-Lyons 1991). It would be difficult to generalise from these types of test as to how candidates might perform on more productive tasks which required construction of a complete text. It would be difficult from these discrete item tests to make direct statements about how good a writer is or what he or she can do in writing. Such indirect tests have an extremely negative washback effect on the teaching that precedes them.

At a very elementary level, microlinguistic features might be all the candidates are capable of being tested on. At higher levels of ability these microlinguistic elements are likely to be subsumed by the informational and interactional operations listed in Table 5.2. In some contexts, however, for the sake of form, they might still be identified separately.

Secondly, more direct extended writing tasks of various types could be employed (see Examples 5–7 below). These involve the production of continuous texts of at least 100 words, with the writer being given some room for individual interpretation. Because these tasks can approximate more closely to the operations and conditions involved in writing academic, social, and service texts in the real world, they have greater construct validity (see Hamp-Lyons 1990 and 1991 for important surveys of assessing second language writing).

*Conditions*

A survey of the literature suggests that there is a particular concern with a number of the conditions in Table 5.1 which have a strong bearing on the reliability and validity of writing tests. These are discussed briefly below.

**Text types**

Taking more than one sample of a student's work can help reduce the variation in performance that might occur from task to task. We know that student performance will vary even on very similar tasks as well as in producing different text types. This argues for sampling students' writing ability over a number of tasks, typical and appropriate to their discourse community. This will give them the best chance of showing what they can do. Setting candidates more than one task has obvious implications for test practicality, particularly in terms of time.

However, both reliability and validity have been found to be increased by sampling more than one composition from each candidate, and there is a widespread feeling that the performance on one writing task is not representative of a candidate's general writing ability (see Hughes 1989: 81, Hamp-Lyons 1990, 1991). In general it is felt advisable to take at least two samples (see Jacobs *et al*. 1981: 15).

The more samples of a student's writing in a test, the more reliable the assessment is likely to be, and the more confidently we can generalise from performance on the test tasks. As we noted in relation to comprehension tests above, the reliability of a test score tends to increase as the number of items in the test is increased, provided each sample gives a reasonable estimate of the ability. We obviously cannot elicit samples of all the operations that candidates may have to perform, even in a closely specified EAP situation. Therefore, we must make every effort to ensure that the tasks we set and the conditions we build in to our tests are as representative as possible in the practical context obtaining. We certainly cannot rely on one sample if important decisions are going to be made on the basis of evidence provided by the test.

The growing interest in portfolio assessment in the United States is worth noting in this respect (see Hamp-Lyons 1991: 261−3). In this system a collection of texts a writer has produced over a period of time in line with the specifications of a particular context are used to assess competence on exiting a programme. This has some similarity with the continuous assessment mode familiar from the former externally moderated Mode 3 examinations, administered by the General Certificate of Education Boards (GCE) in the United Kingdom. It is easy to see how this format might take account of redrafting and other developmental aspects in writing. The issue of reliability remains, however.

**Topic**

Raimes (1983: 266) has forcibly stated that choosing topics should be the teacher's most responsible activity. This applies to testers as well.

As regards selection of topic(s) it is necessary to ensure that students are able to write something on the topic(s) they are presented with. The issue of background knowledge is as relevant in this discussion as it was in the other skills. The task we set candidates should be seen by these writers as realistic, appropriate and feasible (Hamp-Lyons 1990: 53) if they are to attend to the topic as intended. If a task is seen as unrealistic, inappropriate or impossible, then candidates will not perform to the best of their abilities and may challenge or ignore the task.

There is clear evidence (Reid 1990) that different topics elicit different responses which are measurably different. This raises the further issue of whether to allow a choice of topics, for it too could affect the reliability of the test.

According to Jacobs *et al.* (1981: 1), it is generally advisable for all students to write on the same topics because allowing a choice of topics introduces too much uncontrolled variance into the test. Their research raised the issue of whether observed differences in scores are due to real differences in writing proficiency or occur as a result of the different topics. They conclude that there is no completely reliable basis for comparison of scores on a test unless all of the students have performed the same writing task(s). Moreover, reader consistency or reliability in evaluating the test may be reduced if all of the papers read at a single scoring session are not on the same topic.

By basing writing tasks on written and/or spoken text supplied to the candidates or on non-verbal stimuli, it is possible to ensure that in terms of subject knowledge all start equally, at least in terms of the information available to them. In addition Campbell (1990) has recently suggested that practice in reading-into-writing tasks is beneficial later in academic writing, but refers to difficulties this integration may cause when done under time pressure.

In general, then, all students should write on the same topic and preferably more than one sample of their ability should be measured. Where possible they should all be in possession of common information. In addition, as the work of Hamp-Lyons (1991) so clearly demonstrates, we need to be extremely careful in the selection and wording of the prompts we use in our writing tasks, not only in general, but also in relation to the needs and background knowledge of the candidates.

### Amount of time allowed for each writing task/size of output

Apart from examination essays, in the real world, writing tasks would not be timed at all and students would be allowed maximum opportunity and access to resources for demonstrating their writing abilities. When we looked at this issue in connection with the testing of reading in exercises 3 in Chapter 3 above, we discovered many difficulties in fully replicating reality. Considerations such as time constraints, reliability and test security requirements make longer, process-oriented tests impractical in most situations.

The texts we get candidates to produce obviously have to be long enough for them to be marked reliably. If we want to establish whether a student can organise a written product into a coherent whole, length is obviously a key factor.

As regards an appropriate time for completion of product-oriented writing tasks in an actual examination setting, Jacobs *et al.* (1981: 19), in their research on the Michigan Composition Test, found that a time allowance of thirty minutes probably gave most students enough time to produce an adequate sample of their writing ability.

It had been thought in the past that time-restricted test tasks are only a limited representation of what writers usually do in creating written discourse and that it could not lead to work that was representative of anyone's best capabilities. Interestingly, Kroll (1990: 140−54) reports on research comparing the essays written in class under pressure of time and essays written at home over a 10−14 day period. Her results suggest that, in general, time does not buy very much for students either in their control over syntax — the distribution of specific language errors being remarkably similar in both — or in their organisational skills.

### Quality of output:  assessment criteria

The design of writing tests is an iterative process and we need to think of how a test is to be scored, at the same time as we make decisions on tasks in the light of salient conditions and operations in a particular context. Decisions on all three elements of our framework are interactive. The absence of one reflects badly on the others.

The marking of direct writing tasks requires a more carefully worked out set of procedures than the marking of indirect tests. Particular attention is paid below to ways of assessing the output in tests of written production. The criteria of assessment considered important in this area are listed in Table 5.3.

Section 5.3 below is on the marking of writing with particular reference to establishing criteria and marking schemes. The reader is also referred to Sections 1.3.4 on the moderation of mark schemes and 1.3.5 on the standardisation of marking in Part I of this book. The advice given there is particularly relevant to the training of raters.

Table 5.3
*Summary checklist of quality of output: assessment criteria (writing)*

| |
|---|
| Relevance and adequacy of content |
| Organisation |
| Cohesion |
| Adequacy of vocabulary for purpose |
| Grammar |
| Punctuation |
| Spelling |
| Appropriateness of language to context, function and intention and appropriateness of layout |

## 5.2   Formats for testing written production

Before looking at the formats below you might find it useful to refer back to the general guidelines for test construction we developed above in Part I of the course, especially Sections 1.3.3−1.3.5. In any of the tests you write or evaluate you should try to apply the general principles and specific guidelines for test construction discussed there, as well as considering the summary checklists in Tables 5.1−5.3. You need to decide on the features of the target performance that you consider important to incorporate in your test, in terms of the three-part framework for writing outlined above.

We will now turn to some examples of tests designed to measure writing to see how far they take account of our framework and the extent to which they exhibit good practice in test design.

These are examples that have been constructed for specific students in specific contexts. They are taken from a variety of levels·from elementary to advanced. The particular conditions or operations in some examples may well be inappropriate for your students. The purpose of the exercise is to become aware of these formats, their advantages and limitations. It is also to think critically about them in terms of the frameworks so that you can decide what would be most appropriate for the students you are responsible for in your particular context, and how you would need to adapt them in terms of the conditions and operations involved.

## EXERCISE 5B  EXAMINING TEST FORMATS

What follows in Examples 1−7 are some of the available options for testing writing ability along an indirect/direct continuum. Examine critically these formats for testing writing.

For each format:

(a) Think about what operation(s) can be tested through this format. Secondly, consider what conditions the test writer has been able to take account of in designing this task. Refer to the list of operations/enabling skills and conditions in Tables 5.1 and 5.2 above.

(b) Consider the advantages and disadvantages of testing writing through this format. You may wish to comment on the operations involved, the conditions under which the task is performed, or the criteria you would employ in judgement of level. You may also wish to relate the examples to the framework of general principles and specific guidelines for test construction. After each test format you will be given a commentary. Ideally you should try to do each of the items yourself to see what is involved in their completion.

*Formats for testing written production*

**Example 1:  Gap filling**

Fill in the gaps in the passage below:

I'd like to phone my American friend. _____ a newsreader on American television.

He has got a really _____ job. It's seven o'clock here _____ it will be 12 o'clock

in America. I _____ phone him at home. He _____ going to work this evening.

He's on holiday today. There _____ a big storm in America yesterday. It damaged

_____ of the houses and it killed 40 people. It _____ at eight in the morning. News

of the storm was _____ television last night. We _____ the homes the fire destroyed.

ANSWER KEY

I'd like to phone my American friend. *He's* a newsreader on American television. He has got a really *interesting* job. It's seven o'clock here *so* it will be 12 o'clock in America. I *can* phone him at home. He *isn't* going to work this evening. He's on holiday today. There *was* a big storm in America yesterday. It damaged *some* of the houses and it killed 40 people. It *started* at eight in the morning. News of the storm was *on* television last night. We *saw* the homes the fire destroyed.

*Scoring*
One mark to be awarded for each gap appropriately completed.
*Total = 10 marks*

**Comment on Example 1**

In our earlier discussion of the testing of reading we looked at selective deletion gap filling and C-tests, and noted the potential value of these techniques for testing the more specifically linguistic skills such as understanding of vocabulary, structure or cohesion devices.

We found that these were not always discrete tests of reading as such, in that the candidates often had to supply productively in writing the answers to these questions. However, by making the task a selection from a group of possible answers one effectively reduced the importance of writing ability in providing the answer.

It is more accurate, where answers are not provided, to talk of these formats as testing a mixture of both reading and writing skills. There is obviously a problem in reporting on what is being tested in these more specifically linguistic items. It is by no means clear whether the results of such tests should form part of a profile of reading or of writing ability, nor is it clear how they would contribute to such assessments. Many writers (e.g. Hughes 1989) avoid this problem by referring to them as tests of general proficiency. The problem of saying what the results mean still remains, however.

The wider the range of conditions to be taken account of in the test, for example subject areas or topics, the more difficult it is to select discrete linguistic items for testing purposes. In specialised courses, where there is an identifiable, agreed domain, it is easier, but still a choice has to be made as to which items are the most criterial to an understanding of the passage. In those cases where the interest is in achievement related to a course book or a course of instruction, the problems are slightly reduced as lists of structures and lexis covered, and the contexts for these items, are available from course descriptions/syllabi and from scrutiny of materials used by students. The problem of sampling does not go away, even then, and an argued case for selection and inclusion needs to be made.

Having selected our passages, how do we in fact decide which items to delete? If such formats are adopted in tests, the developers must come to a reasoned decision about which lexical items are contributing the most to a reasonable understanding of the passage.

Similar problems occur in the selection of grammatical items. A quantitative survey of the occurrence of the various structural items in the receptive and productive written materials that students will deal with is obviously beyond the scope of most test constructors. What is needed is a more pragmatic, but still reliable method of selecting items to be included.

It would seem sensible to examine the content of existing tests and course books at an equivalent level to determine what experts in the field have regarded as suitable items for inclusion for similar populations (though the circularity of this approach needs some caution and these data should always be subject to critical scrutiny on the part of teachers and their colleagues). Where the test is an achievement test on a course book or prescribed set of materials, the problem of selection of grammatical items and appropriate contexts is not as great. The decision still has to be made, though, on which items to delete. As we have argued above, this is best done through discussing with colleagues the most important items to delete in terms of their contribution to the overall meaning of the passage.

At the lower levels of language ability gap filling is sometimes considered a suitable format for testing 'productive writing ability' in a very guided sense. With the prior acquisition of grammatical and lexical skills beyond a certain baseline level, more extended productive tasks are of course feasible and, as we argue below, more desirable.

It is extremely difficult to say what scores on indirect tests actually mean. They relate to writing ability, but in no sense are they representative of it. In addition the washback effect of such procedures on the teaching that goes on in the classroom may be negative and draw attention away from equipping learners with the capacity for producing extended writing on their own.

It may be sensible to opt instead for carefully graded real writing tasks at a very early stage. These might involve the student initially in simple copying, then, with increased levels of ability, move in a scale of directness to eventual integrated reading into writing or information transfer tasks. Examples of these are discussed below.

### Example 2:   Copying

Ensure that the amount to be copied is within the level of the students, but not too easy for the majority of the class.

Copy the following:

Fawzia likes figs and grapes.

_____

She doesn't like orange juice.

_____

She's going to ride to the market.

_____

She will buy a carpet for her uncle.

_____

Does she live next to the mosque?

_____

**Comment on Example 2**

This is among the very first tasks along the road to productive writing. In this example the test writer has managed to ensure that all the letters in the alphabet are contained in these sentences. The words in the test should be selected from the material covered in the course book and should not be too heavy a burden on the learners. There is some argument as to whether copying is a skill worth testing, but in some situations it may be all the students do in the first year(s) of writing. If no formal attention is paid to handwriting at an early stage, it could also have unfortunate consequences later on in terms of illegibility.

A problem arises in how such a task should be marked. One solution proposed is that an overall global impression marking scheme should be adopted. The marker should take into account:

> the use of the semi-cursive script
> spacing
> writing on the line
> punctuation
> spelling

First take a decision on pass/fail and then locate on the scale below:

> excellent     = 10
> very good     = 8/9
> good          = 6/7
> pass          = 5
> poor          = 3/4
> very poor     = 1/2

A sample of scripts from each level could be collected and a set of specimen scripts might eventually be included in a Test Handbook for Teachers.

**Example 3:   Form completion**

(a) You are going to London for a holiday. Before the plane lands at Heathrow you have to fill in this form.

LANDING CARD

Family Name _____    First   Name(s) _____

Date of Birth _____    Place  of  Birth _____

Address in Britain _____

_____

Signature   _____

(b) Form Completion

Many students in Europe are in a club for young people who want to write to other young people in different countries. You have to fill in an application form giving details of who you are.

1. Family Name _____ Other Names _____

2. Date of Birth _____

3. Address _____

_____

4. Your nationality _____

5. Nationality of person you would like to write to _____

6. Three hobbies you would like the person to have _____

_____

7. Other information about yourself _____

_____

_____

_____

*Scoring*
The emphasis here is on spelling and relevance. A half-mark is awarded for relevance and then, if this criterion is met, a further half-mark can be awarded for spelling.
*Total = 6 marks.*

## Comment on Example 3

Form filling occurs in many examinations which lay claim to being communicative, since it has the outward appearance of being an authentic task which many students might have to perform in real life.

When you examine more closely what operations the candidate is involved in, these would appear to be limited to expressing/giving specific information and the task involves reading as much as writing. In addition the criteria that can be applied to the product of this task are limited. Little more than spelling and lexical knowledge is available for comment.

A real problem in testing writing, particularly in general English contexts, will be the problem of sampling. Given the need to cover a range of appropriate operations and conditions, it might be worthwhile considering whether test tasks, other than Example 3, might be more representative of what students have done in a course or will have to perform in the future target situation. Where a choice has to be made one would wish to ensure that the task(s) selected gave the best available coverage in terms of appropriate conditions and operations and enabled the tester to make the widest range of statements in terms of quality of output.

In achievement testing with mixed-ability classes, it might be necessary to include such a task as this, though, to ensure that the weakest students can succeed at something.

*Indirect EAP tasks*

**Example 4:   Editing**

*Test in English for Educational Purposes editing task*
The following extract contains a number of errors in grammar, spelling and punctuation. Indicate where these are by underlining the errors. Then correct the errors in the space provided under each line, making only the necessary corrections. Do not rewrite the passage in your own words.

Example:

I am <u>an</u> student of <u>Inglish</u>
    *a*              *English*

You have fifteen minutes for this task.

*New Scientist Survey: the Cost of Unemployment*

Nearly all the writers were conscious from the cost of unemployment and the waist

of expensive training Some of the costs may to be roughly estimated, such as

unemployment-benefit payments or the money spended on training these graduates.

a whole range of costs, identified in the letters we reseived, are not so easy to quantify.

Their are, for example, costs to organisations, which, in several year's time, is likely

to discover the disadvantages of not take a steadily flow of graduate into its lower posts

(some respondents said employers were all too awear of the dangers). There is also

the cost to science and universities, through the lost of knowledge that will have been

contribute presumably to the common store. Often, as respondents pointed out, the

drift away from science into other fields is unreversible.

**Comment on Example 4**

Indirect techniques are restricted in terms of their perceived validity for test takers and the users of test results. An interesting attempt to retain the objectivity and coverage of the discrete point approach whilst enhancing validity can be found in the editing task

Example 4 in Paper Two of the TEEP test (CALS, University of Reading).

In this task the student is given a text containing a number of errors of grammar, spelling and punctuation typical of learners in his/her discourse community and is asked to make all necessary corrections.

The task provides an objectively scored measure of linguistic competence, and in addition it may have a good washback effect in that students may be taught and encouraged to edit their written work more carefully. It is certainly more face valid than other indirect techniques we have looked at in this section, and it comes closer to simulating a valuable part of the writing process.

The difficulty in sustaining this argument is that there is some doubt as to whether the ability to correct somebody else's errors equates with an ability to correct one's own. Marking can also be problematic if a candidate alters something which is already correct.

Furthermore, even if this task does relate to part of the writing process, it does not represent what people do when they write. It takes account of a very restricted range of the operations and conditions we have identified as potentially important. Though it may generate objectively scorable data, the difficulty of interpretation remains because of its indirect nature. What do scores on such a test mean? How can they be combined with more readily interpretable scores obtained through more direct measures?

The answer to these questions is that we do not know. If we find it difficult to say what performance on such tests means, we should avoid their use. We will be better served by using more direct tasks which allow us to select and incorporate appropriate operations, conditions and criteria.

*More direct tests of writing*

**Example 5:   Open-ended essay test**

(a) Holidays
(b) Describe what you did on your holidays during the summer.
(c) You have just come back from a disastrous holiday. Write a letter of complaint to the tour operators.

**Comment on Example 5**

The stimulus is usually written and can vary in length from a limited number of words to several sentences. Setting the tasks is a relatively easy affair. The topics tend to be very general and rely heavily on the candidate providing the content either through background or cultural knowledge, or through imagination. The task has no clear purpose. Little guidance is given to candidates on whom the audience is, how they are expected to answer the question, or how their essay will be assessed. It only samples a narrow range of text types. Many of the conditions we identified as important in Table 5.1 above are not taken account of.

The format can be used for testing ability to carry out a range of the operations we identified earlier in Table 5.2, including developing an extended argument in a logical manner, which cannot be tested through any of the indirect formats. The big advantage this task type shares with other tests of extended writing (see more controlled tasks below) is that a sample of writing is produced which, as well as enabling the tester to apply a range of appropriate criteria in determining the quality of the output (see Table 5.3 above), can also provide a tangible point of reference for comparison in the future. A candidate's work at the start of a course can be compared with work produced at the end. This can be most useful in those cases where sponsors or students themselves require a clear picture of progress as a result of taking a course of instruction (videoed interactions can provide a similar picture in speaking).

This type of free, open-ended writing is problematic, however. An ability to write on such open-ended topics may depend on the candidate's background or cultural knowledge, imagination or creativity. If we are more interested in his or her ability to produce neutral, transactional, expository prose in defined situations, these may not be factors we wish to assess. If the candidate is not interested in the topic or does not regard it as appropriate, he or she may challenge the task.

Candidates tend to approach an open-ended question in different ways, and may produce quite different text types, exhibiting a wide variety of operations. Examiners will somehow have to assess the relative merits of these different approaches. This increases the difficulty of marking the essays in a precise and reliable manner. Furthermore, where a selection of topics is provided, it is very difficult to compare performances, especially if the production of different text types is involved.

### Controlled task examples (6(a)–6(h))

Where feasible we must include a direct extended writing task in our tests because it samples important productive skills which indirect forms of assessment cannot. It allows the inclusion of operations and conditions other less direct tasks cannot cater for. To omit a writing task in situations where writing tasks are an important feature of the student's real-life needs might severely lower the validity of a testing programme and have an undesirable washback effect on the teaching prior to the test.

On the face of things, free, uncontrolled writing would seem to be an invalid test of the writing ability required for acceptance into most discourse communities, e.g. academic life, the medical profession or the business sector, and is to be resisted because of this until proof is produced that there is a strong link between performance on such tasks and performance on more controlled tasks. It is also easier to generalise about writing ability from samples of a candidate's performance, when care is taken in specifying for each task the operations required (see Table 5.2 above) and appropriate conditions (Table 5.1) and assessment criteria (Table 5.3). When the task is determined more precisely in this manner, it is easier to compare the performances of different students and to improve reliability in scoring.

We should aim to test a candidate's ability to perform certain of the functional tasks required in the future target situation. For students in general English courses, we can include functional tasks they have been exposed to in their language courses. For doctors in a hospital we might set a task which involves writing a letter to a local GP about a patient on the basis of a set of printed case notes. For a student in an EAP context it might involve search reading of an academic text to extract specified information for use in a written summary (see Example 7 below) or describing information contained in a diagrammatic or non-verbal form (see Examples 6(f) and 6(g)). For those studying English as a foreign language in a secondary school, it might involve tasks similar to those included as Examples 6(a), 6(b), 6(d) and 6(h). For English for Business students, it might involve writing in response to a variety of contextually appropriate stimuli, as in Examples 6(c) and 6(e).

There are various types of stimuli that can be used in controlled writing tasks. Stimuli can be written as in Examples 6(a)−6(e), or non-verbal as in Examples 6(f)−6(h).

## Example 6:   Responding to given information

### Example 6(a):   Responding to a letter

You receive this letter from a friend. Write a short reply to it. Give your friend all the information he asks for. You should write in complete sentences.

Alexandria, Egypt

5th May

Dear friend,

We are going to visit London in September. Can we see you then? What's the weather like then? Do we need to bring our warm coats? Liz would like you to tell us what we could visit in a week. What sort of food will we be able to eat? Finally, can you suggest a good hotel for us to stay in?

Love

Tim

Write your reply here:

London

6th July

Dear Tim,

_____

_____

_____

_____

_____

_____

Love

**Example 6(b):   Semi-scripted**

You've been abroad two weeks on holiday and have lots of news. Write to an English friend who has offered to meet you at the airport on your return. Tell him or her where and when to meet you. Describe what you have done since you last saw each other. Say how you feel about the holiday so far. Your letter should be not more than 150 words.

(Royal Society of Arts)

**Example 6(c):   Responding to given information (letter + comments)**

You work for the Manager of the Management Training and Development of Human Resources Department, Anza (UK) Ltd, 37−42 Tufnell Way, Hammersmith, London.

Your Manager has asked you to write a letter on his behalf to an external training consultant who is keen to arrange an appointment. The consultant's letter ends:

> I suggest that we meet on 6 or 7 May to discuss the arrangement of training modules in Time Management, Handling Stress, and Leadership Skills. I shall telephone you in the next few days to arrange the exact time, and look forward to the opportunity of meeting you then.
>
> Yours sincerely
>
>
> K Vance
> *Training Consultant*

Your Manager's comments included:

1.  I'm in Brussels all week — can't see him.

2.  We don't want those courses this year.

3.  He can send his brochure *before* we meet him!

4.  Who has he done seminars for? We want names & 'phone numbers.

5.  We don't want *him* to ring *us*; we'll ring *him* if we want him!

**Now write a suitable reply to Mr Vance.**

Source: LCCI English for Business, Level 3.

**Comment on Examples 6(a)−6(c)**

The operations demanded of the candidate can be manipulated to suit those covered in a course or required in a future target situation (see Example 6(c) from an English for

Business examination). Most of the interactional and informational operations identified in Table 5.2 could be built into this type of format, even at the lower-ability levels. It is particularly suited to the production of social and service texts.

By careful construction of the input the candidate receives, the conditions under which the task is to be performed can be largely controlled and thus made more appropriate for the candidature than might be the case in more open-ended pieces of writing. The candidate does not have to invent a response out of thin air. There is a person to write to, for a particular purpose. The topics can be carefully selected to ensure contextual appropriateness, and the format provides the means of exerting some control over the organisational, propositional and illocutionary facets required in writing the response to the stimuli.

There is a question mark over the difficulties that having to process a written stimulus might cause, but to the extent that the task represents real-life interaction, this should not trouble the tester unduly. In order to respond to letters in real life we have to be able to read them. It does not seem to be the case that competent writers are unable to read, though the reverse may be quite common.

Most of the criteria we might wish to apply to a writing task can be catered for, with the possible exception of organisational ability in the more structured examples. Controlling the tasks in this fashion makes it easier to make reliable judgements on the relevancy and adequacy of content. There are a number of points in the stimulus material the candidate receives that have to be answered in the response.

## Example 6(d):  Responding to information given in chart form

You have to write a short paragraph for the English Club at your school. Look at the information below where Jordan and Britain are described. Write a paragraph comparing Jordan with Britain.

|  | Jordan | Britain |
|---|---|---|
| Capital: | Amman | London |
| Area: | 96,000 sq. km. | 245,000 sq. km. |
| Population: | about 4,000,000 | 57,000,000 |
| Language: | Arabic | English |
| Exports: | fruit, vegetables | machines |
| Climate: | Mediterranean | wet |
| Currency: | dinar | pound |

**Example 6(e):   Responding to information from a variety of written sources**

## QUESTION 2

As Assistant Manager of Personnel in a British firm employing some 900 staff, you have been asked to look into the possibility of improving the company's dining facilities.

You sent a questionnaire to 100 employees who use the canteen; 63 replied, and the results are below. Using these and the other information you have collected, write a report on the canteen situation, giving your recommendations to the Personnel Manager.

---

### ANALYSIS OF REPLIES TO QUESTIONNAIRE

| *Quality of food* | | *Choice* | | *Dining facilities* | |
|---|---|---|---|---|---|
| Very good | 5 | Good | 4 | Very pleasant | — |
| Good | 19 | Sufficient | 18 | Pleasant | 19 |
| Poor | 26 | Insufficient | 29 | Unpleasant | 33 |
| No view | 13 | No view | 12 | No view | 11 |
| | 63 | | 63 | | 63 |

| *Value for money* | | *Preferred changes* (may choose 2) | |
|---|---|---|---|
| Very good | 9 | Redecoration of dining room | 27 |
| Good | 27 | Wider choice of menu | 32 |
| Poor | 20 | New kitchen facilities | 8 |
| No view | 7 | Covered footpath to dining room | 4 |
| | 63 | Fast-food stall | 12 |
| | | Bar | 18 |
| | | Separate sandwich and coffee area | 22 |
| | | | 123 |

---

| *NOTES FROM PLANT MANAGER* | *VIEWS EXPRESSED BY MANAGING DIRECTOR* |
|---|---|
| 'I estimate approx 1/3 of factory workers eat at the canteen. The rest go home or off the premises at lunchtime. Probably the same for office staff.' | 'I want no alcohol on the premises.' <br><br> 'Approx £5–6,000 available for improvements this year.' |

---

### ESTIMATED COST OF IMPROVEMENTS

| | £ |
|---|---|
| Covered footpath | 1,500 |
| New kitchen equipment | 5,200 |
| Redecoration (dining room) | 2,300 |
| Additional coffee etc. area or bar | 4,600 |
| Provision of wider menu | 3,500 |
| Provision of fast-food facility | 2,000 |

Source: LCCI English for Business, Level 3.

### Example 6(f):    Information transfer task 1

The diagram: Figure 2 illustrates a trap for catching small animals for observation purposes. Use it to help you answer Questions 1 and 2. (Make sure you use different information in each answer.) Write about a page on each.

1.   Write a description of the trap.
2.   Outline how the trap works.

You have 40 minutes for this task. Marks will be awarded for content and organisation of ideas, as well as for accuracy in English.

*Figure 2*

Section

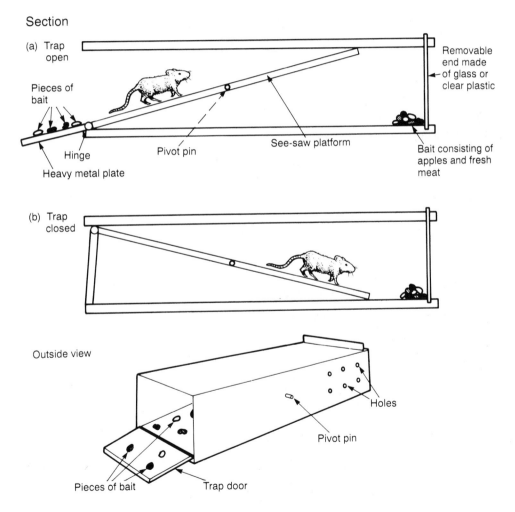

Source: JMB Test in English (Overseas).

## Example 6(g):   Information transfer task 2

---

**Section 1   Writing Skills**

**Answer Questions 1A and 1B in the answer book for Section 1.**

---

**Question 1A (10 marks)**

The map, on page 151, provides information on the weather expected tomorrow in the U.K. A key for this map is provided.

The map below identifies the 4 countries within the U.K.

Write the weather forecast to *accompany* the map (e.g. for a daily newspaper). Write 3 paragraphs using these 3 headings in your answer:

Scotland and Northern Ireland
Northern and Central England and Wales
Southern England

The first sentence has been done for you; continue in the same style. Write about half to three-quarters of a page.

THE 4 U.K. COUNTRIES

N.B. Eire is not part of the U.K.

WEATHER MAP

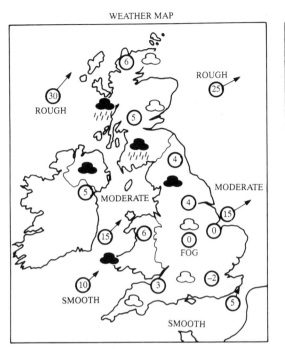

KEY

| | |
|---|---|
| (15) ↓ | Wind direction and strength in miles per hour (mph) |
| (4) | Temperature in degrees Celsius |
| ☁ | Light cloud |
| ☁ | Heavy cloud |
| ☁ ⁄ ⁄ ⁄ | Heavy cloud with rain |

ROUGH
MODERATE    } refer to the sea.
SMOOTH

Source: JMB UETESOL.

## Example 6(h):   Information transfer task 3

A = Railway Station
B = Telephone Box
C = Park
D = School
E = Police Station
F = 23 Balmoral Drive

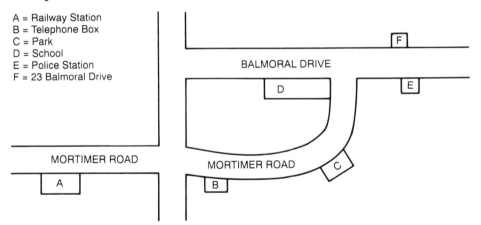

Look at the map. You live at 23 Balmoral Drive. Your friend is coming to stay with you. She is coming by train. Write simple directions from the railway station to your house. Do *not* write anything else.

Source: Pitman Examinations, Elementary.

## Comment on Examples 6(d)–6(h)

With concise, clear, accessible stimuli (tabulated data, graphs, pictures and drawings) the candidate does not have to spend a long period of time decoding an extended written text. The more visual and the less verbal these stimuli are, the more efficiently they can be decoded. These semi-verbal to non-verbal stimuli can be used to elicit written performance of a number of different language operations such as description of phenomena and ideas (see Examples 6(d) and 6(g)), argumentation (Example 6(e)), description of process (Example 6(f)), and also directing (Example 6(h)).

These information transfer tasks, employing a largely non-verbal stimulus, may not prove as suitable in those contexts where the desire is to assess the ability to produce interactional, social and service texts (with the possible exception of directing). The latter tasks would require different prompts (of the type exemplified in 6(a)–6(c) above), and would extract performance under different conditions.

As with prompts in other tasks, care needs to be taken in the selection of topics. Problems have arisen in this format when, in an attempt to avoid bias arising from background knowledge, a test has resorted to extremely specialised, arcane areas for visual stimuli, for example, castle crenellations in the fifteenth century or door frames in the eighteenth century. This is a problem familiar from our discussion of testing reading and the spoken skills. In all skills testing, care must be taken in selecting topics to ensure that candidates are in a position to process language productively and receptively as they would in real-life contexts. This entails that the writing tasks we set students should not make undue or unequal demands on the background knowledge of candidates.

Sometimes candidates are unable to cope with the mental challenge of decoding complex non-verbal stimuli and the equally complex rubrics that sometimes accompany these. The need to understand a very complex set of instructions and/or visual stimuli to produce a relatively straightforward piece of writing sometimes causes the candidate to resist or fail the task. This was a problem we referred to in discussing this format in relation to reading in Chapter 3 above.

Another major difficulty we referred to in that discussion was that the drawing ability required (see Examples 6(f) and 6(g) above) is likely to be beyond the reach of most teachers, and the replicability of such items by teachers is open to doubt. In important national examinations such as the JMB University Entrance Test in English for Speakers of Other Languages (UETESOL), however, the value of items such as 6(f) and 6(g) above is more obvious. The information is presented clearly and the task allows description of both state and process. Equivalent information is available to every candidate. Reading does not interfere with the measurement of writing as it might in the case of Example 7.

## Example 7:    Integrated reading into writing

This is a test of your ability to read in English and to write in English about what you have read. You have two tasks to do in 75 minutes.

### TASK ONE

Read the passage 'Changes in the Position of Women' in the source Booklet and then summarise, in your own words as far as possible,

**What the author says about the employment of women from the 1940s onwards.**

Your summary should be about 200 words in length.

You should use the space below to make notes which will help you to write your summary. These notes will not be marked.

WARNING: some of the sections in the passage are not relevant to this writing task. Remember the topic of the summary is only

**The employment of women from the 1940s onwards.**

You should spend only 40 minutes on this task.

Source: TEEP test, CALS, University of Reading.

## Comment on Example 7

Great care needs to be taken in ensuring that the conditions relating to text type and method factor in Table 5.1 above are discussed rigorously at the moderating stage. The views of subject specialists and of a sample from the test population need to be elicited to try to ensure that any bias is kept to a minimum. The subject specificity of certain input texts might create too many problems for non-specialists in the subject, and the test might prove unsuitable for them. In the end one may have to resort to generally accessible scientific texts of the sort that appear in *New Scientist* for science and engineering students, and topics such as health education if the test population is to include arts and social science students.

Addressing the conditions in Table 5.1 might help improve the task in other ways. It might be enhanced if the candidates were given an explicit addressee for the task, and also if it was made clear which criteria would be applied to their written work (compare

Example 6F in this respect). The criteria would need to match closely those that would be applied in the future discourse community the candidate was seeking entry into. Demonstrating qualities of literary style and imagination might not be entirely appropriate for the budding engineer.

The task needs to match with generalisable EAP writing operations if a subject-specific test is not possible because of heterogeneity of population. A generalised academic writing task should include the following features: provision of topic/assignment prompt; an indication of audience expectation; specified and accessible source(s) of data; lexis constrained (to some extent) by all of the above. The candidate has to search for and extract data relevant to the question. Furthermore, the candidate has to reorganise and encode these data within the conventions of academic discourse so that the reader's expectations of relevance, adequacy, coherence, appropriateness and accuracy are fulfilled (see Weir 1983 for further discussion).

A summary is suitable for testing a student's writing ability in terms of the tasks he or she has to cope with in an academic situation. This example represents one of the few attempts in public examinations to build greater content validity into a prompt for an academic writing test.

A common difficulty with an integrated writing component of this type, however, is making the marking reliable. To assess students' responses reliably one needs to formulate the main points contained in the extract, construct an adequate mark scheme and standardise markers to it using explicit criteria and a script library (see Section 5.3 below). Some subjectivity inevitably remains and it is easy to underestimate the difficulty of marking reliably. Whether such written work should be marked by specialists from the target discourse community or by language specialists needs to be thought about. The simple solution might be to involve both.

## 5.3  The marking of written production

An attempt is made in this section to bring together what is known about the main approaches to assessing writing (see Hamp-Lyons 1990 and 1991 for excellent surveys of this area). The relative merits of global and analytic approaches to marking for improving the reliability and validity of a writing sub-test are examined below.

Before turning to this discussion you should complete Marking Exercises 1−3 below. Much of what is discussed here in relation to the assessment of writing will apply to the assessment of spoken language ability. It is treated here in the writing section because it is possible to provide concrete samples of written work to make judgements about. To do the same for speaking would require videos of candidates taking part in spoken language tasks.

## MARKING EXERCISE 1

For the purposes of this exercise we are assuming that you have considered carefully the operations you want your students to perform in writing and have constructed a writing task in accordance with these which also reflects, as far as possible, conditions appropriate for the test population.

Look again at the writing task, Example 6(f) above. It is an interesting early example of an information transfer task from the JMB's Test in English (Overseas), used to determine whether such overseas students have sufficient writing ability to enter tertiary-level English-medium education in UK. In Appendix C you will find eight scripts from students taking this test.

Mark each of the eight scripts in Appendix C out of 20 and record your marks on a separate sheet of paper. Do this fairly quickly. When you have finished jot down the criteria you employed.

Look below at the marks that 22 MA TESOL students gave to these scripts. In the right-hand column we have indicated the mean mark of each rater and the range used. Below the marks awarded by the raters at the bottom of the page we have provided the range of marks awarded by different raters to each candidate and the overall mean score for each.

Look carefully at the marks awarded. What conclusions can you draw from these data?

Table 5.4  *Scores awarded out of 20 by MA students*

|   | 1 | 2 | 3 | 4 | 5 | 6 | 7 | 8 | mean m | range r |
|---|---|---|---|---|---|---|---|---|---|---|
| A | 8 | 12 | 12 | 13 | 15 | 8 | 14 | 16 | 12 | 8–16 |
| B | 7 | 11 | 12 | 13 | 14 | 7 | 14 | 15 | 12 | 7–15 |
| C | 5 | 12 | 11 | 9 | 9 | 4 | 11 | 9 | 9 | 4–12 |
| D | 9 | 10 | 14 | 14 | 14 | 6 | 16 | 19 | 13 | 6–19 |
| E | 9 | 15 | 15 | 11 | 14 | 8 | 16 | 16 | 13 | 8–16 |
| F | 7 | 10 | 11 | 12 | 13 | 14 | 15 | 12 | 12 | 7–15 |
| G | 4 | 10 | 15 | 5 | 12 | 3 | 18 | 19 | 11 | 4–19 |
| H | 7 | 11 | 10 | 8 | 12 | 6 | 17 | 11 | 11 | 6–17 |
| I | 12 | 14 | 17 | 10 | 19 | 10 | 17 | 17 | 15 | 10–19 |
| J | 5 | 2 | 3 | 2 | 5 | 1 | 18 | 5 | 5 | 1–18 |
| K | 8 | 12 | 14 | 5 | 10 | 13 | 6 | 10 | 11 | 6–15 |
| L | 8 | 9 | 11 | 11 | 13 | 9 | 15 | 15 | 11 | 8–15 |
| M | 5 | 12 | 15 | 8 | 15 | 9 | 16 | 14 | 12 | 5–16 |
| N | 4 | 10 | 12 | 12 | 15 | 3 | 18 | 20 | 12 | 4–20 |
| O | 7 | 10 | 10 | 10 | 12 | 15 | 16 | 18 | 12 | 7–18 |
| P | 4 | 7 | 12 | 9 | 10 | 3 | 14 | 17 | 10 | 4–17 |
| Q | 5 | 7 | 10 | 8 | 9 | 3 | 11 | 13 | 8 | 3–13 |
| R | 3 | 8 | 9 | 9 | 7 | 4 | 17 | 15 | 9 | 3–17 |
| S | 8 | 10 | 15 | 10 | 12 | 8 | 15 | 15 | 12 | 8–15 |
| T | 3 | 3 | 5 | 5 | 6 | 2 | 8 | 14 | 5 | 2–10 |
| U | 12 | 14 | 16 | 13 | 12 | 3 | 19 | 18 | 13 | 3–18 |
| V | 10 | 14 | 17 | 14 | 13 | 8 | 18 | 18 | 14 | 8–18 |
| r | 3–12 | 2–15 | 3–17 | 2–15 | 5–19 | 1–15 | 6–18 | 5–20 | | |
| m | 7 | 11 | 12 | 10 | 12 | 7 | 15 | 15 | | |

*Comment on Marking Exercise 1*

There is a great deal of variability in the marks awarded by the different raters. The most likely reasons for this are the lack of explicit agreed criteria for carrying out the marking task and perhaps also the speed with which it was done. Whatever the reason, candidates would have been seriously affected by the choice of rater assigned to mark their script. Compare the marks of rater *T* with those of marker *I*. Who would you prefer to be marked by? Some of the raters have high average marks (see under *mean* right-hand column) and some have quite low average marks. Some use a narrow band of marks (rater *S*) and some use the full mark range (rater *N*).

The picture is even more disturbing if we look at the range of marks given to each script (see first set of figures at the foot of the column). Take script 8. The mark range is 5−20, and that for script 6 is 1−15. In nearly all cases the worst scripts, 1 and 6, if they had been marked by certain markers, might have been given higher marks than the best scripts, 7 and 8. This degree of unreliability cannot be tolerated. We must seek ways to bring raters closer together in the marks they award.

## MARKING EXERCISE 2

Re-mark the scripts using Mark Scheme 1 (Table 5.5 below). This is an early draft of a global impression band scale being developed with Don McGovern and John Trzeciak at CALS, University of Reading, for marking the scripts of overseas students entering our presessional programme. Record your grade on each script and then rank the eight students in order of performance. The one with the highest grade is first, etc.

Either with a colleague or by using the comments below:

(a) Determine where you agree on the grade and position of a particular candidate. Establish where the biggest differences are.

(b) Discuss: why there are differences in the grades awarded; what you understand by the various criteria; whether you paid special attention to a particular aspect of the script.

(c) See if you can now come to an agreement on a final ranking and grades for the scripts.

Table 5.5
*Mark Scheme 1: Global assessment scale (writing)*

GRADE 1
A text which significantly fails to achieve the task in terms of content and organisation. It may be quite short. High incidence of errors in grammar, vocabulary and spelling. Frequently incomprehensible. Argument falls into incoherences. Expression not appropriate to the situation or context. May lack control over syntax. Overall impression is of somebody using the language with considerable difficulty. ( = IELTS 4)

GRADE 2 –
The text may either be under-developed or contain irrelevant information. Organisation is flawed or lacking in control. Student may be 'over-cautious' about exposing weaknesses. May be *occasionally* incomprehensible. Expression largely or consistently unidiomatic. Occasional gross inadequacy of grammatical usage. Cohesion barely adequate, unsatisfactory use or absence of connectors. Confusion of tenses evident. Overall impression is of someone using the language with difficulty. ( = IELTS 5 – )

GRADE 2 +
Content may be relevant and given some degree of development but is probably rather simplistic. Likely to show at least a modicum of skill in organisation. Occasionally more ambitious use of vocabulary. Unidiomatic expression evident, though simpler uses may be accurate. Relatively satisfactory use of connectors. Simple sentences without much variety of structure. Some lapses in coherence, but errors do not seriously interfere with comprehension. Overall impression is of someone able to communicate at a superficial level with limited accuracy. ( = IELTS 5 + )

*GRADE 3
Content is relevant, adequately-developed and organised. Communicates meaning without undue demands on the reader. Expression is occasionally unidiomatic, though lapses from standard English are not gross. Mostly coherent and cohesive. Appropriate to the context in terms of expression. Largely accurate in the use of relative structures, where appropriate. Overall impression is of someone who operates competently within a limited range of language and has some command over style and expression. ( = IELTS 6: Just Adequate)

GRADE 4
Content is relevant and well-developed. Shows clear competence in organisation. Very few if any errors of grammar, vocabulary or spelling. Language is largely idiomatic, though there may be occasional minor lapses. Points are interesting, appropriately-expressed and coherently-organised at both paragraph- and essay-level. Fluent command over style and expression. ( = IELTS 7/8)

GRADE 5
Content is relevant, fully-developed and comprehensive. May be imaginative in its approach. Organisation is excellent. Virtually indistinguishable from the English of a well-educated native speaker. Literate, coherent, interesting and of some length. High degree of fluent command over style and expression. ( = IELTS 9)

*Comment on Marking Exercise 2*

Average band scores awarded by 22 MA students:

    8:  4
    7:  3+
    5:  2+
    4:  2+
    3:  2+
    2:  2−
    1:  1
    6:  1

Most colleagues who have taken part in marking exercises on these scripts would place script 8 at the top of the list with a score of 4 on the band scale, closely followed by script 7 at the top end of the 3 band. At the lower end, scripts 1 and 6 would probably be placed at the bottom in the 1 band. Script 2 for most people would just about scrape into the 2− band.

Most disagreement occurs over scripts 3,4,5 which are placed either at 2+, or on the 3 band borderline. They were deliberately included in the batch of scripts because of the disagreement they cause. The reasons for disagreement may relate to the marginality of the scripts themselves, to insufficient clarity in the band descriptors at the 2+/3 mark boundary, or to the fact that these scripts exhibit configurations of criteria that are not exactly matched by the band profiles.

Certainly more work has to be done in developing the band descriptors, especially at the 3/2+ borderline. This is most important as non-native speakers attaining this grade would be deemed to have nearly reached the minimal, acceptable standard for entry into English-medium study at a British university. In any assessment of writing it is the boundary between pass and fail that should be the starting point, and the focus for development of assessment criteria.

It is essential that in developing such descriptors they are based on real performances. Mark Scheme 1 is an attempt to define levels of proficiency, in this case for academic writing. To the extent that the levels are based on real-life performances, then we can have confidence in their applicability. Teachers of similar year groups can set common tasks and develop criteria-based descriptions to fit different ability levels. Over a period of time it should be possible to develop profiles of ability levels in writing for the students you teach in your context. A similar approach should be adopted for the development of band scales for assessing the other skills as well.

Investigation of linguistic profiles based on the actual written work will tell us about possible configurations in terms of specified criteria. It may well be, after sufficient research and development, that at each level 2−, 2, 2+, 3−, 3, 3+ in the band scale above we will have a number of different but clear configurations, in terms of the criteria we might wish to apply. This would provide further evidence of the variability of language acquisition. If this variability is unmanageable, i.e. the pattern of acquisition is too complex or too varied, then we might have to resort to breaking writing down into its constituent parts, as we do for reading. We would then be able to provide a multi-trait profile of a script in terms of analytic features, such as organisation and grammatical accuracy (see comment on Marking Exercise 3 below).

Script 3 creates problems for marking in that by choosing a more narrative-based description the candidate avoids the more normal process description (and needs to be penalised in terms of content and perhaps also organisation). If the candidate can avoid doing the task set this will certainly present problems in marking. This illustrates a common occurrence in most marking exercises, where ground rules have to be developed in advance to cater for rogue performances. This can include, for example, what to do if a candidate writes a very short piece of work, what to do if he or she writes a prepared script which is only tangentially connected to the task set, what to do if the candidate does not take risks and uses an extremely limited structural range. A ground rule is also necessary for plagiarism in those cases where common information is made available to candidates in the form of verbal text.

## MARKING EXERCISE 3

Take scripts 3, 4 and 5 and mark each of them according to the analytic TEEP profile scale (Mark Scheme 2) below.

| Script | 3 | 4 | 5 |
|---|---|---|---|
| Relevance and adequacy of content | | | |
| Organisation | | | |
| Cohesion | | | |
| Vocabulary | | | |
| Grammatical accuracy | | | |
| Punctuation | | | |
| Spelling | | | |

Compare the marks you have given for each script with colleagues (or with our suggestions on page 160).

Table 5.6
*Mark Scheme 2: TEEP attribute writing scales*

**1.** *Relevance and adequacy of content*
0   The answer bears almost no relation to the task set. Totally inadequate answer.
1   Answer of limited relevance to the task set. Possibly major gaps in treatment of topic and/or pointless repetition.
2   For the most part answers the tasks set, though there may be some gaps or redundant information.
3   Relevant and adequate answer to the task set.

**2.** *Compositional organisation*
0   No apparent organisation of content.
1   Very little organisation of content. Underlying structure not sufficiently apparent.
2   Some organisational skills in evidence, but not adequately controlled.
3   Overall shape and internal pattern clear. Organisational skills adequately controlled.

**3.** *Cohesion*
0   Cohesion almost totally absent. Writing so fragmentary that comprehension of the intended communication is virtually impossible.
1   Unsatisfactory cohesion may cause difficulty in comprehension of most of the intended communication.
2   For the most part satisfactory cohesion though occasional deficiencies may mean that certain parts of the communication are not always effective.
3   Satisfactory use of cohesion resulting in effective communication.

**4.** *Adequacy of vocabulary for purpose*
0   Vocabulary inadequate even for the most basic parts of the intended communication.
1   Frequent inadequacies in vocabulary for the task. Perhaps frequent lexical inappropriacies and/or repetition.
2   Some inadequacies in vocabulary for the task. Perhaps some lexical inappropriacies and/or circumlocution.
3   Almost no inadequacies in vocabulary for the task. Only rare inappropriacies and/or circumlocution.

**5.** *Grammar*
0   Almost all grammatical patterns inaccurate.
1   Frequent grammatical inaccuracies.
2   Some grammatical inaccuracies.
3   Almost no grammatical inaccuracies.

**6.** *Mechanical accuracy I (punctuation)*
0   Ignorance of conventions of punctuation.
1   Low standard of accuracy in punctuation.
2   Some inaccuracies in punctuation.
3   Almost no inaccuracies in punctuation.

**7.** *Mechanical accuracy II (spelling)*
0   Almost all spelling inaccurate.
1   Low standard of accuracy in spelling.
2   Some inaccuracies in spelling.
3   Almost no inaccuracies in spelling.

## Comment on Marking Exercise 3

Average marks awarded by seven presessional course teachers at Reading University:

| Script | 3 | 4 | 5 |
|---|---|---|---|
| Relevance and adequacy of content | 2 − | 2 + | 2 |
| Organisation | 2 − | 2 | 2 |
| Cohesion | 2 | 2 − | 2 − |
| Vocabulary | 2 | 2 | 2 − |
| Grammatical accuracy | 2 − | 2 | 2 − |
| Punctuation | 2 + | 2 + | 2 − |
| Spelling | 2 + | 1 + | 2 |

By asking markers to be explicit about individual aspects of a piece of written work it is possible to provide a more detailed profile of a candidate's strengths and weaknesses. The complexity of an individual performance is indicated in the results from Exercise 3 above (to the extent that we can rely on these assessments). These assessments illustrate the different configurations of ability that make up the three pieces of written work, which markers using the global assessment scheme had difficulty in distinguishing. The variability in terms of performance on different criteria may also help explain why markers differed in placing them on the global band scale in Exercise 2.

Analytic mark schemes have sometimes been found deficient in the choice and delineation of appropriate criteria for a given discourse community. In the design work for the TEEP test it was felt that the assessment of samples of written performance should be based on behaviourally described, analytic criteria, appropriate to the academic discourse community.

The criteria needed to be comprehensive and based on data, collected from the academic discourse community. The criteria in Mark Scheme 2 above resulted from a survey of a large number of academic staff at tertiary-level institutions in the United Kingdom (see Weir 1983). Academic staff were in favour of procedures that would assess students, particularly in relation to their communicative effectiveness, and in such a way that a profile containing details of candidates' strengths and weaknesses could be made available.

The empirical investigation suggested the criteria of relevance and adequacy, compositional organisation, cohesion, referential adequacy, grammatical accuracy, spelling and punctuation as the most suitable for assessing writing tasks. Of these the first two were rated as highly important and the last two mechanical accuracy features of very little importance. The remaining criteria were rated as being of medium importance. Serious thought might be given in future to omitting any concern with the last two mechanical accuracy features.

As was reported in Weir (1990: 69−71):

> ... To apply these 'valid' criteria reliably an attempt was made to construct an analytic marking scheme in which each of the criteria is sub-divided into four behavioral levels on a scale of 0−3 [see Table above]. A level 3 corresponds to a base line of minimal competence. At this level it was felt that a student was likely to have very few problems in coping with the writing tasks demanded of him or her by his or her course in respect of this criterion. At a level 2 a limited number of problems arise in relation to the criterion and remedial help would be advisable. A level 1 would indicate that a lot of help is necessary with respect to this particular criterion. A level 0 indicates almost total incompetence in respect of the criterion in question ...

> The nature of the problems encountered in the evolution of the criteria provide useful background for the development of similar schemes for assessing both spoken and written production. The first problem in earlier versions of these assessment criteria was that in some an attempt was made to assess two things, namely communicative effectiveness and degrees of accuracy. As a result great difficulty was encountered in attempting to apply the criteria reliably. It was necessary to refine them so that the first four related to communicative effectiveness and the latter three to accuracy. It may well be that the latter three criteria contribute to communicative effectiveness or lack of it, but attempts to incorporate some indication of this proved unworkable.

> Secondly, distinctions between each of the four levels were only gradually achieved, and it was also necessary to try to establish roughly equivalent level distinctions across the criteria. Great problems were experienced in the trial assessments in gaining agreement as to what was meant by certain of the descriptions of levels within the criteria. Most sources of confusion were gradually eliminated, and this seemed inevitably to result in a much-simplified scale for these descriptions of level, particularly in the accuracy criteria 5−7.

In those cases where the candidates are provided with information, as in Example 7 above, or as in the TEEP test, where the candidates have to extract specified information from an article provided, it may be problematic to employ certain of these criteria.

Where all the lexis is provided for the candidates, either through labelled diagrams or in available text, the likelihood is that most candidates will score reasonably well on the adequacy of vocabulary criterion. They might in fact score disproportionately better on this criterion than on other criteria, where this degree of help is not available. One could argue, however, that this help is available in real life, as it is for spelling through spellcheckers on computers. Perhaps this is a strong argument for reducing our criteria accordingly.

A similar argument is put forward in terms of content in those tasks where candidates are given this assistance. One might wish to argue more strongly in this case that information is available in real life and what is at issue here is candidates' ability to demonstrate that they can convey relevant and adequate information in their own words.

An important issue is, how many distinctions can you make in respect of each criterion? If it is felt that further distinctions can be made, for example between levels 1 and 2, then it will be necessary to provide copies of actual scripts to exemplify these. These concrete exemplifications should assist us in talking about stages, which are really only invented conveniences to help us talk about performance on a continuum. More obviously the scale might be altered by providing a level 4 which would be a perfect performance in respect of a particular feature.

A decision must be taken on how the individually assessed traits relate to each other. In the absence of any indication to the contrary it is probably sensible to weight each facet equally. A possible alternative would be to weight in accordance with proficient users' intuitions. We must also establish what composite mark is equivalent to what level of performance.

The most crucial decision relates to determining the base line for passing a candidate, the most important of mark boundaries. If task conditions and operations are appropriate to the context, and the criteria are approved and seen as criterial by the discourse community the candidate is entering, then we can be reasonably confident in the decisions we take. This approach ensures a close match between the writing to be done and the skills and test facets to be evaluated. Once these have been established, raters, in collaboration with end users of the information in the discourse community, can determine where to draw the line in terms of pass and fail. This is a matter of defining a minimally adequate candidate in terms of the tasks being carried out, under specified conditions, to a certain level of output on specified criteria. The selection of sample scripts from these tasks to form a script library illustrating the various distinctions we wish to make, can enable us to be even more confident in our subsequent judgements.

### Single global impression versus multi-trait analytic marking procedures

The relative merits of single, global impression and multi-trait analytic approaches to marking, for improving the reliability and validity of a writing sub-test, are examined briefly below (see also Hamp-Lyons 1991: 241−76). Many of the points raised are also applicable to the testing of spoken language.

In discussing the examples of extended writing above, it was argued that, by controlling the writing tasks, we might improve their validity and reliability. We concluded that there was a need for 'controlled' writing tests, in which the context and scope of a feasible, acceptable, appropriate writing task were determined for, and made clear to, the candidate. It was felt that this would facilitate marking and allow a more reliable comparison across candidates. We will now examine how the application of single, global impressionistic and multi-trait analytic approaches to marking might also aid us in our attempt to improve the reliability and validity of our writing tasks.

In the global impression method of marking, candidates are placed at a single level on a scale, based on an impression of their written work as a whole. In global marking no attempt is made to evaluate a text in terms of separate criteria. Each grade on the scale is usually equated with a distinct level of achievement which is closely described in terms of a number of criteria.

The method is quick to use and this often encourages the use of two markers who have to agree on a final single grade. It has found favour with admissions tutors because the descriptions are easy to handle administratively, e.g. all candidates at band 7 or above can be accepted. No interpretation or computation is required.

One danger is that a marker's impression of the overall quality might have been affected by just one or two aspects of the work. In some ways this is similar to the halo effect reported in relation to analytic scales where the possibility exists that the rating of one criterion might have a knock-on effect in the rating of the next. If a major preoccupation of a marker is with grammar, and the candidate exhibits a poor performance on this criterion, are the marks awarded in respect of other criteria contaminated by the grammar mark? With careful standardisation of markers and checking of marking it should be feasible to counteract this possibility.

A more deep-rooted problem is that the global approach fails in practice because it does not cater for learners whose performance levels vary in terms of different criteria. ESL writers quite often acquire differential control over the components of writing ability, e.g. some have much greater fluency than accuracy and vice versa, some have greater syntactic control than lexical, etc.

The major problem with most global impression band scales is that they are not empirically derived. They appear to represent levels of proficiency, but as yet we do not have a clear idea of the order of acquisition of various skill attributes in writing or even whether there is such an order. Until adequate research is carried out, and scales are empirically founded on the scripts produced by real candidates, then they are at best tentative in their implications

In multi-trait, analytic marking, a level is recorded in respect of each criterion, and the final grade is a composite of these individual assessments. This method avoids the potential flaw in global impression band scales of uneven development in the different criteria. Hamp-Lyons (1991: 242) has argued:

> In order to reach a reasonable balance among all the essential elements of good writing, readers need to pay conscious attention to all those elements. A detailed scoring procedure requiring the readers to attend to the multidimensionality of ESL writing is needed.

It would then be interesting to see if the judgements produced matched the global impressions of proficient users. One would hope that judgements of a good piece of writing resulting from the analytic approach accorded with what reliable native writers thought was a good piece of writing.

This method has the added advantage that it lends itself more readily to full-profile reporting and could perform a certain diagnostic role in delineating students' strengths and weaknesses in written production. It can tell the end user of the information whether a candidate has a flat profile or whether it is in any sense marked by particular strengths or weaknesses (see Hamp-Lyons 1991: 253–5). This information cannot be supplied through a global impression scheme.

This diagnostic function, when based on more than one sample script, might be particularly beneficial for placement purposes, opening up the possibilities of targeted remedial tuition. It might also be of value in a formative role during a course of instruction.

Such a diagnostic function might also help to provide clearer information on the areas of language gain during a course of instruction. Thus it could be useful in providing educational, illuminative information, as well as establishing evaluation data for accountability purposes.

Hamp-Lyons (1990: 81) emphasises the importance of a further dimension of assessment. She stresses that we need to investigate ways of rater training to improve on the present situation. This will involve careful consideration of the context in which training occurs, the type of training given, the extent to which training is monitored, the extent to which rating is monitored and the feedback given to raters.

Although analytic schemes may facilitate agreement amongst examiners as to the precise range of qualities that are to be evaluated in an essay, in many schemes the actual amount of individual marker variation involved in the assessment, i.e. degree of unreliability, may be reduced very little if there is a lack of explicitness with regard to the applicable criteria, or a use of vague criteria. Hamp-Lyons' work on the development of multiple-trait scoring procedures for specified topics, in particular contexts, shows how these dangers can be avoided (see Hamp-Lyons 1991: 248−61).

She argues that the raters should focus only on the most salient criteria as established through careful test development, well grounded in actual data, in the context where measurements are to be made (see discussion of the establishment of the TEEP assessment criteria above).

Weir (1990: 68) reported that a multi-trait analytic mark scheme is seen as a useful tool for the training and standardisation of new examiners. By employing an analytic scheme, examining bodies feel they can better train and standardise new markers to the criteria of assessment (for an extended discussion on the standardisation and training of examiners see Section 1.3.5 in Part I above and Murphy 1979). A measure of agreement about what each criterion means can be established, and subsequently markers can be standardised to what constitutes a different level within each of these criteria. Analytic schemes have been found to be particularly useful with markers who are relatively inexperienced.

It is often argued that work marked independently by two different markers, with their marks being averaged, is a more reliable estimate than if it were marked by a single marker. This is of course true only if the markers are equally consistent in their own marking. If this is not the case the reliability of the more consistent marker on his own might be better than the combined reliability estimate for two markers who exhibit unequal consistencies. With an adequate marking scheme and sufficient standardisation of examiners, however, a high standard of inter-marker and intra-marker reliability should be feasible (see Sections 1.3.4 and 1.3.5 in Part I). The advantages of a double as against a single marker system would then be clear.

Hamp-Lyons (1990 and 1991) and Jacobs *et al.* (1981) provide valuable overviews of the issues in assessing writing, and the reader is referred to their work as useful and stimulating further reading.

Hamp-Lyons concludes (1990: 82)

> ... there are no easy answers. Each aspect — task, writer, scoring procedure, and reader (marker) — interacts with the other, creating a complex network of effects which to date has eluded our efforts to control. We will not, I believe, solve the problems of writing assessment until we look at this total picture rather than each facet in isolation.

# Chapter Six

## Language testing for teachers: overview and way forward

### 6.1  An important and developing field

Much has happened since Alan Davies wrote an important state-of-the-art article on language testing (Davies 1978). In the past decade we have seen the founding of the *Language Testing Journal* and the appearance of three newsletters on language testing. Teachers can now take an MA Course option in testing at many universities, or even whole MAs specialising in testing and evaluation. Books and articles on testing have appeared in abundance in the 1980s.

Two recent review articles (Skehan 1991, Alderson 1991) have provided excellent surveys of developments in language testing and, interestingly, most of the references cited are from the 1980s. Both surveys make important contributions to the current debate in testing and many of the points made below arise from their illuminating discussion.

At seminars, conferences and in the applied linguistics and language teaching literature, there has been a greater demand over the last decade for the public demonstration of the value of tests in the areas of validity and reliability. It is strongly felt by practitioners that it is now necessary to demonstrate through appropriate validation procedures how good a test actually is in measuring specified performance. Faith validity — the intuitive belief on the part of the test constructor that his test is a good one — is no longer sufficient. The recent comparative study of Cambridge/TOEFL examinations (Bachman *et al.* 1988) has been a major step in this direction and has clearly signalled to other examining boards the path to be taken if tests are to gain international currency.

### 6.2  Focus on understanding language proficiency in the 1980s

The concern of Davies (1978), in his survey article looking back on the 1970s, was mainly with the *how* of testing: discrete items versus integrative formats. Skehan's 1988 state-of-the-art article is concerned mainly with the *what* of language testing and the focus in the 1990s will remain with this.

The 1980s were marked by investigations into the structure of general language proficiency. They witnessed the declining importance of conservative, linguistic models and a developing interest in, and description of, the different competencies that might be involved in using language (see Bachman 1990 and Skehan 1991).

In the wake of developments in English language teaching, the last decade has seen a general decline in the prestige of psychometric, statistically driven, approaches to testing. There is far greater concern now with validity as opposed to an earlier overriding concern with test reliability. Most noticeable in recent years has been the importance given to the washback effect of a test on the teaching that precedes that test. There has been a growing interest in the importance of context, in defining performance conditions: in short a growth of interest in the real-life school of testing (see Canale 1983, Canale and Swain 1980, Hughes 1989, Morrow 1977 and 1979, and Weir 1990).

This communicative/real-life approach in testing might be said to be characterised by the following features (in no particular order): focus on meaning, contextualisation, activity has an acceptable purpose (reasonable suspension of disbelief), realistic discourse processing, use of genuine stimulus material, authentic operations on texts, unpredictable outcomes, interaction based, performance under real psychological conditions, e.g. time pressure and in assessment of performance on a task, judgements made on achievement of communicative purposes.

Most teachers are teaching language for eventual use in real life, for real-life purposes under real-life conditions. The ability to use 'real-life language' will need to be tested. We cannot build into our tests *all* the features of real life *all* the time. But we should maximise the involvement of these features.

Along with this approach has come ESP/EAP test development: the development of tests based on prior specification of desired performance through empirical needs analysis of the future target situation. This needs-driven approach can be seen in many current EFL/ESP examinations: UCLES/RSA, TEEP, IELTS. All bear witness to the importance of context.

However, most of this work has been carried out in the field of large-scale or institutional proficiency testing. Relatively little has permeated through to the area of classroom-based achievement testing.

## 6.3   Neglect of achievement testing

Information on student achievement is crucial to teaching and learning. As teachers we need information on student progress. We need to monitor achievement of objectives as part of course implementation. We need to monitor the functional ability of students; what they can do. This can lead to a descriptive profile of a learner's communicative performance or a record of achievement.

Teachers need to evaluate formatively, to make appropriate decisions concerning modifications to teaching procedures and learning activities. Is new material being introduced too quickly or too slowly? If it is, the effectiveness of learning may well be diminished.

Teachers need to decide when to move on to the next unit. If the next units are dependent on what has gone before then the teacher needs to be sure the students have mastered the objectives of a particular unit before proceeding on to the next one. This can lead to necessary modifications in the programme.

Formal tests devised for monitoring achievement can also be extremely helpful to individual students, can help identify areas of strength or weakness and provide focus for future learning objectives. They can also be motivational, by providing an idea of progress.

The inclusion of published tests at the end of each unit of teaching materials would greatly facilitate this monitoring of student achievement. If easily replicable they could also help teachers design their own tests or quizzes which might be used en route through the unit.

The washback effect on teaching and learning could be extremely beneficial.

Achievement tests can also help in making decisions about changes to programmes if they are to be run again. They can help determine which objectives have been met and where changes might have to be made; an important contribution to curriculum improvement.

However, despite the value of more formal assessment procedures, there has been a general neglect of the formal means for establishing goals and standards for courses and syllabi; a lack of progress in formal measurement of the growth and development of learners' proficiency in using the language.

With few exceptions (most notably Geoff Brindley (1989) and David Nunan from the National Centre for English Language Teaching and Research, at MacQuarie University, Sydney, in the Adult Migrant Education Programme in Australia) this crucial area has been mostly neglected by researchers, syllabus designers, textbook writers and teachers.

Brindley (1989) in a study of 131 teachers in the Australian Adult Migrant Programme found a tendency to rely on informal methods of ongoing assessment, e.g. observation followed by recycling of work, and verbal feedback in informal discussions with learners about their progress. Brindley found (p.43) that:

> this does not seem to be sufficiently explicit to meet the expectations and requirements of either administrators or learners for more formal information on learners' achievement of the objectives of a course or a unit . . . The informal methods of ongoing assessment favoured by teachers do not provide the kind of explicit information on achievement required by learners and administrators.

Most of the teachers Brindley surveyed regarded formal assessment as someone else's job and a potentially threatening process. His research evidenced a strong teacher reaction against external accountability and a feeling that data were for internal consumption in the classroom only.

Brindley stressed the need to develop criterion-referenced procedures to measure learner's achievement of the communicative objectives of a given course or unit of instruction. He argued (1989: 45) that the use of criterion-referenced, communicative assessment procedures would help satisfy learners' demands for formal instruments. They would also allow for the aggregation of information in the form of a summative profile of achievement, thereby allowing interpretation by external agencies. If the objectives, tasks and criteria can be specified in user-friendly terms, learners, teachers and outside parties could, he argued, all be involved in their development.

There is a pressing need for a great deal more work on formative as against summative testing in the 1990s. As Skehan (1988) points out, this would help provide the information which feeds into the process of learning and which could enable learners and teachers to modify their behaviour in an ongoing way during instruction.

There is a need to focus on the development of progress-sensitive performance tests for use during courses. Empirical work is required on the parameters and descriptions used in association with band scales to increase their validity and to make them more sensitive to smaller performance differences. Testing must be related to the developmental stages in language learning: in this sense bridge building with SLA theories and findings will become an extremely valuable feature of the next decade.

## 6.4    How can we make advances in the 1990s? A framework for test development for both teachers and researchers

As a profession we badly need a framework for research into language proficiency which will be accessible and relevant to the needs of teachers, testers and researchers. Most crucially this framework would need to take into account real-life conditions, the context in which language is used for communication, as well as a more theoretical account of the skills/abilities that might be involved in language use.

We need a coherent framework within which to work. We must build on the models of Canale and Swain (1980), Canale (1983) and Bachman (1990) and encourage a move from abstract theory to build in context. As well as the operations that our students will have to carry out, we need to investigate the conditions under which these activities are carried out. There is a pressing need to incorporate work from other areas of applied linguistics into the development of language testing. Tests must be theory driven.

Teachers need to relate classroom tasks to the tasks their students will have to cope with in tests. But equally, testers need to relate their tests to a frame of reference used by teachers. Otherwise the language teaching profession could be forever divided in what it considers good performance to consist of. More crucially both sets of tasks need to bear a systematic relationship to the tasks students will be required to do in life after the course. The aim is to improve the match between teaching, testing and target situation behaviour.

This book represents an initial attempt at developing a framework which is consistent with a wide range of theoretical insights and which will form a systematising framework for generating connected research activity. It is argued that such a framework can provide an account of the construct which tests should be aiming to assess, and that it is desirable that tests should take account of these features in the tasks they use whenever appropriate. The intention is also that it should provide teachers with the means for writing better tests, joining with colleagues in carrying out action research in this area.

A three-part framework has been suggested for use by teachers as a checklist in designing tests or by researchers as a framework for a concerted body of research in this area. This framework specifies the operations to be tested, the conditions under which the operations should be performed, and the criteria for assessing quality of output (level).

### Need for validation

An attempt has been made in this book to map out what features the test writer might want to consider in the construction of tests. It remains for empirical research to determine the relative importance of the elements of our framework in all three sections : operations, conditions and criteria for assessing quality of output. It would be presumptuous, given the present state of knowledge, to offer prescriptive advice on which conditions, operations or criteria are important and which are not. This may well vary from context to context and what holds true for an ESP situation may not fit a general English teaching situation.

We simply do not know at present and must look to research to provide the answers.

To take the frameworks further we need help from teachers and researchers in taking specific elements of the framework and determining their importance. We need to find out if the categories are of use to teachers. What do they make most use of to write items? Underlying all of this is the important research issue: which categories make a difference? In seeking to answer these questions we may contribute to a clearer understanding of what language proficiency is and the order in which our students acquire it. This is what makes testing so worthwhile and so crucial.

# Appendix A
## *Transcript of lecture on issues in the Women's Liberation Movement*

I want to talk to you now about some issues in the Women's Liberation Movement. It was during the early 70s that people first became, really active in what has become, really active in what has become to be known as the 'Women's Liberation Movement'. Um ... the sort of women who were involved this, in these discussions, in these early meetings were often older women, typically women who had been educated at university or college and who were facing ah ... the unexpected frustrations of life, looking after small children. Um ... they tended to meet in small groups at first to, to read about and to discuss issues which they felt to be important to women. Um ... these small groups have continued until now there are discussions groups which, for women which go in every town, and village in the country. But um ... they also began to grow together ah ... to form regional groupings and national groupings and these regional groupings themselves from time to time mounted regional and national campaigns and these campaigns um ... marked for and concentrated on four central demands:

Firstly they demanded equal pay for women, that is that they demanded that women should be paid at the same rate as a man, as men um ... if they were doing the same work.

Secondly ah ... they demanded equal education and opportunity that is women should not be discriminated against in any way ah ... or treated in any any differently simply because they are women.

Thirdly um ... the demand was for 24 hour nurseries ah ... that is child care should be available at any time of the day or night. This would mean of course that no woman would be stopped from doing her job simply because she had to look after her children.

Fourthly, um ... the demand was for free contraception and abortion on demand. So that women do not have to have children if they did not want to have them. This would then free them to work normally in the same professional areas as men are already working in.

But um ... today I want to talk particularly about a couple of issues which relate to all of these. Um ... which are rather more general. Um ... Firstly, um ... it's something women in the movement particularly resented from the beginning this is perhaps one of the issues which made the, brought the women's movement to operation in the first place. Particularly resented the fact that in every day life, in all spheres of activity, um ... women were always expected to operate in a clearly defined subordinate role, that is, it was always the women that made the tea, the women who typed the leaflets, the women who sold the papers and so on. But it was the men who organised, the men who spoke at meetings, the men who took the decisions. So all the major, dominating roles were filled by men. In fact um ... even in the early meetings of the Women's Liberation Movement itself um ... where men were included, they tended, it was the men who dominated the discussion, not simply because they were trying to dominate it, because the women lacked confidence in themselves and they allowed the men, they almost expected the men ah ... to dominate.

In fact, one of the crucial early experiences in the Women's Movement uh ... was at one of the earlier conferences in Skegness in 1971. Um ... when a group including several men tried to take the political leadership of the meeting, and the men were playing a very dominant role in that take over bid. This caused a great deal of resentment and hostility among the women present.

So after these initial experiences, men were excluded not only from discussion sessions at conferences and so on. But also from the social events they were totally excluded in other words from the activities of the Women's Liberation Movement. This doesn't mean to say that ah . . . men's participation in the fight for, fight over certain issues was not welcomed, it was ah . . . but during, but in the specific activities of the Women's Liberation Movement itself men were excluded. Um . . . this exclusion ah . . . was part of an attempt to find ways of developing and extending the political and social confidence of the women involved.

This question of relationship with men and the relationship and the Women's Liberation Movement and male dominated organisations is one which has remained a subject of debate ah . . . some people within the movement feel that all Women's Liberation Movement activities should take place apart from men ah . . . but it has to be said that this is certainly not the view of the majority.

A second issue which I'd like to talk about um . . . and which is very widely discussed in women's groups is the question of wages for housework. Many women feel that the work they do in the house ah . . . does not receive and has never received proper recognition. They feel that the man usually goes out to work in an office or factory, and he is paid for that work and he uses the money he receives to support the family, what is usually called his family, and this is particularly the case when the wife herself does not go to work, but works in the home. This automatically puts the man in a dominant position and makes the woman dependant on him.

But it is argued that this is not a fair arrangement, the work the woman does in the home is every bit as important as the man's work. It is also in every way real work, it is necessary and the whole family benefits from it. In fact, it could be said that in some ways it's less pleasant than the man's work as the woman house worker doesn't have the pleasure of working together with colleagues. She's working alone, she's shut-up, shut-up in the house for most of the time ah . . . so it's not surprising that many women suffer from acute loneliness.

Perhaps the one major thing which separates woman's house work from the man's work is that the man is paid for his work, but she is not paid for hers. So it is that some women have suggested that the State would pay wages to all women for doing housework. But most women have shown themselves to be against this idea, for a number of reasons. In particular, they're against the idea, firstly because um . . . such an arrangement would not change the fact that mothers with young children tend to be socially isolated in the house during the day. They would still be isolated, they would simply be paid for being isolated.

Secondly, ah . . . they are against the idea because such a system would implicitly accept that it would be the woman who would stay at home confirming what she already feels that her role is simply subservient, subordinate to the man.

And finally, ah . . . many women are against the idea of wages for housework because this would give the State a means of tempting women to stay in the home and produce large families. That is, it would be treating them and leading them to a role of being baby machines and little more. And so it would be reducing them as full human beings. In fact, the only situation where something similar to wages for housework has ever been introduced ah . . . was in Nazi Germany ah . . . where it was used to get women out of the work force so that they can provide large families to safeguard the future of the fatherland.

Of course, the State does already pay mothers family allowance to help feed and clothe the children. And some people have argued this would be the basis of um . . . ah . . . a system whereby wages would be paid for housework, to be clearly stated that this is a very different matter from a wage for housework um . . . a family allowance is a recognition of a social responsibility. Whereas a wage for housework would in effect serve as a means to maintain, what many women feel is an oppressive situation.

Source: Don Porter CALS, University of Reading

# Appendix B
## *Example of invigilator's instructions*

**1.** Before you visit the school you need to have a clear list for each class you are to visit. Make sure that all concerned (headmaster, teachers, pupils ...) know that you are going to need approximately three hours' class time in total to administer the tests and that pupils are expected to turn up on time for all parts of the test. Ensure that the candidates have been informed exactly what they need to bring with them (pencils, erasers, etc.) and are aware of all relevant details of the test. Establish clearly when and where the tests are to be administered beforehand. Try and ensure that other teachers will keep their classes reasonably quiet while the tests are administered. Ensure students are advised to arrive in good time for the test. Make it clear that latecomers will not be admitted. Check the suitability of the facilities for the examination in advance (size and location of room, acoustics, number of desks, clock, etc.).

Before administering the test familiarise yourself completely with it: be clear concerning the directions you have to read out concerning the conduct of the test and the filling out of details on the answer papers; work out the papers you need to distribute and the order; how you are going to collect them in; what you have to check such as names, etc.; how the tape recorder works; what tapes you will need; what papers you need and whether you have the right number; what you will do in cases of cheating; how students are to secure your attention quietly during the conduct of the examination; what happens at the end of the examination such as all remaining seated until everything has been handed in.

Before you administer the test check against the class list to ensure that only the pupils who are registered for the examination are actually taking it.

**2.** Before starting the test advise pupils that if they attempt to copy from each other their papers will simply not be marked. Keep the pupils as far away from each other as is possible.

**3.** Keep a clear record of each visit. You should each have a field notebook for this purpose. Make sure you note for each part of the test:

(a) which pupils are absent;

(b) the names of pupils who are obviously cheating. Indicate this on your master class list and also write it across the top of the pupil's papers (mark with a large 'C' on the candidate's script'). Remove this student's papers from the file for that class.

(c) the start time and the stop time of each part of the test;

(d) any irregularities that occur in the administration of the test, interruptions, etc.

**4.** At the start of each part of the test check that candidates fill in their names and roll numbers correctly and clearly at the top of the paper. You should double check this as you collect each script in at the end of each part of the test. At the end of each part make sure you collect both question and answer paper from each candidate.

Before you administer Part I of the test advise students not to write on the question sheets as you will need to use the question papers again at the next school. You should check beforehand to make sure none have been written on before you hand them out. If you number the question papers in sequence before you hand them out it will make it easier to check you have collected them all in. Check this before you allow pupils to go at the end of the test.

**5.**  Make sure each test lasts for the exact period specified. Nobody should leave or enter the examination room while the test is taking place. The pupils should be silent during the conduct of the test until the papers are collected in. Nobody is to leave the room until all the papers have been collected in. Anyone distracting other pupils should however be ejected and they are to be removed from the class master list and the research study.

Where feasible a short break should be given between each of the three parts of the test.

**6.**  After the whole test battery has been administered ensure that you have three part tests for each candidate. Make sure the scripts are collated in the order that pupils' names appear on the class list. Number each one sequentially to match the class list.

**7.**  Make sure that all the papers from a particular school are clearly identified and kept separately from the papers of other schools.

## *Paper 1   Reading and gap filling*

Make sure all candidates have a pencil, question paper and answer paper. Explain carefully the instructions for taking the test. Make sure they understand that they have to write the answer against the corresponding number on the answer paper. Make it clear that they have sixty minutes for this part of the test and seventy-five items to complete in passages A−D. When you have introduced the test task check to see if they have any questions on the conduct of the test. Answer any queries. Start the test.

After fifteen minutes tell them they have had fifteen minutes and are a quarter of the way through the test.

After thirty minutes tell them they are halfway through and have thirty minutes left.

After forty-five minutes tell them they have fifteen minutes left.

After sixty minutes tell them to put their pencils down and not to write anything more.

Be vigilant for cheating during the exam. Any candidate suspected of cheating should have a large 'C' written on his/her answer sheet and this fact clearly recorded on the class master sheet/exam register. All papers for those candidates caught cheating should be removed from the master file for that class and the candidates are to be eliminated from the study.

Collect in both question and answer papers. Make sure each student has written his name and roll number clearly on the answer paper. Collate in the order that pupils' names appear on the class master list.

## *Paper 2   Dictation task* (approximately 30 minutes)

Before administering the test check that the tape recorder works (always carry spare batteries); check that the tape is audible and that the acoustics of the room the test is to be held in are OK. Make sure that the tape can be heard clearly from all corners of the room. Do this before candidates enter the exam room.

First hand out the answer sheets and explain to the students what they will have to do. Emphasise that they will only hear the dictation once and they are not to worry if they cannot understand everything. They are to write down all they can.

Make sure they know they have to write each new utterance on a new line opposite the right number. If they do not understand an utterance tell them not to worry and to leave that line blank, wait for the next utterance and then write this on the next line down opposite the correct number.

See if they have any questions on the test. Warn them that the tape will not be stopped until the end of the test. They are to remain silent throughout. Start the tape.

When the tape is finished they can have two minutes to check through what they have written. Be vigilant for cheating during this period. Anyone suspected of cheating should be treated in accordance with the general instructions regarding this outlined above.

Collect in all the scripts and ensure that the personal details at the head of the page have been filled in correctly; ensure each candidate has legibly written his or her name, roll number, etc., on the answer paper.

## *Paper 3   Guided writing* (approximately 80 minutes)

Read out the instructions to candidates and make sure they understand that they have to write forty sentences in eighty minutes. Advise them that the sentences will be marked for accuracy and adequacy of content.

See if there are any questions regarding the conduct of the examination. Start them off on the first writing task (five sentences).

After ten minutes have elapsed tell them to go on to the second task of five sentences. After twenty minutes tell them to go on to the third task. After thirty minutes tell them they have ten minutes to do task 4. After forty minutes tell them to do task 5. Advise them they have ten minutes for this. After fifty minutes tell them to start the last task and warn them they have thirty minutes for this. Collect in all the scripts and ensure that candidates have written their names and roll numbers legibly at the top of each sheet.

## Appendix C

*Scripts for marking of writing exercise in Section 5.3*

① Trap is open and the maoss is trying to find anything to eat. Inside the trap are a piece of apple and a piece of frish meat. The animal goup on the platform to get The a piece of apple and the a piece of fish meat.

When he arrived to the end of platform sure he press the otherside of platform and go down inside the Trap and because the animal press the otherside trape, The first side go up and close the entry of trap, then the animal will become inside the trap and it cant to go outside again He it will be inside to eat the apple and meat which have put as a trick by us.

Then it will eat the apple and meat and we can see him throgh the holes and then we can Catch him because he can't go out and if to it has inside then he is going to dead: a piece of apple and meat have a bait and a bait will catch him and then he can't go autside the trap.

② Trap works as alrich it has a pieces of Bait and along plat form and we usually put a picece of anything to eat and abait on the apicece the platform is fenced on the a pivot pin and the platform inside the box. animal usuly smell anything to eat and it trys to get it so it goes up the platform to find the piece of apple or anything then it will press the platform to get inside the trap then the other side of the platform will be closing and it will tray to eat a piece of apple whicl have put and we usnally put some bait on them the bait will catch him and the other side of the will be closeing and hcit. Cant see the go out again. because the trap door has closed by the pressing of anima on the platform.

(1)   THIS TRAP IS LIKE A BOX AND JUST ONE OF THE SIDE IS OPEN IT HAS A SEE SAW PLATFORM WHICH IS HOLDING FOR THE PILOT PIN. AT ONE OF THE ENDS OF THIS SEE SAW PLATAFORM THERE ARE A HEAVY METAL PLATE, WHICH WILL WORK LIKE A LOOK TO KEEP THE ANIMAL INTO THE TRAP. THIS HEAVY METAL PLATE IS HOLDING BY A HINGE WITH ONE OF THE ENDS OF THE SEE SAW PLATFORM. ONE OF THE END ON THE IS BOX IS MADE OF GLASS OR CLEAR PLASTIC. ONE OF THE CORNER HAS LITTLE HOLES.

(2)   IN ORDER TO CACH LITTEL ANIMAL
I AM GOING TO EXPLAIN HOW THE TRAP
WORKS.

FIRST THE TRAP IS OPENED AND SOME
PIECES OF BAIT ARE PUT ON THE HEAVY
METAL PLATE. OF COURSE THERE ARE
SOME MORE BAIT NEAR TO THE GLASS
OR CLEAR PLASTIC. AFTER THAT WE
HAVE TO WAIT UNTIL A LITTLE ANIMAL
SMELLING THE TRAP. AND TAKE FIRST
PIECES OF BAIT ON THE HEAVY METAL
PLATE. THEN THE MOUSE BEGING TO
GO INTO THE BOX ON THE SEE SAW
PLATFORM AND WHEN THE MOUSE
RISE THE HIGHES POINT THE PLATFORM
WILL DROP DOWN WITH THE MOUSE WEITH
AND THE HEAVY METAL PLATE WILL WORK
LIKE A LOOK IF THE MOUSE TRY TO
GO OUT THE SEE SAW PLATFORM WILL
NOT DROP DOWN BECAUSE IS JAM WITH
THE HEAVY METAL PLATE. AT THE END
IT IS POSSIBLE TO GET A MOUSE WHICH
IS ALIVE.

1. The trap shapes a square box. Inside the box there is the platform supported by a pivot pin at the middle of it to make it see saw. One side of the platform is hinged with a heavy metal plate ∧ (to fix it before a mice is trapped). The end of the box inside was made of glass ∧, to make a mice believe as though there were no wall at the end (wall).

There is a bait in front of the glass wall. On a heavy metal at the entrance there are ∧ (also) some pieces of bait to attract the first attention of a mice.

On the ∧ (both) side walls near the end there are some halls for a mice to breathe when he is trapped.

The wall of the glass is removal, so he can be relieved through it after he is catched.

2  At first a mice may be attracted by pieces of
   bait at the entrance. After a mice finishes eating
   them, he will notice another bait inside
   the box. Then he will try to come in order ^the box^ to have it.
   At the entrance the platform is fixed 'because of a
                          ^a mice has to pass^
   heavy metal plate, so he won't notice this is a trap.
   Therefore he will try to run the platform to the other
   end of it ^to gain the food^ But when he passes the middle of the
   platform, it will recline to the other side due to
   the weigh of a mice itself, because the platform is
   see-saw and the weigh of a mice is heavier then
   a heavy metal at the entrance Necessarily the trap
   door will be closed by a heavy metal plate and
   he will loose the place to run through.

The trap consists of two ^main parts. One
is moveable and others ^is are not movable.
The un moveable part can be considered
box has a removable end made of
glass or clear plastic In ~~are~~ the middle
of the ^plate ~~pin~~ there is a pivit pin that
~~makes the platform moveable)~~ At one ~~his platform~~
~~too  id  platform~~    end of ~~opposit side of~~
(u/up/down) opposit to the side which is removable, there is a
heavy metal plate that is hanging and can be
moved easily to inside if the second was
pressed down by anything heavier than the
metal plate

The box can be divided into two parts,
The first part is open and there is ~~put~~ some
pieces of bait to ~~thicker~~ ^ensure the animals. the second
part is to continue the trick and to catch
the animal ~~bail~~ because it ~~not~~ ~~has~~ ^contains bait.

The trap works as follows: Firstly, let the trap open and ~~put the~~ that means let the heavy metal plate laid down. Put some pieces of bait on it to attract the animal and also to ensure him to go deep in the box. Then, Remove the removal end which is in the other side to put some bait consisting of apple and fresh meat and after that close it properly. When an ~~that~~ animal came in or saw the bait he try to eat them or first test it if there is a trick. Then, he will be ensured, so, he will continue to go inside in purpose to get the bait which is in when the animal ~~goes~~ walks on the see-saw platform and eates the baits on it he reach the interior of plate form and thus make this ~~~~ side ~~~~ laid down. Directly the another side goes up and + of heavy metal plate close the opening. ~~~~ By This way the animal can't go out

1.  The trap is for catching mice has long
box shape.
The length it is longer than the hight
and the hight is the same as the width.
One of the ends of this box is normally
opened to allow mice to enter, and another
is removably shut by the plate of glass or
clear plastic.
From the open end to the out side there is
a moval heavy metal plate which connect,
with hinge to this box. From the open
end to inside of this box, there is a
see-saw platform of which has a pivot pin
in the middle. You can see the pivot
pin from outside in the both narrow
and long sides of this box.
Finally, there are many holes in the
both narrow and long sides, near the
closed end.

2. Firstly,
there are some pieces of baits, on
the heavy metal plate from the open end,
which attract the mice to enter this
trap. after a mouse enter it it go
on to clime the see-saw platform
to get foods which are put on the
bottom of this box near the closed
end.

Secondly, soon after it climb up the
see-saw platform and clime over the
pivot pin, this platform change
the angle and the top side of it
go down to the floor
while, the another bottom side of
it comes up to the ceiling of this box.
as the result of it, the metal plate
shut the open end and the mice
cannot escape from this box.

① <u>Description</u> of the trap

The trap is lock like not big and not small box it size like two box of cegarets. The trap have bottom ~~and~~, wall and in front of the door which made of ~~heavy~~ heavy metal plat have removable which made of glass or clear plastic. Tolled ~~plat~~ platform

In side of the trap have flat which V ~~and~~ made of wood and in the middle of the flat have door can be closed or open by hinge.

(2)

When the muse smell a food ~~is~~ ,
the ~~to~~ door of the trap and when
the muse go inside the box at the
first time ~~when the muse made~~ a
the muse ~~of~~ can go the door of the
box and eat some food on it ~~-~~ that
the muse go to the see-saw platform
at the first time the platform have
one posetion. One side of platform is
on the bottom of box and the of
saide ~~is in the~~ the platform can tuch of
walk.

When the muse acrros the middle of
the platform sunt side of the flat
dive to the bottom and the other side
is go up.

1.    The trap for catching small animals for observation is made from a simple box with an open end and a removable end. The open end is made with a heavy metal plate as a weight to keep the door open. This metal plate door is fixed to an hinge which enables the door to close. The metal door is also the place where you put the pieces of bait to attract small animals. ~~The hinge~~ The other side of the hinge is ~~connected~~ connected to a ~~pivot pin~~ see-saw platform. ~~The platform is fixed to a pivot pin to allow rotation of the platform~~ A pivot pin is fixed in the middle of the platform to secure to the sides of the box. ~~To allow full rotation of the other end of the box. To where the removable door is.~~ But consisting of apples and fresh meat will place at the other end of the box where the removable glass is. Holes are provided at this end    on the sides of the box to allow air into the box. That is the trap for catching small animals for observation purposes.

2

In order to trap a small animal, first of all, let the trap open, you'll see the heavy metal plate at the end of the trap box. Then, put some pieces of bait on the trap door to attract the small animals. As the metal plate is heavy, it keeps the door open and it keeps the see-saw platform as a bridge for the small animal to go straight. Once the ~~it~~ small animal is attracted the door and finishes the pieces of bait, it ~~will~~ probably will try to enjoy ~~the~~ bait at the ~~a~~ other end of the box. As it walks along the see-saw platform, it adds on weight ~~the~~ toward the other end of the platform and leads to ~~the~~ a rotation of the platform. ~~The platform will the the~~ The movement of the platform close the door of the trap straight the hinge. The small animal is then trapped as you can see straight the glass at the other end. ~~The removable glass allow you to take you~~

Title: A trap for catching wild animals

A trap for catching small animals like rabbit etc. can be made by using ordinary materials and hand tools as can be seen from the figure 2. The main portion of the box type trap is the "see-saw platform" which can rotate about the pivot pin. The see-saw platform is hinged to a heavy metal plate so that in normal position when the trap is said to be "open", the heavy metal plate touches the bottom of the box type trap. To ensure the metal plate to touch the bottom of the box, one may place some pieces of bait on it.

Care must be taken into consideration that whenever a small animal crosses the pivot point from the traps entrance end to the removable end, the total weight of the animal plus the weight of the portion of the see-saw platform at the removable end must be higher than the other side containing the rest of the see-saw platform with its heavy metal plate and also with the pieces of bait.

So the difference between the weights of portions about the pivot determines the weight of the small animal to be trapped by this trap.

"How the trap works :    Steps to be followed .

1. Normally the trap should be in "open" position, that is the heavy metal plate end touches the bottom of the box of the trap .

2. Bait consisting of apples and fresh meat is to be placed on the removable end by removing the glass or clear plastic .

3. Some pieces of bait ~~should be~~ placed on the heavy metal plate depending upon the weight of the animal to be trapped ; if the animal is big enough ~~one may~~ put heavier pieces .

4. Attracted by the pieces of bait when small animals starts going up ~~the~~ along the see-saw platform and crosses the pivot point, the weight on the removable end becomes higher than the other side. Thus the see-saw platform rotates about the pivot and the ~~open~~ portion of the see-saw platform on the open end moves up to close that end with the heavy metal plate thereby closing the trap.

5. Then by removing the glass or clear plastic the animal can be taken out for observation .

# Tapescript for JMB listening test, March 1990

*Joint Matriculation Board, University Test in English for Speakers of Other Languages.*

Good afternoon.

This is the start of your Listening Skills test for March 1990.

I would like you to make sure that you have written your name, surname, centre number, and the name of your school or college on the front of your answer book.

Now, I would like you to follow the general instructions at the bottom of this page, as I read them out to you.

This test of your understanding of spoken English is in two parts. In the first part you will hear a conversation and part of a radio programme, and in the second part you will hear a talk. You should take notes as you listen. These notes will not be marked.

Now turn to page 2 of your answer book for Part One of the test.

In this part of the test you will hear a conversation and part of a radio programme about olive oil. You will hear them once. You may take notes as you listen. Then:

(i)     On Figure 1, page 3, label the parts of the olive using words from the conversation.

(ii)    On Figure 2, write a colour to show each stage of the olive's development.

(iii)   On Table A, circle the correct letter or letters in each column.

(iv)    Complete Tables B and C.

(v)     Tick any correct answers, 1−6 below, about Ray's attitude.

You will have $1\frac{1}{2}$ minutes to read these instructions again, and to look at the tasks on pages 2 and 3.

[Pause $1\frac{1}{2}$ minutes]

The conversation is about to begin.

Ready?

## *March*
## *JMB Aural 1990*

### Part One

| | |
|---|---|
| *Text* | *Olive Oil* |

Pauline: Hello Ray, come in. I haven't seen you for ages. You do look well. How was your holiday in Italy?

Ray: Great. The weather was fantastic. Oh, by the way, I brought you a present.

Pauline: Thank you. A bottle of olive oil. Italian Extra Virgin. You know that I enjoy trying different kinds of olive oil.

Ray: Yes, I know.

Pauline: Did you see the book Peter got me for Christmas? About the olive. Its history, its use, where it grows . . .

Ray: Uh, no.

Pauline: Here, come into the kitchen and have a drink and an olive.

Ray: Great. Black olives. Umm.
Let's have a look at the book then. Oh yes. You're lucky to have a husband who manages to find interesting presents!

Pauline: Yes, I am. Mind you, I'm going to bore you with everything I've learnt so far.

Ray: Really. Must you?

Pauline: Yes, I must. You want to know, really, don't you?
Well, for example, you're just biting into the flesh or mesocarp of the olive.

Ray: 'Meso', Greek for middle. Right?

Pauline: Correct. Now mind you don't break your teeth on the endocarp.

Ray: As in 'stone'.

Pauline: I can see you're going to show off as usual.

Ray: Yes, because I'm going to tell *you* that that only leaves the skin which is called the epicarp.

Pauline: You've been reading my book!
All right, if you're so smart, tell me how many different kinds of olive there are.

Ray: How should I know. I'm not an expert on olives. I just like eating them.

Pauline: Have another one. Now, did you know that black olives and green olives are the same?

Ray: Really. What do you mean?

Pauline: *All* olives are green at first and black by the time they ripen or mature; from young green olives they become brown and then purple and you might have seen reddish, dark red ones which is just before they properly mature.

Ray: So the one that I'm eating is just a mature olive.

Pauline: Yes, that's right.
Oh, I almost forgot. There's a programme on the radio, an interview with the woman who wrote this book. Do you mind if we listen?

Ray: You do that. I'll just finish off the olives.

Pauline: Oh dear, it's already started.

*Radio programme*

Interviewer:
(David)        . . . so olives are a bit like grapes?
Speaker: (Jane) That's right. There's almost 200 varieties of olive, and some are grown for eating, and others for pressing into oil. You can pick them green or when they are black.
David:         So green olives are unripe black olives. How interesting. Olive groves must be an impressive sight all around the Mediterranean.
Jane:          Oh yes, rows and rows of them on hillsides in Italy, France, Spain, Greece and of course North Africa.
David:         Does the tree need a Mediterranean climate?
Jane:          It does really. Extreme cold would kill it. Mild winters and hot summers are best.
David:         A bit like me really. *Long*, hot summers, no doubt.
Jane:          That's right. But David, I suspect *you* need to drink a lot more than the olive tree. It needs very little water.
David:         Now then, Jane, I'm not sure I like that reference to my drinking habits. So I'll ignore that. Of course, olive groves in North Africa grow in arid areas with little or no rain.
Jane:          Yes, so we're talking about survival in poor soil. Rich, clay soil isn't necessary for the olive tree.
David:         Uh, huh. Now what about life span. I was amazed to read the other day that the Bonsai tree, you know Japanese miniature trees, can live for up to 300 years.
Jane:          Well I can better that; the olive tree can live for up to 600 years.
David:         Really? And does it yield fruit all that time?
Jane:          It can. You see it takes between 5 and 8 years to mature. Once mature, it bears fruit from June to October. Then every year it will produce olives during that period. The technical term is fruition, bearing fruit from June to October.
David:         Marvellous. Can we go back to talking about olives grown to produce oil? They can be harvested after fruition from October onwards. Is that right?
Jane:          Yes, picking starts in October and goes on till March but remember different types of olive produce different flavours, of course.
David:         Olive oil has many labels, pure, fine, extra virgin, all very confusing.
Jane:          I know that people get confused by all those labels on shelves in supermarkets, but it's quite simple really. We're talking about quality and corresponding price, I'm afraid.
David:         So what's the best kind? And what's the most expensive kind?
Jane:          Let me answer that by telling you a little bit about how it's made. All cold-pressed, or first pressed oil is virgin. Can I be a little technical again here? I mean that young, green, unripe olives are crushed into a paste and the oil is extracted by centrifugation, or spinning the paste around at high speed. Neither heat nor chemicals are used. And for just 1 litre of oil you need about 5 kilos of olives, so you can see why virgin oil is so expensive.
David:         That makes sense. And extra virgin, that's the very best, I suppose?
Jane:          Yes. Extra virgin has an acidity of less than 1%. You see they're all categorised according to their acidity level. Now, 'pure' olive oil has a much higher acidity, more than 3%, and may not be pure at all, because it may have had chemicals added to it. So 'pure' is a bit of a misnomer really.
David:         I see. So that's quite low down the scale in quality. Are there any other gradations?

| Jane: | Yes, in fact you can buy fine virgin or even semi-fine virgin oil. The former, fine virgin has an acidity of less than 1.5%, I should say between 1.00 and 1.5% while semi-fine, which is obviously cheaper than fine, has an acidity of less than 3%. I mean between 1.5 and 3%. |
|---|---|
| David: | This is getting technical, but I think I'm keeping up! All right I've understood that acidity determines the quality of the oil. But how do you choose the right oil for the right thing? Say for frying or mayonnaise? |
| Jane: | Well it's up to you really. You have to experiment with taste. Different countries produce differing flavours and colours of oil. Take for example Southern France. In Provence, the oil is soft, mellow and golden. But the Tuscan variety is different, rather sharp in taste, with a peppery flavour. And this Italian oil has a different colour too; dark green and rather cloudy. Nothing wrong with that, of course. It just means that a lot of olive has been left in it, that is, there are bits of skin and flesh, to be 'technical' the epicarp and mesocarp of the olive can be seen in the oil. The oil hasn't been filtered or 'cleaned' up, you see. |
| David: | Do some producers filter their oil then, to make it clear? |
| Jane: | Yes they do. It's all to do with preference really. Spanish oil, for example, is often lighter in texture. A pale, clear oil. Better for mayonnaise perhaps. Whereas Greek oil, which I particularly like, is fruity and full of flavour. It's also dark green, a bit like Tuscan oil, but not so full of sediment, not so cloudy in fact. I like it on salads, or just on tomatoes. |
| David: | You're making me hungry. I think this is a good time to take a break. Well thank you Jane for a most interesting chat. |
| Jane: | Thank you David. |

[Music]

\*    \*    \*    \*    \*    \*    \*

| Pauline: | I found that quite fascinating. How about you Ray? |
|---|---|
| Ray: | Oh, it was alright. At least you know that I brought you a top quality present. It says 'extra virgin' on the bottle so according to our Jane that has a low acidity level, and so it must be good. |
| Pauline: | That's right. Extra virgin, let's see . . . less than 1% acidity. I was writing some of this down you see, for future reference. |
| Ray: | Oh really, hum . . . |
| Pauline: | And 'pure' isn't pure at all but has a high acidity. More than 3%, the others were in between. |
| Ray: | Were they? |
| | Sorry. I wasn't listening properly. |
| Pauline: | Never mind. You bought me a lovely present. |
| Ray: | Good. |
| | Glad you like it. Well then, I must be off. See you soon. |
| Pauline: | Thanks for dropping in Ray. Bye. |

That is the end of the conversation about olive oil.

You will now have 2 minutes to complete the tasks on pages 2 and 3.

[Pause 2 minutes]

Now turn to page 4 of your answer book for Part Two of the test.

In this part of the test you will hear a talk about the design of English drinking glasses. You will hear the information once, followed by a question and answer session. As you listen you should take notes. Then:

(i)    Identify the glasses on page 5.
       Write the name of each glass in the large box below each illustration.
       The names are listed in Table 1 below.

(ii)   Indicate the order in which the glasses were developed.
       Write a number 1−7, in the small box below each illustration.

(iii)  Write the name of the drink served in each glass in the circle on each illustration.
       Write (AL) for ale, (CH) for champagne, (CO) for cordial, (ME) for mead, and (WI) for wine.

(iv)   Choose a reason, or reasons for the design of each glass.
       Write a letter from a−g below, on Table 1.

You will now have $1\frac{1}{2}$ minutes to read these instructions again, and to look at Table 1 and the phrases below it, and to look at the illustrations of glasses on page 5.

[Pause $1\frac{1}{2}$ minutes]

The talk is about to begin.

Ready?

## Part Two

*English drinking glasses*

Lecturer:    Over the last few weeks we have discussed the concepts of design in quite a lot of detail and we have decided that design is concerned not only with the way things look, but also with how easy they are to use. They should be suited to their purpose and fit into their surroundings. Remember the three main requirements of design — use, appearance and cost. Design reflects such things as social, economic or even political influences. And that's what I'd like to talk about today.

Perhaps the best way to illustrate the connection between design and changes in society is to take a particular object and examine it in its historical context. If you turn to page 5 of your handout, you'll see eight illustrations — these are all English drinking glasses. Together they form a potted history of English glasses from the Dark Ages right through to the 19th century. The illustrations are not presented in chronological order, I'm afraid, but I'll take you through them and explain which is which. Let's start with the earliest glass. This glass here — the tall conical one. It's called a mazer — that's M-A-Z-E-R. Its design is supposed to reflect the decline of Britain during the Dark Ages. The Romans had brought with them quite sophisticated glass making techniques but then glass making in Britain fell into a primitive state. It seems that even the art of making and attaching a foot was forgotten. In fact, all 8th century English drinking vessels are footless. As I said before, they are usually of a tall conical shape with varied decoration on the body.

On this one, the upper part is ornamented round with threads of glass. Now these were not just decorative but gave the user's hand a firm grip. And these raised hollows on the lower part, they're called prunts by the way, prunts — served the same purpose. Yet, look at the base. It's uneven. You couldn't stand it upright could you? In fact, you might say that this glass doesn't fulfil the basic requirement of use. But let's consider the user.

He's probably someone rich with waiting men in attendance. He would be handed the glass, he would take a drink and return it to his servant. So, you see, it was never meant to be set down. The uneven base does not affect the function.

Let's move on. The Normans came to Britain in 1066, a new race of people with a new language and new customs. One Norman custom was that of offering a cup of welcome to guests. The host would first take a drink to show that the drink was wholesome. The glass was then passed from guest to guest. Hence, it's name — Passglass. It's the tall straight-sided glass with threads of glass at intervals down its body. Do you see? The idea being that each guest drank down to one of those lines. In this way, they knew how much to drink. Like the mazer it usually contained mead. Perhaps you've heard of mead. It's a slightly alcoholic drink made of honey and spices. In fact you can still buy it in the North of England. But it's not as popular as it used to be. Then, some centuries later, with the religious wars in France, French glass workers emigrated to Britain, bringing with them their manufacturing skills and designs.

In their glass works in Surrey they produced a design which was a vessel with a globular bowl and a straight sided stem. It was decorated with raspberry shaped prunts and supported on a sloping foot. Now, this type of glass was made of low quality soda or Roman glass — giving it its name — Rummer.

The decorative ribbing that's invariably found on the bowl, stem and foot had a specific purpose to disguise or hide the sediment or dregs that the wine often contained.

Unfortunately, many of these glass works were shut down in the late 16th century because they were in competition with shipbuilders for supplies of wood, and the Queen thought that shipbuilding was more important than glass making. So that was that.

Let's move on to the next stage of development. Now, I'm sure you know a little bit about the Civil War in England. The monarchy was restored in 1660, and then there was a new period of intense research and scientific inquiry which resulted, amongst other things, in the discovery of a new type of glass. Flint glass. You probably know it as lead crystal. It was heavier, superior in colour and brilliance and had completely different working qualities. Now, English glass makers were forced to design shapes that were more suited to the new material. Initially, decoration of this new type of glass was confined to the stem, which was blown into different shapes. But lead glass is difficult to blow and later, during the next century, decoration was done first by engraving, usually the bowl of the glass, and later by facetting, which became popular in about 1770. Let me explain. We cut lead glass to produce flat surfaces which reflect the light. This is facetting. This stirrup glass here is an early example of facetting. It's a cup-shaped glass which has facetting around the lower section of the bowl. You can see that the stem is also facet cut and ends in a ball. Notice there is no foot. This made it impossible to put the glass down until it was emptied of all its wine and could be turned upside down. Now why did the stirrup glass have to be emptied?

Well eighteenth century wine would leave bits of grape skin, in other words the sediment in the bottom of the glass. Now unless this was drunk or drained at every toast, you would end up with a glass full of sediment.

Now where were we? O yes, let's just go back for a moment to the earlier form of decoration I mentioned — engraving. This came into use after the Excise Act of 1745.

We'll discuss the importance of this act later. But don't worry about it for the moment. Engraving: now a good example of engraving is this ale glass here. Ale glasses usually had quite small, narrow bowls, somewhat conical in shape. You can see that they often had a stem with a ball shaped knob in it and a flat foot. They were more often than not engraved with either hops or barley, the cereals used to make ale. They are quite small, aren't they compared to our beer glasses. That's because 18th century ale was much stronger than beer is today. These particular glasses are called Dwarf glasses, because of their small size, no doubt.

Okay, on to the beginning of the 19th century and the industrial revolution. England was much more prosperous. The middle classes were growing richer. Men's clubs were flourishing.

A feature of many of these places was the use of the firing glass which appeared in about 1820. It was short, with a small, plain, trumpet-shaped bowl and a specially solid foot and thick stem. These glasses would have been thumped on the table you see, in support of a toast and so they needed the thick base to withstand such treatment, otherwise they would have broken.

The noise made by banging the glass on the table was thought to be like gunfire and that's how we get the name firing glass. Since there were likely to be many such toasts in one evening, the glass is designed to take only a very small quantity of wine, although wine was not considered a strong drink, unlike the ale of the 18th century.

Now another type of glass that was being developed at the same time as the firing glass was the champagne glass. So they represent the same stage of development for the same reason — to supply the newly rich middle class. Champagne had always been popular with the aristocracy ever since it was introduced to the English Court. Now, at the beginning of the 19th century its popularity spread to the middle classes. One problem with champagne at this time was the unsightly sediment that fell to the bottom of the glass. To disguise this, the flute glass was made with a globe shaped bowl with heavy vertical facetting on its lower section. Can you see it? Notice also that this particular example has a plain cylindrical hollow stem on quite a high domed foot. In fact, I had always thought that a flute was a tall, narrow, tapering glass on a short stem but I was wrong; it seems that nearly 200 years ago all champagne glasses were called flutes. Now, of course, it means one particular shape of glass and most people would know what you meant by a 'flute' glass.

Okay, the late 19th century. Mechanization was here to stay. The Americans had developed a method of mass producing glass which meant that it was cheaper and more readily available. And look at this example; here we have a 19th century artefact with a recognisable 20th century quality.

Disposability: this is a glass that you can throw away after you have drunk from it. In the context of today's talk, it represents the final stage of development. As you can see, it has a small trumpet shaped bowl with an extremely thin stem that was meant to be snapped between the fingers. Yes, really. The idea being that once a toast had been drunk, the stem would be broken so that the glass would never be used for a less worthy toast. An expensive habit perhaps, but that's the reason for the design of the Ratafia glass. It was known as a Ratafia because of the particular cordial drink that it usually contained. This cordial, often drunk with almond flavoured biscuits, Ratafia biscuits, was a strong drink and so the glass was designed to hold only a small amount like the firing glass, because of the large number of toasts that would be drunk in one evening. Clearly an example of glass makers and brewers *not* working hand in hand, or hand-to-mouth might be a better way of describing it.

Okay, let's stop there. We're due to meet again this afternoon so I'll go over the main points again. You can check your notes and we'll talk about your next assignment.

That is the end of the talk. You will now hear some of the information again in a question and answer session.

| | |
|---|---|
| Lecturer: | Right. Is everyone back? Good. Any questions about the work on glass design? |
| Ben: | Yes. In my notes I've written down 'Mead' for mazer, but I think there was another glass which served mead. |
| Lecturer: | You're right. The passglass was used for serving mead. Any more questions? |
| Jane: | On cost. You said the Ratafia was an 'expensive habit'. Why? |
| Lecturer: | Well, what I meant was that you threw it away every time you had used one. Hence the thin stem, which could easily be snapped in half. You can see from the illustration how easy it would be to break. |
| Ben: | And could you just repeat what you said about facetting? |
| Lecturer: | Certainly. Lead glass or crystal is cut in such a way that it reflects light. You can see it on both the stirrup cup, used for wine, and the champagne drinker's flute glass. Facetting started in the 18th century. |
| Ben: | Thanks. I also wanted to ask about prunts and threads of glass. |
| Lecturer: | So that's the passglass, the rummer, the mazer. Uh huh, I see. The reason for prunts and threads was that the glasses were easier to hold, in the case of the passglass it was possible to see how much each person was supposed to drink. O.K.? |
| Ben: | Yes. Oh, there were prunts on the mazer and the rummer, weren't there? And the rummer served wine. |
| Lecturer: | That's right. Any more questions? |
| Jane: | There's two small glasses, the dwarf . . . |
| Lecturer: | And the firing glass. Yes. |
| Jane: | One was used for wine, and the other one for ale. That's this one with a pattern on it: am I right? |

| | |
|---|---|
| Lecturer: | It's actually got hops and barley on it. To show what the drink was made from. Any more questions? |
| Jane: | Oh, yes can we just go back to the Ratafia. Sorry about this. I must have fallen asleep. It was the last stage of development we talked about, wasn't it? And it served? |
| Lecturer: | Cordial. A very potent drink, served in small quantities. Is that all then? Good, and now I've got a short test for you, based on last week's work. |
| Ben: | What ... |
| Jane: | Oh, dear ... |
| Jill: | I didn't know ... |

That is the end of the talk on English drinking glasses.

You will now have 4 minutes to write your answers on pages 4 and 5.

[Pause 4 minutes]

That is the end of Part Two of the test. And that is the end of your Listening Skills Test for March 1990.

# Bibliography

Adams, M.L. and J.R. Frith (eds.). 1979. *Testing Kit*. Washington D.C.: Foreign Service Institute.

Alderson, J.C. 1978. *A Study of the Cloze Procedure with Native and Non-native Speakers of English*. PhD Thesis, University of Edinburgh.

Alderson, J.C. 1990. 'Testing reading comprehension skills (Part One)'. *Reading in a Foreign Language*, 6(2): 425–38.

Alderson, J.C. 1991. 'Language testing in the 1990's: How far have we come? How much further have we to go?' In S. Anivan (ed.), *Current Developments in Language Testing*. Singapore: SEAMEO Regional Language Centre. Anthology Series 25.

Alderson, J.C. and A. Hughes (eds.). 1981. *Issues in Language Testing*. ELT Documents 111. London: The British Council.

Alderson, J.C., K.J. Krankhe and C.W. Stansfield. 1987, *Reviews of English Language Proficiency Tests*. Washington D.C.: TESOL.

Alderson, J.C. and B. North (eds.). 1991. *Language Testing in the 1990s*. London: Macmillan.

Alderson, J.C. and A.H. Urquhart (eds.). 1984. *Reading in a Foreign Language*. London: Longman.

Anderson, A. and T. Lynch. 1988. *Listening*. Oxford: Oxford University Press.

Anivan, S. (ed.). 1991. *Current Developments in Language Testing*. Singapore: SEAMEO Regional Language Centre. Anthology Series 25.

Bachman, L.F. 1990. *Fundamental Considerations in Language Testing*. Oxford: Oxford University Press.

Bachman, L.F., A.K.S. Vanniarjan and B. Lynch. 1988. 'Task and ability analysis as a basis for examining content and construct comparability in two EFL proficiency batteries'. *Language Testing*, 5(2): 128–59.

Beretta, A. 1983. 'A comparison of three tests of listening in the context of English for academic purposes'. University of Edinburgh MSc Applied Linguistics Assignment.

Brindley, G. 1986. *The Assessment of Second Language Proficiency: Issues and Approaches*. Adelaide: NCRC Adult Migrant Education Program Australia Research Series.

Brindley, G. 1989. *Assessing Achievement in the Learner Centred Curriculum*. Sydney, Australia: National Centre for English Language Teaching and Research, Macquarie University.

Brindley, G. and D. Nunan. 1992. *Draft Bandscales for Listening*. IELTS Research Projects: Project 1. Sydney, Australia: National Centre for English Language Teaching and Research, Macquarie University.

Brown, G. 1991. *Listening to Spoken English*. London: Longman.

Brown, G. and G. Yule. 1983. *Teaching the Spoken Language*. Cambridge: Cambridge University Press.

Buck, G. 1990. *The Testing of Second Language Listening Comprehension*. Unpublished PhD Thesis, University of Lancaster.

Buck, G. 1991. 'The testing of listening comprehension: an introspective study'. *Language Testing*, 8(1): 67–92.

Buzan, T. 1974. *Use Your Head*. London: BBC.

Bygate, M. 1987. *Speaking*. Oxford: Oxford University Press.

Campbell, C. 1990. 'Writing with others' words: using background reading text in academic compositions'. In B. Kroll (ed.), *Second Language Writing*. Cambridge: Cambridge University Press.

Canale, M. 1983. 'On some dimensions of language proficiency'. In J. Oller (ed.), *Issues in Language Testing Research*. Rowley, Mass.: Newbury House.

Canale, M. and M. Swain. 1980. 'Theoretical bases of communicative approaches to second language teaching and testing'. *Applied Linguistics*, 1(1): 1–47.

Candlin, C.N. 1987. 'Towards task based learning'. In C.N. Candlin and D. Murphy (eds.), *Language Learning Tasks*. Prentice Hall.

Carrell, P.L. 1984. 'The effects of rhetorical organisation on ESL readers'. *TESOL Quarterly* 18(3): 441–69.

Carrell, P.L., J. Devine and D.E. Eskey (eds.). 1988. *Interactive Approaches to Second Language Reading*. Cambridge: Cambridge University Press.

Carroll, B.J. 1980. *Testing Communicative Performance*. Oxford: Pergamon.

Clark, J.L.D. and S.S. Swinton. 1979. *Direct Testing of Speaking Proficiency: Theory and Application*. Princeton N.J.: Education Testing Service.

Cohen, A.D. 1980. *Testing Language Ability in the Classroom*. Rowley, Mass.: Newbury House.

Cohen, A.D. 1984. 'On taking tests: what the students report'. *Language Testing*, 1(1): 70–81.

Cook, G. 1990. *Discourse*. Oxford: Oxford University Press.

Crookes, G. 1986. 'Task classification: a cross-disciplinary review'. *Technical Report*, 4. Centre for SLCR, Honolulu: University of Hawaii.

Davies A. 1965. *Proficiency in English as a Second Language*. PhD Thesis, University of Birmingham.

Davies, A. 1978. 'Language testing. Survey Article Parts I and II'. *Language Teaching and Linguistics Abstracts*, II, 3(4): 145−59 and 215−31.

Davies, A. 1990. *Principles of Language Testing*. Oxford: Blackwell.

Dunkel, P. 1991. 'Listening in the native and second/foreign language: toward an integration of Research and Practice'. *TESOL Quarterly*, 25(3): 431−59.

Faerch, C. and G. Kasper. 1987. *Introspection in Second Language Research*. Clevedon, Philadelphia: Multilingual Matters.

Fulcher, G. 1987. 'Tests of oral performance: the need for data-based criteria'. *ELTJ*, 41(4): 287−91.

Grabe, W. 1991. 'Current developments in second language reading research'. *TESOL Quarterly*, 25(3): 375−406.

Grellet, F. 1987, *Developing Reading Skills*. Cambridge: Cambridge University Press.

Hamp-Lyons, L. 1990. 'Second language writing: assessment issues'. In B. Kroll (ed.), *Second Language Writing*. Cambridge: Cambridge University Press.

Hamp-Lyons, L. (ed.). 1991. *Assessing Second Language Writing in Academic Contexts*. New Jersey: Ablex.

Heaton, J.B. 1975. *Writing English Language Tests*. London: Longman.

Henning, G. 1987. *A Guide to Language Testing Development, Evaluation and Research*. Rowley, Mass.: Newbury House.

Henning, G., N. Gary and J.O. Gary. 1983. 'Listening recall — a listening comprehension test for low proficiency learners'. *System*, 11(3): 287−94.

Hughes, A. (ed.). 1988. *Testing English for University Study*. ELT Documents 127. Oxford: Modern English Press.

Hughes, A. 1989. *Testing for Language Teachers*. Cambridge: Cambridge University Press.

Hughes, A. and D. Porter (eds.). 1983. *Current Developments in Language Testing*. Academic Press.

Hughes, A., D. Porter and C.J. Weir (eds.). 1988. *Validating the ELTS Test: A Critical Review*. Cambridge: The British Council and University of Cambridge Local Examinations Syndicate

Hymes, D. 1972. 'Models of the interaction of language and social life'. In J.J. Gumperez and D.H. Hymes (eds.), *Directions in Sociolinguistics*. New York: Holt, Rinehart and Winston.

Jacobs, H.L., S.A. Zinkgraf, D.R. Wormuth, V. Faye Hartfiel and J. Hughey. 1981. *English Composition Program. Testing ESL Composition: a Practical Approach*. Rowley, Mass.: Newbury House.

Klein Braley, C. 1985. 'A cloze-up on the C-test: a study in the construct validation of authentic tests'. *Language Testing*, 2(1):76−104.

Klein Braley, C. and U. Raatz. 1984. 'A survey of research on the C-test'. *Language Testing*, 1(2): 134−46.

Kroll, B. (ed.). 1990. *Second Language Writing*. Cambridge: Cambridge Univeristy Press.

Long, M.H. 1989. 'Task, group and task group interactions'. *University of Hawaii Working Papers in ESL*, 8(2): 1−26.

Long, M.H. and G. Crookes. 1992. 'Three approaches to task-based syllabus design'. *TESOL Quarterly*, 26(1): 27−56.

Morrow, K.E. 1977. *Techniques of Evaluation for a Notional Syllabus*. Centre for Applied Language Studies, University of Reading (for the Royal Society of Arts).

Morrow, K.E. 1979. 'Communicative language testing: revolution or evolution?' In J.C. Alderson and A. Hughes (eds.), *Issues in Language Testing*. ELT Documents 111. London: The British Council.

Murphy, R.J.L. 1979. *Mode 1 Examining for the General Certificate of Education. A General Guide to Some Principles and Practices*. Guildford: AEB.

Nunan, D. 1989. *Designing Tasks for the Communicative Classroom*. Cambridge: Cambridge University, Press.

Oller, J.W. 1979. *Language Tests at School: a Pragmatic Approach*. London: Longman.

Portal, M. (ed.). 1986. *Innovations in Language Testing*. London: NFER/Nelson.

Raimes, A. 1983. 'Anguish as a second language? Remedies for composition teachers'. In A. Freedman *et al.* (eds.), *Learning to write: first language/second language*. London: Longman.

Raimes, A. 1991. 'Out of the woods: emerging traditions in the teaching of writing'. *TESOL Quarterly*, 25(3): 407−30.

Reid, J. 1990. 'Responding to different topic types: a quantitative analysis from a contrastive rhetoric perspective'. In B. Kroll, *Second Language Writing*. Cambridge, Cambridge University Press.

Richards, J.C. 1983, 'Listening comprehension: approach, design, procedure'. *TESOL Quarterly*, 17(12): 219−40.

Rost, M. 1990. *Listening in Language Learning*. London: Longman.

Ruth, L. and S. Murphy. 1988. *Designing Writing Tasks for the Assessment of Writing*. New Jersey: Ablex.

Sarig, G. 1989. 'Testing meaning construction: can we do it fairly?' *Language Testing*, 6(1): 77−94.

Shohamy, E. and O. Inbar. 1991. 'Validation of listening comprehension tests: the effect of text and question type'. *Language Testing*, 8(1): 23—40.

Skehan, P. 1984. 'Issues in the testing of English for specific purposes'. *Language Testing*, 1(1): 202—20.

Skehan, P. 1988. 'Language testing: Survey Article, Part I'. *Language Teaching Abstracts*, 21(4): 211—21. Cambridge: Cambridge University Press.

Skehan, P. 1989. 'Language testing: Survey Article, Part 2'. *Language Teaching Abstracts*, 22(1): 1—13. Cambridge: Cambridge University Press.

Skehan, P. 1991. 'Progress in language testing: the 1990's'. In J.C. Alderson and B. North (eds.), *Language Testing in the 1990s*. London: Macmillan.

Stansfield, C.W. (ed.). 1986. *Towards communicative competence testing: proceedings of the second TOEFL invitational conference*, TOEFL Research Report 21, Princeton N.J. Educational Service.

Weir, C.J. 1983. 'Identifying the language needs of overseas students in tertiary education in the United Kingdom'. Unpublished PhD Thesis, University of London Institute of Education.

Weir, C.J. 1988. 'The specification, realisation and validation of an English language proficiency test'. In A. Hughes (ed.), *Testing English for University Study*. ELT Documents 127. Oxford: Modern English Press.

Weir, C.J. 1990. *Communicative Language Testing*. Hemel Hempstead: Prentice Hall.

Weir, C.J. and M. Bygate. 1990. 'Meeting the criteria of communicativeness in a spoken language test'. Paper presented at the RELC Conference on Testing and Evaluation, Singapore.

Weir, C.J., A. Hughes and D. Porter. 1990. 'Reading skills: hierarchies, implicational relationships and identifiability'. *Reading in a Foreign Language*, 7(1): 505—10.

Williams, E. and C. Moran. 1989. 'Reading in a foreign language at intermediate and advanced levels with particular reference to English'. *Language Teaching*, 22(4): 217—28.